T0374535

Is Praise What You Do?

Developing a Passion for Praise, a Will to Worship

LL. White

Cover Design by LL. White
Cover photo of Spottswood A.M.E. ZION Cross taken by LL. White
Author photo taken by Patricia A. Lawrence

WestBow Press books may be ordered through booksellers or by contacting:

WestBow Press
A Division of Thomas Nelson & Zondervan
1663 Liberty Drive
Bloomington, IN 47403
www.westbowpress.com
1 (866) 928-1240

ISBN: 978-1-4908-7612-2 (sc)
ISBN: 978-1-4908-7614-6 (hc)
ISBN: 978-1-4908-7613-9 (e)

Library of Congress Control Number: 2015905695

Print information available on the last page.

WestBow Press rev. date: 07/28/2015

Foreword by
Marichal Monts

Dedicated to
Bishop Samuel and Mother Rosetta White

Thank you.

Contents

Foreword

Psalm 22:3 declares "But thou art holy, O thou that inhabitest the praises of Israel." I have often said if you really want to know where God is, He is somewhere blessing a praiser! It takes incredible faith to praise a God that you cannot see, for something that you need to see. It takes a deeper faith to simply honor His name just because of who He is.

As we navigate through life in search of its meaning and our divine purpose, the authenticity of our praise not only causes God to bend toward us, He will actually dwell in the midst and become what the hymn writer called "the center of unbroken praise." What a beautiful image! God in His rightful place - where every created thing acknowledges His holiness!

The true scholar of life, however, has recognized that we cannot make it by ourselves, and we serve The Creator God who has created a destiny for every one of us to walk in. It is in genuine relationship where we bless God for His righteousness; and in His righteous decisions toward us that He then makes clear our next move.

Many people are broken, discouraged, confused and have not yet come to the place where they realize that not only is there a release in praise, not only will God give answers in praise, but praise will cause you to gain the victory every time! God is simply delighted when His children exalt, extol, celebrate, honor and appreciate Him for who He is - everything. He actually shares His ability to be all that we need when He instructs Moses to tell Pharaoh that "I AM that I AM" sent him. He was simply saying that whatever you need me to be, I already AM! When we understand this principle, then when we call on God, we call on all of who He is and celebrate His ability to be ALL that we ever need. Who wouldn't serve a limitless God like ours?

I am convinced that praise will sustain you when everything else fails. I have been so privileged to live a life of praise and see the results time and time again. I have also seen LL. White do the same. From the old fashioned "devotional" service in a small Pentecostal church, to sharing the stage with her before countless people....we knew that our ultimate goal was to embrace our own praise and subsequently lead people into the Presence of God. Her dedication to God, ministry and her assignment qualifies her to write this book. The depth of love that she has to see The Body of Christ in its rightful place in reverence to our King, is paramount in her thinking. Her keen sense of the importance of personal intimacy has allowed her the privilege to tap into some very important revelations that I believe will catapult us to a deeper understanding of our purpose. So open up your heart and prepare to embrace the richness of heaven that can only be experienced when we surrender true, unbridled and passionate praise.

Be Blessed

Marichal Monts, Senior Pastor
Citadel of Love, Hartford
Author, *Ordered Steps*

Preface

Is Praise What You Do? A Passion For Praise, A Will to Worship began as a workshop in 2004. In that year God was drawing me into relationship with Him. I began to examine myself and draw close to God in praise because I realized that the purpose of our existence as God's creation is to praise and worship Him. I had begun to see that it is downright shameful to believe on God and His Son Jesus, and not show forth adoration and acclaim His name. God resides in those words of adoration that we send up to Him. We have so much to praise God for; above prosperity, over money, problems, and issues. If we think about praise, is it not logical and the very least courteous to thank someone for a kind deed or to compliment someone for doing well? All the more, we owe God for His acts of Love, mercy, and kindness toward us.

Next we need to know that praise is the mode by which we have intimacy with God. Praise is that process in which we draw nigh to God in humble recognition and favorable expression of who He is, His acts, His attributes, and His character. Praise is our verbal and physical appreciation and celebration of God the Father, Son, and Holy Ghost.

Additionally, this book was written out of a need to challenge believers and people that will believe on the Lord Jesus Christ to pursue – that is chase down a life of praise. I hastily admit the Word of God and the revelation of God by the Spirit should be the primary sources of knowing God's will, this book serves as a commentary to ignite critical thought on the subjects of Praise and Worship.

Perhaps you are a person who has no problem clamorously praising God. Maybe you attend a church that is already vibrant with praise, and His train fills the temple every week. You do not attend a Dead Zone of a church. I trust these writings will encourage you to continue in faith (Col. 1:23), in Grace (Acts 13:43), in truth of the Gospel (Gal 1:50), His goodness (Rom. 11:22), and "*By him therefore let us offer the sacrifice of praise to God **continually**, that is, the fruit of our lips giving thanks to his name" (Heb. 13:15).*

I am a witness that experiences boosts praise. I began writing this book and from that moment on, my life, my faith, my steadfastness in God has been tested. The same year I began the workshop-turned book, I had a brain aneurism which rendered me paralyzed on my left side, nearly blind and a short term memory deficit. I had several strokes related to the aneurism. God healed me completely while my doctor's other patients died that week.. Though my doctor called me his miracle patient, I was not certain I would ever be able to articulate ideas with the pen. Like so many reading this, after a long period where money was a non-issue, I endured financial hardship which left me at times with only pennies in my accounts, homeless and living out of my vehicle. Some days I wanted to write a note to someone and die. There was no one to whom to write the note and I could not settle on the method that would bring me the least amount of pain. I'd been through enough. Seen enough.

This is not a belly ache but a testament to God's grace. He did not allow the devil to devour my soul. And through it all, I maintain that God is awesome and I refuse to complain. I praise. The Devil doesn't like it but I continue to witness in praise. I am determined to do no less by God. Though I have suffered tremendously on an emotional level: disappointment in the church, being called everything but a child of God by people of God, loss of friends, family, substance – yet in this wilderness, I still believe in the faithfulness of God that He will keep His promises and that He "who began a good work in me will be faithful to complete it."

We never know from whence our praise will emanate. As we mature in Christ, our praise must evolve to become personal and independent of the collect or the corporate setting. Our praise must be subjective beyond the hearsay of the worship leader or preacher. The evolution of our passion to praise is unavoidable and consists of countless experiences that often involve suffering. Trust me; you can get through whatever you are going through. If you haven't been through tribulation, keep living. And when you are in the midst of having no other choice but to trust God - because no other help you know and if He "withdraws His help from you, whither shall you go?" Passion for praise develops beyond perhaps even the understanding or ability to resist. It is that state of desperation for – not just deliverance from God – but to know and be in the company of the One who loves us enough to extend that hand of deliverance.

As you will see this book emphasizes *relationship* with God. Accepting Jesus Christ as Lord and Savior is just the beginning of a relationship with God. As we seek to know God, He carefully and methodically shapes (crafts) us into vessels that He can pour into and pour out. In this process, I liken myself to a body of clay. God cut, shaped, pressed, squeezed and pulled, then centered my vessel. Centering is the most important stage in pottery making because the pot is only as strong as its center. Firing is what makes the clay irreversible pottery. The pot must be fired or it is rendered fragile and easily broken. Firing forces out impurities. Then there is glazing and then more firing at 2100°. "Glaze fired on a clay body, combined with the uniqueness of the design of the piece is what identifies the pot as belonging to a certain potter." However, before the glaze is applied, there is the removal of imperfections.

Therefore, becoming a praiser is a process. I have literally been through the fire. (That's another story!) Becoming the vessel that is pleasing unto God is a process linked to getting to know God. In praising, I recognize I am not yet complete. And so I keep on pursuing God to become that vessel made fit for use; to be poured into and to pour out godly exclamations.

All over the world saints are pouring out to God in praise, but it must spread so the countenance of the church illuminates a message to the world, the passion we have in knowing Jesus. We must broadcast to the world about the attributes of our God. This is not the time to be quite. Praise cannot and must not be our private thing. As the Holy Spirit fills our purified vessels; He anoints us to minister to God and edify one another by pouring out what He has poured into us.

To those of you who have a non-existent or luke-warm praise life, I trust this book will help transform your will and inspire a path to exuberant, uninhibited, passionate praise. In other words, freedom. I urge you not to let your issues or guilt keep you from praising God. If you have issues, put the 'T' in front of issue, grab a tissue and get on with the privilege of developing your praise! As you will discover we praise by calling out His names and showering Him with compliments. It's that simple. However, no one can praise God for someone else. Every person must express adulation for God out of one's own mouth. The preacher cannot make us do it nor does his or her praying or lying on of hands replace praise. God expects everything that has breath to praise Him. The choir, the praise and worship team, nor the musicians can praise God for anyone. Praise is an individual thing. Praise and worship are keys to a healthy and vibrant relationship with God the Father, Son, and Holy Ghost. I pray you read this book you will allow a passion for praise and a will to worship to develop in you and make you a witness so God will do the same in everyone you know.

In the Service of the King,

L.

Acknowledgments

Special thanks to my ever-loving, ever-merciful Savior, Jesus Christ. I cannot believe I am still here to say 'thank you.' To the host of individuals who have sustained me through my years of trying; including but not limited to my Big sister, Deborah Anita Conyers, Elder Nicole Watson, Mrs. Helen Dear. No matter how much I believe, I needed someone else to love me enough to believe as much as a river needs the rain, and so I thank my Dad, Bishop White for steering me to utilize what God has placed in me; Pastor Marichal Monts: years ago you told me that I could find happiness in praising God and that I must 'trust God'; Pastor Alice Echols for your constant prayers and encouragement; Presiding Elder Timothy Howard - my biggest cheerleader and PR man, for calling on me to serve over and over - no one encourages like you; Rev. Elvin Clayton and the endless list of Pastors, Apostles, Prophets and ministers of the gospel who opened your doors, showed me favor and appealed to the Throne of Grace on my behalf; Pastor John and Mrs. Marcella Morris and the church family at Spottswood A.M.E. Zion Church for your smiles, applause and prayerful support during my tenure; to my 'lil sis. Markesha Knight-Gonzalez; Thanks to James A. Floyd and Jessica Gagne for not billing for all your respective IT consulting; and finally but not least, to my dear friend, Ms. Patricia Lawrence for your tireless support and unconditional love in the beauty of holiness. You have truly been a life line. Thanks to Nicole and Ms. Linda Vickers for taking the time to read portions of the manuscript over and over. Love you all.

Acknowledgments

[illegible]

Part One

Praise

Introduction

As a child growing up in Akron Ohio, I attended a church where the typical order of services was Sunday school, followed by a session where the deacon would lead the congregation in a series of songs and testimonies called 'devotional service.' The devotional service would go on until one of those repetitious songs became frenzied, and people broke into what is called shouting (dancing). Songs like "I'm A Soldier in the Army of the Lord" and "You Don't Know Like I Know What He's Done for Me," "Glory, Glory Hallelujah (Since I laid My Burdens Down)" and "Can't Nobody do Me Like Jesus." As a musician, you could theoretically play those old songs continuously and not change the key (usually Cm, Gm or A^{b}m) beat, tempo, or chord. The only element that changed was the lyrics.

Over time, these call-and-response songs of the devotional service gave way to songs that reflected praises to God. The shift toward a more optimistic political and economic climate outside the church impacted music within the church, and testimony service became known as 'Praise and Worship.' Songs like the bluesy, "I Will Trust in the Lord," and "Amazing Grace" had offered a suffering people hope, but the message of the praise and worship experience came to center on commending God, than on problems and situations.

Trends have evolved in the church, but are the present actions praise according to God's expectations?

Is what we do praise, or is it worship?

A popular expression now is 'worship experience.' Worship experience sounds so hip and pious at once; like something deeply sacred or spiritual happened, but with little action or participation on the part of the worshiper. The congregation observed as the choir sang, the minister prayed, and the preacher preached amid virtually no initiative rendered on the part of the congregation. In other cases, depending on the style of service, the worship leader has had to prompt, urge and plead for people to do the equivalent of Simon-says with zero fruit-of-the-lips response.

Mixed results in praise and worship experiences have prompted the need for understanding related to what the Word of God says about the role and practice of praise and worship. *Is Praise What You Do?* points to the distinct acts of praise and worship as the most proficient methods to increase faith and intimacy with God, beginning with knowing who God is.

As a body of believers, the church ought to be clear on what we are doing when we do what we do.

Specifically, praise and worship are separate acts, intricately connected in truth, but vertically directed heavenward. We should aspire to the status of a true worshiper, acquainted with who God is, and how God is identified by His names, His character, His attributes, and His mighty acts. The universal church ought to appreciate the essence of praise and worship as separate acts of adoration so our time spent with God is constantly transformative, and progressive. We must begin to see praise as more than an abstract idea, relegated to four walls. We need to view praise as fundamental to our survival in this world, and the world to come.

I began by telling you about my experience growing up.

I have no excuses.

I should have understood what was required beyond that initial moment of accepting Jesus Christ as Lord. It was not for lack of example. My parents prayed, sang, held bible studies in our home, and spoke of God's goodness to everyone they met. What it comes down to is being open to knowing God and always pursuing a deeper relationship with Him.

I get it.

How can you possibly be expected to have a relationship with someone you cannot see?

We are constantly called on to have faith in God. Have faith in God. We are called on to love God, and to trust God.

God help us.

Meeting expectations as a believer is difficult. What a dilemma! I will not lie.

Sometimes I feel the sense of desperation that Moses must have felt when he begged God repeatedly: "show me your glory."

Moses wanted more. Even though Moses was closer to God than anyone (other than Jesus) he wanted more; like a man and a woman who share a friendship but one of them wants more.

When you are the one who wants more, you suffer such a deep ache that cannot be satisfied. Nothing can take the place of being in the presence of the one you love. And if you have been in love, you want the benefit of the complete experience; not just an occasional text message. No. you need that person to pick up the phone so you can hear the voice that – to you- sounds like no other. As time progresses you need encounters that involve sharing meals, trips, walks, or whatever 'godly' activity of interest. As time passes, you want to hear "I love you" along with an exchange of compliments.

God wants nothing less than for creation to glorify Him.

What I love so much about God is the knowledge that He seeks us out. No other faith can make the claim that a Living God seeks the company of worshipers. I love that our relationship with God never has to be one-sided.

So how do we glorify God?

We glorify God by lavishing Him with praise and worship.

We begin this examination by distinguishing the separate acts of praise and worship, followed by unveiling who God is. We must know God in order to praise God.

Praise is action. Praising God in action involves incorporating the names of God according to His attributes and His mighty acts. We praise God by lifting up hands, lifting the eyes, with a dance, in singing, on the instruments, and with a shout. We praise God by clamorously making noise to show that we are unashamed, and we are victorious. God deserves all the praise and honor. Therefore, spiritual leaders, angels, or Jesus' blessed Mother, Mary have no place alongside God in praise.

Praise may lead to worship, but our account points to praise as motion, while worship involves being still and surrendering to the

Most High God. Praise is what we do when we pay tribute audibly or physically.

Worship is the disposition of surrender. Worship is adoration, reverence, adulation, to deify, to esteem, and to exalt another higher than one's self to the extent there is no one higher. In every instance in the bible, worship required bowing one's self down or the bowing of one's head or face to the ground. Bowing to God signifies obeisance with the most earnest reverence and willingness to submit to the brightness and strength of the glory of God. In bowing, there is humility. In bowing there is meekness and surrendering of our nature to His greatness to His majesty, and to his absolute perfection.

By contrast, praise is physical, audible jubilation to the Lord God. Praise is to compliment or to laud. Praise is the outward expression of our love and appreciation of God.

I trust as you read this book, the Holy Spirit will deposit in you an unquenchable passion for knowing God in praise, and invigorate your will to worship. If your praise is already active, then may the Holy Spirit breathe into you new inspiration every day. There are helpful tips throughout this book for those of you in ministry. As you read the next pages, begin to contemplate on what the Word of God has to say about praise. I entreat you all to take the contents to heart, and put it into practice immediately. The benefits are joy overflowing and life eternally, praising and worshiping God!

Chapter 1

Praise v. Worship

For the greater part of my life as a Christian, I subsisted in the shadows. I don't mean to use the word 'shadows' like some obscure Shakespearean figure of speech, but shadows accurately describes the state of living while knowing *there's gotta be more to it than this.* Psychologically, I had outgrown my 'triangle' existence of church-school-home, and a life defined by adhering to an endless list of do's and mostly, don'ts.

The term 'life' or 'alive' should suggest vitality and the ability to move. But over time I found new life in Christ had become old, and honestly I did not know how to transcend going through the motions of the initial invitation to accept Christ, to the place of a relationship with Christ.

The idea of a relationship with the Living God is a contemporary notion and wasn't spoken when I was coming up. But back to that word 'alive.'

Alive has to do with breath, blood, water, and heat. Alive means mind, body, and soul are completely and inextricably engaged.

I am captivated by the word "alive" because of its relationship to what happens when we praise. Praise always involves action. Our Christian lives are not meant to be random, but deliberate. Over and over we find ourselves clinging to the Christian life solely because of the promise of eternal life; or perhaps to ease the conscience, or for a bucket full of reasons. But if we were to get real, sometimes we are living double lives. Can we get real for a moment?

Some days living as a Christian is weird because of the daily challenges to live in this world with 'alien' status; that is to live in the world, but not of it. So what's a Christian to do?

I submit that God has given us weapons to survive spiritual warfare – that is, the warring between fleshly desires, and the things of God. Praise is a spiritual weapon. The desires of the flesh are strong and can separate us from God. Spiritual weapons help us to resist the influence of the adversary, overcome complacency, and then equip us for this Christian journey. The best benefit of all is a relationship with the Living God.

Spiritual weapons consist of love, prayer, praise, worship, fasting, and the Sword of the Spirit - which is the Word of God. This list may not represent a complete inventory of available weapons, but we want to focus on praise and worship as gifts that God has given to us as conduits to an effervescent relationship with the Living God. I assure you, active praise makes a difference in an otherwise mundane life encumbered by religiosity and sameness.

Have you ever experienced days when no one called, texted, or emailed you? Are there days when no one 'likes' you, no one 'follows' you, nor do you feel 'Linked' to anyone?

Relationship Issues

For most of my adult life (and even as a child), I was more inclined to appreciate the company of the setting sun or a full moon, than socializing. For more than ten years I had no desire to even get a phone, or mechanisms to connect me with other people, such as a computer.

One day it hit me. I had grown tired of 365 days of meals alone. I was exasperated by sameness. I wanted the company of another person. I longed to share in conversation, laughs, and the variety that a day could bring.

As Christians, we are not called to exist in the safety of religion.

We are called to the sanctity of relationship.

A Christian life that is focused around praise is a life that deliberately and purposefully seeks the presence of God. A life focused on praise sends the message to heaven that *God I acknowledge you, I love you and I want you.* Our lives as Christians should be exciting because when we praise and worship, we are communing with the Living God.

The reality of the living God is the most potent aspect of our faith, which indelibly distinguishes us as believers from other faiths. This book is not about preaching against other faiths; however, I want to be clear in the stance that God is alive and that He invites us to commune with Him in praise and worship as a part of an awesome, thriving relationship.

Check out this truth: It is entirely possible to live the Christian 'way of life' and be otherwise detached.

Serving as the Minister of music and organist in my father's church for nearly 25 years was the extent of my involvement in actual worship. I had worked in many capacities: as an usher, as devotional leader, Sunday school teacher, toilet washer, grounds sweeper and wallpaper hanger, but when it came to praising, I was silent. As far as church goes, I took the straightest way in and the shortest route out. I simply did my job. Don't get me wrong, I have always been a student of the Word of God. I loved the rightly-divided-Word-of-Truth sermons, loved playing down home gospel music and the church was somewhere I felt secure.

Breaking news: serving or working in the church is not the same as relationship.

I used to get so agitated when a friend of mine used to say, "L. you gotta spend [invest] time with God. You gotta have relationship beyond intellectual knowledge." I thought, *really*? I attended church practically every time the doors were opened. I had keys to the church for God's sake. How could she say I needed to spend more time with God? I didn't get it.

I only wish it hadn't taken me so long to learn the lesson of what she was talking about.

My friend was not talking about the role of religion, daunting duty, or the confines of custom - all of which have a place in the order of things if you are so inclined. She was talking about a new Life in Christ demonstrated in praise and worship. She was not talking about asking God for stuff and going to Him with a hand out, but rather with hands up! She was not talking about a "season" or the cliché du jour in the body of Christ. She was talking about a relationship where we commune with God like Moses did; as we do our fellow human beings until something happens in the supernatural.

Another News Flash: Relationship requires willing participation on the part of both individuals.

You have to actively participate with God in giving Him praise.

I have never been married, but on occasion, I have heard married people repeatedly make references to "give and take," or "fifty-fifty" as it relates to roles and expectations of the individuals involved in the relationship. Those views always gave me cause to pause because I see relationships as having a greater chance for success when the emphasis demands that both individuals give sacrificially, rather than assigning percentages.

Relationships must involve connection by blood, adoption, contract, commitment or affection.

Relationships necessitate a series of encounters for the purpose of becoming familiar with one another. Hence, the passage *"come close to God and He will come close to you..."* (James 4:8, NLV). God is willing, but we must want to get to know Him in the atmosphere of praise, worship, and reading the Word.

Have you ever been 'involved' in one of those friendships where you were the one who did all the calling and makes all the effort to progress the relationship? The good news is that God will not leave you hanging. He will respond with His presence when we invite Him with our praise. He will not ignore your call or disregard your show of affection.

As was the case in my life, many things happen within the context of either praise or worship while there's been effectively, no participation on the part of the person.

Is praise what you do?

Church Programs say 'worship experience' but at best, the service was either a clearing house for A-Z, or a virtual Simon-says with a lot of prompting and pumping people up. The other choice is 'straight up' sameness (which I find most frustrating).

We should also know that serving or working in the church on those year-in and year-out events do not constitute relationship.

Is praise what you do?

I'm going to blow your mind.

Our works do little to define relationship with God. Just because you *do* stuff, does not mean you are praising or worshiping.

Serving on the various ministries and committees, visiting the sick and the shut-in, feeding the homeless, or handing out gently used clothes and diapers – all pertain to works and is good stuff – do not make up a relationship. You are probably thinking, "but I washed the toilets, volunteered to clean the carpet, and made cakes for the bake sale!" Hey wait! "I *paid* my tithes, offerings, and my assessments."

Sorry. Not a relationship.

Is praise what you do?

Don't get me wrong, works is not a bad thing, but works do not make a relationship. Concentrating your Christian life on works is like a man who works three jobs to provide for his family, but never sits down to enjoy a meal with his wife and children; he never hears the children talk about their day, nor for that matter, about their dreams or difficulties.

That man would quickly present the argument, "but I work hard for this family."

True. But your children want to see you. They want to play catch with you. That daughter wants to lay her head on your shoulder, or sit at your feet. She wants to study the lines in your hands and the features of your face. Your wife (possibly) wants to be caressed by the timbre of your voice; she wants to make love to you and cuddle.

To have relationship, people have to talk to one another, touch each other, embrace, and share moments. The same principle applies to our relationship with the Living God. We must talk to Him, learn of Him, listen out for Him and spend time with Him on a daily basis. Only then will our love for Him grow and He will grace us with His presence, and His peace.

Another point about relationships specifically: relationships are sustained by frequency of interaction. The further along the intervals of interaction, the farther apart people become, and we call that condition 'movin' on" or 'going separate ways.'

What I love about praise and worship is the function of liberation. Even in my capacity as a musician, my spirit is free from works and tradition because I have a personal relationship with God made possible by constant contact. Just like the old song "I Come to the Garden," my personal relationship means "He walks with me and He talks with me, and He tells me I am His own."[1] But before we go too far...

★★★★★

We need to understand that praise and worship are two separate and distinct acts. Both acts are directed vertically toward God. Praising God involves speaking well of God or complimenting Him for His names, His character, His attributes, and His mighty acts. Praise is not about airing our problems or difficulties - nor is praise a petition or a competition. You may be in such bad shape that you need to borrow from the guy collecting cans. You may find yourself envying the girl with the coffee cup of quarters, but your condition does not exempt you from directing your attention towards complimenting God audibly, verbally and visibly.

Praise is to tell of God's worth and His works. Praise means to celebrate God by lifting up hands, lifting the eyes, going forth in the dance, singing, shouting, and playing on the instruments.

Praise is Action.

Comparatively, worship is humble adoration. Worship is the disposition of bowing down one's face, head, or knees to the ground in earnest reverence to God. Worship involves bowing down or laying prostrate in humble submission to Almighty God.

The Word of God says that God resides or lives in our praise. Praise and worship act as spiritual vital signs to show that there is new life in Christ. Praise acts as a spiritual gauge of our devotion to God. Praise is a demonstration that we are alive and moving in the Spirit and the Holy Spirit breathing on us.

Moreover, praise expresses favorable views of someone or something; to speak well of; to pay tribute in a complimentary way. Praise is linked to 'value' or 'price' or "to invoking blessings on a thing."[2] Thus, praise speaks of something's merit or worth. Deuteronomy 10:21 (ESV) says, *"He is your praise, and he is your God that has done for you these great and terrible things, which your eyes have seen.*" The language in the verse denotes God's worthiness of our praise and our worship.

Praise requires action, and if there is no action by way of words, song, or dance that recognizes or compliments God, then what has happened was something other than praise. Praise involves making positive statements about a person, object or idea - either publicly or privately.

I think all of us can appreciate a compliment now and then, when we've done well or when we look good. Compliments encourage us to continue doing what we do and to do it better. Praise is typically - but not exclusively - earned relative to achievement and accomplishment. In all spheres of life, praise celebrates good news. Praise compliments.

Secondly, praise consists of exclamations that come as a result of us thinking good and Godly thoughts; especially when those thoughts credit the hand of God.

Genesis 29:35 records the first instance of the expression, praise. The passage tells the story of Jacob, who had two wives, Leah and Rachel. The scripture says that Rachel was barren and for that reason she hated Leah. Leah gave birth to Reuben, then Simeon, then Levi, and then Judah. The scripture says "*when she gave birth to Judah, Leah said 'Now will I praise the Lord.' Therefore, she called his name Judah and left bearing.*"

Leah was tired of bearing children for Jacob so that he would love her as he did Rachel, and proceeded to have a 'waiting to exhale' moment. She declared Judah to be her last child and went into praise! [Note: The scriptures depict Judah as a person of integrity. He saved his brother, Joseph's life; was a patriarch according to customs, also saved his brother Benjamin's life and pleaded to Joseph on behalf of his evil brothers. Jacob (Israel) rewarded Judah - the fourth child - with his birthright over Reuben, the firstborn, and prophesied that his brothers would bow to him. Later, the tribe of Judah split from Israel and Judah became a nation in its own right. Read Genesis chapters 29, 35, 37- 45.]

Thirdly, praise - that is, the exclamation of good and Godly thoughts – in turn, produces prophecy and proclamation.

Luke chapter 1 records the chain of events that serve as evidence. In this passage, we find that the angel of the Lord appeared to Zacharias to tell him that his wife Elizabeth would give birth to a son, and he was to call his name John. Zacharias did not believe, resulting in God shutting his mouth so he could no longer speak. God muted Zacharias. But when the angel appeared to Elizabeth, the Holy Spirit fell upon her, and she praised, prophesied and proclaimed.

The same phenomenon happened to Mary.

When the angel Gabriel appeared to Mary, she began singing the praises of God and talking about His wonderful works. Mary then went to see her relative Elizabeth, and when she spoke, Elizabeth was filled with the Holy Ghost, the babe leaped inside her, and Elizabeth began to prophesy.

How do we know Elizabeth prophesied?

Elizabeth proceeded to speak prophetically when she referred to Mary as "*The mother of my Lord.*" Mary and Elizabeth had church service right there in Elizabeth's tent! Those words were prophetic because there is no record that an angel had given her the 'heads up' that Mary was pregnant with Jesus Christ, the Messiah. No one got on the cell phone or Facebook or put out an email blast that Mary was coming, and that she too was pregnant. The Holy Spirit revealed what was concealed, and Elizabeth spoke the revelation of God.

Mary remained with Elizabeth three months. Elizabeth gave birth, and the nosey neighbors began to give unsolicited advice that the child's name should be Zacharias, after his father. Elizabeth said "No. His name is John." The meddling townsfolk went to Zacharias and asked, "What is the baby's name?" Someone gave him ink and tablet, and he wrote *His name is John.* Immediately the Holy Spirit fell upon him, and Zacharias' mouth was opened. He was no longer mute, and he began to praise, prophesy, and proclaim.

Next, praise establishes an audience with God for the purpose of giving back to God what He has placed in us because we no longer hold the status of estrangement. When we praise, we reflect the image of God. We give back to Him what He has placed in us. We are the beneficiaries of His image and likenesses and in turn, the best we can offer is to acknowledge God. We acknowledge God by making known that He is, and giving back to Him what He has placed in us.

In May of 2014, I graduated with a B.A. from the University of Connecticut as the second oldest student in a class of thousands, after starting more than 30 years earlier. Unequivocally, Graduation day was the happiest day of my life. I was so proud - not in the sense of pride - but because for years I'd wanted to give that moment to my mother and father. The diploma was my way of giving back to them what they had placed in me.

I remember sitting on the bleachers watching the commencement ceremony and glancing up to see if my parents were safe and looking back at me. It was no different than if I had been twenty. If I could have given a speech that day it would have been in their honor for the life they had given to me. The diploma was the best thanks I could offer my parents at that moment.

The same principle applies to God. God wants us to look up to Him and brag about Him; to give Him credit for what He has done. Just know that He is looking back at us and beaming with great joy.

So, there are many facets of praise: expressing favorable views, commendation, prophesying, proclaiming, celebrating and reflecting the image of God unto His joy and glory. I have already talked about expressing favorable views, commending, and prophesying. Also, consider that the Biblical context of praise is in reference to proclamation.

Proclamation is another level of praise that requires believers to make a public declaration of what we believe in our hearts. Proclamation means you're out there, and you don't care who knows it; you're no longer keeping your love for God a secret. "While the bible contains frequent injunctions to praise God, there are also occasional warnings about the quality of this praise. Praise is to originate in the heart and not become mere outward show (Matt. 15:18)."[3]

Is praise what you do?

Mostly, praise is the fruit of one's lips. God basks in the words of adoration from our mouths to His ears, and so do other hearers. As believers, we are edified by one another's proclamation. Not only that, proclamation is contagious. Proclamation or public commendation breaks down walls of resistance. As you begin to praise God you will find proclamation catches on, and others will follow your example.

Proclamation is defined by the fact that it is heard publicly. Proclamation is not a whisper or whimper. Proclamation is bold and forthright. Proclamation leaves little room for shyness or protecting your dignity. Proclamation in praise is like the *Star Trek* mantra: 'boldly go where no one has gone before." The Psalmist said, "*I will tell everyone about your righteousness. All day long I will proclaim your saving power, though I am not skilled with words*" *(Psalm 71:15, NLT).*

The Hebrew language recognizes the following terms for praise and its various uses:

> **Hala**l: to make a loud clear sound of praise. The original Hebrew also carried the meaning of being clamorously foolish; to rave, or to celebrate. The Hebrew term halal means unbridled, exuberant praise.
>
> **Barak:** comes from the root berech (knee); it means to kneel down and thereby to bless God. It can also mean to congratulate, salute, praise, or thank. It implies giving reverence.
>
> **Tehillah:** coming from the verb halal which means to praise, celebrate… Tehillah means to sing… specifically with a hymn or song of praise. It may also mean spontaneous singing.
>
> **Zamar**: it has the root Hebrew meaning of touching the strings or parts of a musical instrument, that is to play upon it or make music, accompanied by the voice; to celebrate in song and music; to give praise or sing forth praise with instrumental accompaniment.
>
> **Towdah**: confession, praise, thank offering, thanks thanksgiving; comes from the same root meaning as yadah but more specifically to extend the hands with adoration.

Shachach: As an expression of worship means to bow, stoop or to prostrate one's self in submission, obeisance to fall down (worship).

Yadah: means to extend the hands.

Shabach: means to address in a loud tone; to laud, praise (make) proclamation; commend glory, extol.[4]

The *Strong's Concordance* lists praise in the English translation 348 times and the word worship 164 times. "Other terms such as 'rowmah' (#7318) is exaltation, praise be extolled; 'shbach,' corresponds to 'shabach which means to adulate i.e. adore.[5] Another term (somewhat obscure) is 'oz oze' which means strength, boldness or loud in various applications."[6]

Praise may take place prior to worship; other times a person can spontaneously fall to their knees at the precise moment of recognizing the Lordship of Christ, or lay prostrate before the Lord in contemplation and reverence. In both praise and in worship, God is above the Praiser. Worship is the lowest place that gives God the highest reverence.

There are six distinct characteristics of praise: 1) Praise must entail action, 2) Praise is complimentary, 2) Praise is audible, 3) Praise is verbal, 4) Praise is visible, 5) Praise has to do with complimenting God in motion. God is the single focus of our attention. The act or acts of praise have everything to do with demonstrating our appreciation of God, our love for God, our affection for God and knowing God. 6) True praise is vertical. The focus of praise is completely a declaration of who God is, His names, His acts and confessing how we feel about Him. In a manner, praise is our witness – our testimony about the goodness of the Father, Son, and Holy Spirit. Isaiah 43:10 states, *"You are my witnesses, declares the LORD, And My servant whom I have chosen, so that you May know and believe me, and understand that I am He. Before me no God formed, nor will there be after me. I, even I, am the LORD and apart from me there is no savior.* (Isa. 43:10, 11 NIV).

Again, praise is not about airing problems or difficulties, nor is praise a petition or a competition. There is a song that says "We have come into this house, gathered in His name to worship Him." The next verse is "So forget about [disregard] yourself, concentrate on Him and worship Him."[7] You have to be willing to make your issues small in the sight of God. Your condition does not exempt you from praise. You may think you haven't a friend in this world, and that everyone has forsaken you, but you still must praise. You must forget about yourself and focus on Father, Son, and Holy Ghost to truly praise in your lonely hours.

Comparatively, worship is the ultimate condition of self-denial. To worship means to bow, lay prostrate, or to bow one's head, or submit an attitude or demeanor of bowing down in awe of, and surrender to Almighty God.

Praise is the act of distinctively and shamelessly boasting in the Lord. "*My soul shall make its boast in the Lord and the humble shall hear thereof, and be glad. O magnify the Lord with me, let us exalt His name together*"(Psalm 34:2-3, NASB*)*. In boasting, we speak favorable words about the Father, Son, and Holy Ghost. Worship is that state of awe of the glorious magnitude of God.

A beautiful example of a worshiper honoring the matchless supremacy of God is the prayer of King Solomon. Solomon had completed building the temple where God's name was to dwell. The great King knelt down in worship and spread his hands toward the heavens and praised God thusly:

> *Then he knelt on his knees in the presence of all the assembly of Israel and spread out his hands toward heaven.*
> *And said, "O Lord, God of Israel, there is no God like you, in heaven or on earth, keeping covenant and showing steadfast love to your servants who walk before you with all their heart (II Chron. 6:13-14, ESV).*

The responsibility of building the temple had been passed down to Solomon because God had said his father, David was a man of war and moreover, had ignited the anger of God when he became lifted up in pride and numbered the fighting men (I Chron. 21). David had a heart for building the temple, but God said, *no.*

Solomon could have bragged that he was 'the one' picked. He could have been prideful and attributed the occasion to himself, to his ability, wisdom, and power. He could have switched gears on God and ordered the people to bow down and worship him, but instead he praised AND worshiped. Solomon demonstrated wonder of God in bowing down.

The story of Solomon teaches us what it means to worship. The subject of worship will be discussed in more detail later, but praise and worship require humility, a reverential attitude and brokenness. Absent from the above verses is petition or request, rather the focus is on God.

II Chronicles 6, verses 13 and 14 also illustrate humility. The bible says that Solomon kneeled down before the congregation of people. In this instance, Solomon led the people in praise and worship. He did not just look on as the people engaged in praise, exempting himself; nor did he make an entry at a later point in the worship service and then preach praise to everyone else. King Solomon initiated and showed forth praise and worship before the people.

Take a moment and envision the scene of the great and wise Solomon - tall, muscular, handsome, shoulders above everyone else – becoming submissive before Almighty God and the people. Solomon was not only unafraid to become weak before God and the people, but he was emotional and vocal in his expressions about God, as his father before him. Solomon built the temple, but he gave God credit.

Corporate Praise

Corporate praise involves people gathering in one place and complimenting God in various ways together in praise. The scriptures require believers to offer praise in chorus, but the corporate praise experience shifts to a deeper dimension when we pursue God individually.

We must have personal time with God in praise. An individual life of praise does not mean isolation, or avoiding attending church by staying at home listening to the radio or watching television ministries as a sufficient substitute, if you are able to get up and go to the house of the Lord. The Scripture says, "*Not neglecting to meet together, as is the habit of some; but encouraging one another: and all the more, as you see the Day drawing near"* (Heb. 10:25, ESV).

I have a niece who took up gardening as a hobby. One day we were having a conversation about people who have reclusive tendencies. She told me that she was experiencing difficulty growing some of the beans in the garden. In the process of trial and error, she repositioned the tomatoes and some herbs next to the beans. She continued to watch and tend the garden and within days noticed the beans growing like trees. She concluded that humans need other humans in order to flourish and not die.

Apostle Paul encourages the saints to hold onto the profession of their faith (v.23) by coming together and building up one another. Consider the following passage:

> *Behold, how good and pleasant it is when brothers dwell in unity! It is like the precious oil on the head, running down on the beard, on the beard of Aaron, running down on the collar of his robes! It is like the dew of Hermon, which falls on the mountains of Zion! For there the LORD has commanded the blessing, life forevermore" (Psalm 133:1-3, ESV).*

Brothers (and sisters) dwelling in unity is synonymous with corporate praise and worship.

Breakdown of the passage In Psalm 133:

Aaron was a priest. He was a man of high position who offered sin sacrifices for the people of God. The verses speak to unity and brotherly love. David said brotherly love was so special that it was like precious ointment.

Ointment. The ointment was made with oil as its base. Note the passage states, "ointment" opposed to oil. The oil, first mentioned in Genesis 28:18 where Jacob poured oil on the place he believed to be holy, was symbolic and indicative of the Holy Spirit or the anointing. In those days a compound was specifically designed by God in terms of the ingredients (see Ex. 30: 31 – 38) usually with olive oil as its base. In addition, God instructed the people that they were not to use the oil of anointing for any other purpose. The description in the verses below established a standard of set-apartness early on:

> *And thou shalt anoint Aaron and his sons, and consecrate them, that they may minister unto me in the priest's office. And thou shalt speak unto the children of Israel, saying, this shall be an holy anointing oil unto me throughout your generations. Upon man's flesh shall it not be poured, neither shall ye make any other like it, after the composition of it: it is holy, and it shall be holy unto you. Whosoever compoundeth any like it, or whosoever putteth any of it upon stranger, shall even be cut off from his people. And the Lord said unto Moses, take unto thee sweet spices, stacte, and onycha, and galbanum; these sweet spices with pure frankincense: of each shall there be a like weight. And thou shalt make it a perfume, a confection after the art of the apothecary, tempered together, pure and holy: And thou shalt beat some of it very small, and put of it before the testimony in the tabernacle of the congregation, where I will meet with thee: it shall be unto you most holy. And as for the perfume which thou shalt make, ye shall not make to yourselves according to the composition there: it shall be unto thee holy for the Lord.*

The verses in Psalm is sufficient with references as "Aaron's head" to his beard down to the "skirts of his garments" as the dew of Hermon.

Let's view Aaron's head as symbolizing the high office in the church such as the Pastor, Overseer, or Bishop. His beard corresponds to the ministerial subordinates.

Garments symbolize the people in general. Garments were designed specifically for economic classes and position in society; for service in the temple, mourning, violence (Psalm 73:6) and weddings. Materials used were leaves, skins (Adam & Eve) linen (priest) wool, and linen with purple and white garments. The priestly garments were no joke in those days. Consider a portion of the description from Exodus 28 below:

> *Have Aaron your brother brought to you from among the Israelites, along with his sons Nadab and Abihu, Eleazar and Ithamar, so they may serve me as priests. Make sacred garments for your brother*

> *Aaron, to give him dignity and honor. Tell all the skilled men to whom I have given wisdom in such matters that they are to make garments for Aaron, for his consecration, so he may serve me as priest. These are the garments they are to make: a breastpiece, an ephod, a robe, a woven tunic, a turban and a sash. They are to make these sacred garments for your brother Aaron and his sons, so they may serve me as priests. Then use gold, and blue, purple and scarlet yarn, and fine linen. (Ex. 28:1-5, NIV)*

The attention to detail was to solidify God's requirement for set-apartness, purity, and excellence.

God wants the best of what we can offer Him. God does not want our sloppy seconds or thirds. The garments strictly marked the priests as servants of God for the temple. Every instruction for the pieces had a purpose. The engraved stones were to memorialize the names of the tribes after the sons of Israel [Jacob], which Aaron the high priest was to bear on his shoulders, and was symbolic of bearing the sins of the people. The breast piece made of gold, jewels, and yarn ensured that the priests would feel the weight of their service.

An interesting contrast is found in Isaiah 61:3, where the prophet references the "*garment of praise for the spirit of heaviness.*" Rather than the priests bearing the burdens, praise becomes the solution to heaviness in spirit. In other words, praise becomes the covering, hence the answer to the dilemma of sorrow and mourning.

Exodus: 31-43 goes on to describe the design of the priestly garments in elaborate detail as engraved with gold, embroidery, special purple, and blue sashes and tunics all the way down to the undergarments.

The covering of the priests was relevant to the manner of approaching God with reverence. There was no come-as-you-are-just-as-I-am scenario. The Levitical priests were not permitted go before God slovenly and 'throwing on a little something to wear.'

A few more points from the passage in Psalm 133.

Hermon refers to a mountain range whose snowmelt supplies the water for the Jordon River. In the O.T. it was used as a high place for Baal worship; in the N.T. it was the probable sight of Christ transfiguration.[8]

The mountain is considered sacred as evidenced by the twenty odd temples built there. Hermon was the mountain of Zion, a place of worship. Throughout biblical times people loved to go to the mountains. Moses was drawn to the mountain by a burning bush phenomenon. When he desired to confer with God concerning the people, he climbed the mountains. Jesus habitually went to the mountains to pray to the Father. The mountain was considered to be a place of strength, strategy, and triumph - in the event of confrontation.

If we think about it, the mountain represents the exact opposite of the corporate worship experience.

The mountain was a place of solitude; a secret closet. Again, Moses and other leaders of Israel notoriously retreated to the mountain to talk to God and wait in His presence. Jesus withdrew to the mountain to confide in His Father about his innermost feelings.

Mt. Hermon in Psalm 133 speaks to the order of things in the corporate setting of worship. Typically, in nature, precipitation runs down the mountain onto the land below.

The scriptures in the above entries show that the anointing ought to spill out of the person holding the most noteworthy office in corporate praise. As such, the sheep ought to see their shepherds with hands up-raised like Solomon; they should hear a halal and a shabach praise out of the pastors, Apostles and Bishops, and people in ministry.

When church leaders go forth in song or a dance unto the Lord, a change happens in the atmosphere. I have seen countenances change in the congregation when people hear and see the 'Angel' in the house go forth in praise. Though no one is exempt from praise, praise ought to begin with the spiritual leaders in the corporate setting.

Corporate praise is everyone in one place, of one mind, of the same activity.

It doesn't matter whether your church seats ten or ten thousand; whether you meet in a state-of-the-art cathedral or a store-front or someone's basement. I believe if you render to God praise with your whole heart, He will reside in your praise.

I have been in the position to help out churches that met in unlikely places such as a hotel conference room, a community room in a government housing project, the YWCA, a police sub-station, a back yard, and a storefront. Those people praised God with all their might, and God dwelled in the midst of their praise. As a matter of fact, those worship settings were some of the most spiritually fulfilling, perhaps because the move of God didn't have to contend with so much formality.

Pastors and leaders drive the helm as worship leaders of a lively, thriving church. If you want a church ignited with the fire of the Holy Ghost become vulnerable, contrite, and broken before God and the people. Give God the fruit of your lips, sing, clap your hands, and fall on your face before the Lord. Let it begin in you. Allow the anointing of God to overtake you as you offer the 'pineapple and oranges' of your lips, and this will stream to the people. Matthew Henry explicates the passage in Psalm 133 as a reference to love:

> This ointment was holy. So must our brotherly love be, with a pure heart, devoted to God. We must love those that are begotten for his sake that begat, 1 Jn. 5:1. (2.) This ointment was a composition made up by a divine dispensatory; God appointed the ingredients and the quantities. Thus believers are taught of God to love one another; it is a grace of his working in us. (3.) It was very precious, and the like to it was not to be made for any common use. Thus holy love is, in the sight of God, of great price; and that is precious indeed which is so [sic] in God's sight.[9]

I believe God wants to manifest Himself among a people united in readying themselves for His presence.

Imagine people – who having spent personal time with God and contemplated Him all week – entering the temple with expectancy (will) of experiencing the Glory of God! Time would not be an issue. Nothing else would matter but dwelling in the presence of God.

What I am about to say is not intended to be a scolding, but I also believe it was never God's intention for the temple to be a place of socializing and engaging in a chat-fest about everything but God before the designated time of worship. The temple was meant to be a place for God's name to dwell. His name dwells in the temple by way of our mouths.

I repeat: His name dwells in the temple by way of our mouths.

Is praise what you do?

As we begin to speak His names and his attributes and to lavish him with compliments, He will grace us with His presence. The Presence of God is the manifestation of the Holy Spirit, who abides and works to anoint and convict the heart. God is well-pleased when we create an atmosphere favorable to the working of the Holy Spirit.

Ideally, corporate praise should begin when we awaken with a "*this is the day that the Lord has made, I will rejoice and be glad in it,"* praise or "*I was glad when they said unto me; let us go into the house of the Lord"* praise.

Corporate praise is tied to individual praise, so that when there are a push and a pull in the service, usually it is because the assembly lacks oneness of mind and spirit, and there are likely activities going on which are out of order. I have had occasion to visit churches where the atmosphere was more like a mall with people walking and talking, texting and checking cell phones, playing computer games, etc. throughout the service. As soon as the Word of God came forth, people had things to do. God will not dwell in confusion.

(I trust by now this discussion has provoked your thinking on whether praise is what you do.)

Corporate praise begins with individuals bonded together in praise.

Please be mindful that demonic forces will challenge you in your personal time of praise, as well as in the corporate setting. The devil is always working to distract, attack and draw attention away from glorifying God. Consider yourself forewarned that you will become a threat to the devil's agenda when you praise, and if you are not under the blood of Jesus and paying attention, you are vulnerable. These are very real spiritual issues and the reason adhering to protocol according to the Word of God is critical to facilitating the flow of the Holy Spirit, and not warring spirits. Enter as David suggested: with thanksgiving and a mouth full of praise, praying in the spirit. Habitual individual praise makes corporate praise easy.

Once in a while we ought to find ourselves praising in the corporate setting like we're home alone. I don't know about you, but I love to put on a good old song and have a dancing good time as I go about the house. We should praise God in public like we do in the shower or going about household activities. Praise should be easy and free.

Pertaining to the atmosphere, musicians are charged with setting the atmosphere for worship.

Can I vent?

Increasingly, my experience is that some musicians arrive early and get set up to play meditative songs and hymns; the singers sing as people gather and wait for the clergy to lumber out of the office. As we play to kill time waiting for the arrival of the minister, we are competing with a rising pitch of an anxious congregation. I have heard laughter elevate to a roar – over the music. No matter how often Psalm 100:4 is read, people still enter with conversation and then complain when the service fails to reach their level of entertainment expectations. These are conditions beyond a musician's control and are better addressed by the cleric. Ironically, people know how to conduct themselves in a court room, in a library, or at a wedding but when it comes to worship service, a sense of protocol is absent in the house of God.

The Fruit of Our Lips

What should we render unto God? Psalm 116:12 says that we can render the fruit of our lips unto God.

At last, I addressed the notion of individual praise versus the corporate worship experience. Giving God praise individually and when we come together defines what the scriptures refer to as "fruit of our lips."

I think this reference is exciting and in keeping with something that is fundamentally nutritious for the soul; the same as "bread of life" and "living water" and "fruit of the Spirit." Our spiritual health relies on the complimentary words we give back to God.

In Psalm 116, the Psalmist acknowledges that God had done things, and then asks the question, "*what shall I render unto God for all His benefits*?" He answers his own question in that he "*will lift up the cup of salvation, call on the name of the Lord and pay his vows in the presence of the people*," all of which consists of commending and proclaiming because the name of the Lord was complimented publicly.

The fruit of our lips is the foremost manner of praise to directly convey approval, to thank and to show love.

Sometimes praising God is a sacrifice because you may not feel like doing it. You could be discouraged or feel as though praising God is like talking to yourself and answering yourself back. Other times you may want to spend time in praise and worship but your mind is crammed with thoughts like adding and subtracting available funds to pay the bills, the 'To Do' list, the phone calls you need to make that day, news reports, or health issues, etc.

Praising a God you cannot see or feel takes faith and sacrifice when you can think of a hundred other options and see instant results. Continue to delight yourself in the Lord with the fruit of your lips by faith. "*By Him therefore let us offer the sacrifice of praise to God continually, which is the fruit of our lips, giving thanks to His name*" (Heb. 13:5). For example, in this day of technology, text messaging, and social networking, the most special thing that someone can give to me is a quick phone call or a good ol' fashioned card or letter with straightforward words of love and appreciation, or kindness. I save those cards and once in a while just sit back and re-read them. Taking in those words allows me to revisit the moment, see the face and feel the heart of the giver.

Our passion for God is made known with the mouth; with our mouths we confess who He is – that He is the LORD God; with our mouths we bless His names and speak of His attributes and mighty acts. Also, God appreciates words of adoration. He loves to hear sweet sounds of appreciation in His ears. The exception is when individuals do not possess the ability to speak due to physical impairment. (Obviously, the same immunity applies to persons who may suffer physical disadvantage, as it relates to dance or lifting up hands.)

Perhaps you feel as though you need to be an eloquent communicator or that you don't know enough about the Word of God to praise. Can I tell you this? (And please don't take what I am about to say the wrong way.) You need to quit making excuses and start somewhere.

Praise is not about what you are inclined to do within the scope of your personality, eccentricities or intellectual knowledge. The bible is the same for everyone.

You may be able to 'break the ice' by writing down how you feel about God. Write a love letter to God. Read the letter back to yourself out loud. Then read it to God. Add to the letter as you learn more about God. Trust me, He will take seriously what is offered unto Him. The bible states that God created praise. *"By him therefore let us offer the sacrifice of praise to God continually, that is, the fruit of our lips that acknowledge [confess, openly profess - NIV] his name (Heb.13:15,* ESV*).*

Love and Forgiveness in Praise

Love is synonymous with unity; for we cannot have unity without love. Unity in corporate worship begins with love and a spirit of cooperation with one another. We should set our sights on the continuous dwelling or enduring presence of the Holy Spirit, over mere visitation. The bible asks, how can we say we love God whom we have not seen and not love our brother or sister (I John 4:20)? Our worship begins and ends with an attitude that exposes the heart.

God desires people who love Him, but also love each other. Love draws and love binds -even in the instance of separation.

I am inspired by stories of adult children, who set out to find a parent who has abandoned them. Abandonment makes for a different type of separation than separation by another means. Nonetheless, the adult child is left with feelings of unanswered questions, hurt, alongside the residue of rejection in the absence of a father or mother. Although the quest carries no guarantees of a desired result, the child persists in seeking out that parent. The child is drawn to know and to be embraced and loved the way no one else can love them. Children (even grown children) will forgive parents who do the ugliest things.

God entreats believers as his little children. We are connected to God and to each other by our love.

I encourage you not to allow un-forgiveness or bitterness to sever the bond of love. Un-forgiveness and bitterness are adversarial to a prosperous life of praise. Un-forgiveness oppresses; un-forgiveness weighs individuals down. We need to be liberated from the custody of un-forgiveness.

The notion of forgiveness is crucial to the progression of our relationship with God and one another. When we are granted early release from un-forgiveness and the events of the past, something happens in the *soulish* realm that manifests itself in praise.

When I think about the grace (love) of God that set me free from un-forgiveness, I begin to smile and just want to start flapping my arms and moving my feet.

I have a memory of experiencing an emotional hurt. My letting-go process entailed taking letters, cards, poems, etc. and burning them in the sink of my apartment (please do not try this at home). Thankfully, I no longer execute such drastic measures; instead I say out loud, *I forgive so-and-so,* and *God please forgive Joe Blow,* to expedite my own forgiveness in heaven, and so there is nothing between me and my Savior in praise.

Summary

At this juncture we should understand that praise consists of Godly thoughts manifested as exclamations, proclamation and prophesy. Praise is to express favorable views of someone or something, physically, or audibly.

Throughout this book you will see that praise and worship are two separate acts.

Praise is verbal, visible, physical, and audible.

Worship is humble adoration. Worship is the disposition of bowing down one's face, head or knees to the ground in earnest reverence to God. Worship involves bowing down or laying prostrate in humble submission to Almighty God.

It is important that we see praise as a gift given to us by God as a mechanism to facilitate relationship with Him. This is a fancy way of saying we were created to praise God and to give Him glory. We glorify God by telling of His goodness; acknowledging who He is, what He has done His attributes and His character. In other words, we praise by giving God the fruit of our lips, clapping, singing, dancing, and lifting up hands.

Later, we will expound on the various manner of praise, but all praise ought to be directed vertically. Praise takes the attention off of us and redirects our thoughts toward God.

Praise must be individualized. There is no getting around it. No one can praise God on our behalf or on their own terms. As individuals within the body of Christ, begin to develop a passion for praise and a rich praise in the corporate setting will follow.

When we think of praise, we need to constantly be thinking about relationship over religion and ritual. Relationships advance based on a series of purposeful encounters that include communication. Praise is one of the methods by which we communicate with the Living God. When we praise, God will grace us with His presence (encounter).

Although the scriptures command us to do good to our brothers and sisters, good works is not praise. Serving in the various capacities within the church also does not constitute praise. Praise is not about airing problems and difficulties. Praise is not a grievance, but un-forgiveness and bitterness can obstruct effective praise. We should use the same approach in praise as we would in prayer: penance, praise, petition, praise – which will ensure God will hear us.

Is praise what you do?

Chapter 2

The Purposes of Praise

For God's Good Pleasure
The Presence of God
To Strengthen Relationship
Praise Is Our Witness

Why is it necessary that we praise? Why does God require us to glorify Him with words of adoration when an angelic host encircles the throne singing "holy, holy, holy eternally?" Why can't people go to church and hang out, nod their heads to some tunes, take in a sermon, and then resume their normal lives? Why must they spend time at home in praise and worship?

The principal purposes of praise are for God's good pleasure, to invite His presence, to strengthen relationship with the living God, and allow the Word of God to manifest through praise as our witness.

Witnessing doesn't necessarily mean indoctrinating, preaching, teaching, or passing out tracts – all of which are awesome and proven tools for winning souls for Christ. Witnessing serves to validate, prove, attest, or confirm the truth. The truth of God needs no validation, but from a human perspective, praise broadcast a person's experience with God, to whom an individual belongs and to convict the hearts of unbelievers. Moreover, praise is another way of proving our love for God because when we do it, we are compliant with the command to glorify Almighty God.

For God's Good Pleasure

What a wonderful thing to know that we are pleasing God when we speak that He is worthy to receive honor and glory, wisdom and power. Revelations 4:11 foretells the scene in heaven with the twenty-four elders bowing before the throne of God exclaiming, "*Thou art worthy, O Lord, to receive glory and honour and power: for thou hast created all things, and for thy pleasure they are and were created.*"

The pinnacle of our purpose is to glorify God. The above passage in Revelations should first make us understand that the praise we give God on earth is just a glimpse of what we will do for eternity. And secondly, what David meant when he responded to Michal's criticism of his rejoicing in the Lord with the dance, that he was doing it "*unto the Lord.*" David meant *I'm doing what pleases and honors the Lord.* David meant that he could care less what Michal or anyone else thought. The only one that mattered was God. Also, The psalmist states *"You will make known to me the path of life; In Your presence is fullness of joy; in Your Right hand, there are pleasures forever" (Psalm 16:11, NASB).*

The two passages are joined by the notion of glorifying God eternally with praise.

Praise is pleasurable for God and for us. Only when we please God will we enjoy the Presence of God.

The Presence of God

I love to cook. I especially like a good, hearty meal, which usually includes spicy beans and rice with sweet potatoes. Now and then when I have the house to myself, I just want to throw a little something into the microwave and chomp it down while watching football.

One day, such an occasion presented itself and I decided to have a snack that didn't involve a production: cheesy fries. So I ran down to the kitchen, put on a little pot of grease, dashed down to the basement to throw a load in the washing machine in the interest of multitasking, and bounded back up to the kitchen. To my surprise, when I arrived at the doorway of the kitchen the pot of oil was smoking, and there was a flame riding on top of it. I panicked.

I don't know if you've ever had the occasion to experience true panic, but in that state a thousand possibilities race through your brain.

I was wide-eyed and frozen. I had only been downstairs two or three minutes, tops.

My instinct was to grab the pot and throw it out the side door, but when I opened the door, the flame only raged more.

I set the pot back on the stove. I had this thought to go to the sink and put the pot under the faucet, but for some reason - unapparent to me at the time - that idea was scrapped in favor of grabbing a tall glass and filling it with water. In the mean time, the flame was growing like a child.

I had to do something. I confronted the fire, armed with the glass of water. My heart was racing as I tried to think beyond that moment of terror. I stood back and threw the glass of water into the flames. Poof! The flame exploded and within seconds the entire kitchen was engulfed with angry, fighting flames. I bolted for the side door but again, for an unapparent reason, I froze.

Instead, I stood on the wall next to the door watching the inferno. I could not leave that house. The house was not my house.

The house belonged to my friend and her children. I stared as white flames crawled like scorpions up the walls and to the ceiling and foraged over my head.

I whispered, *Jesus.*

I lie not. When I whispered that name; the only name given to save us, I saw the fingers of fire that threatened my head like a claw, back down as though a strong wind chased it away.

When the fire died, every inch of that kitchen was black as death - except the spot where I stood against the wall next to the door. Every inch.

Time seemed to stand still. I was awestruck. I could not believe what had just happened, but mostly I was in awe that I was still alive and the house, standing. I'll be honest with you, nowhere in the minutes before or after did I reason about the Presence of God, nor did I praise. I was grateful but much too shaken to be all deep and theological.

Later, I thought about one of the most preached passages of scripture: the story of Shadrach, Meshach and Abednego in the fiery furnace. I had just been in the fiery furnace. But guess what? God was in there too! *Glory to God!*

The very Presence of God was a buffer between me and the grave, and I am still here to tell you about it as a testimony to the power and presence of the Living God. I couldn't call 911 without braving hellish flames to get to the phone; there was no fire extinguisher, and I was too overcome to call out to a neighbor for help. The prince of the power of the air does not want me to witness that the name of the Lord is a Strong Tower.

As the righteousness of God, you and I have the right to declare that the Presence of the Lord will keep us safe from harm.

Before I get carried away and caught up in the Spirit, I should tell you that the Presence of God has been with me since the moment I was born. My life has been a succession of miracles. My dad tearfully tells the story of how I was born with no holes in my nostrils. *The Presence of the Lord was there.*

Inches from falling off a cliff on a camping trip. *The Presence of the Lord was there.*

Another time when I nearly drowned in a school pool. *The Presence of the Lord was there.*

Three separate occasions when my vehicle was pinned under an eighteen wheeler, and I walked away without a scratch. And those accidents are only three of fourteen when my vehicle was totaled virtually beyond recognition and I walked away - without a scratch.

The Presence of God stayed with me as I lay unconscious on the floor of my apartment, from a brain aneurism. All along God was saying *I'm not trying to take you out of here, I just want your attention.*

No doubt you have a personal testimony. God is saying, *I want your praise; I want your worship.* God wants to get the glory out of your life and for you to walk uprightly before Him. He wants you to see firsthand, the power of His hand. God wants you to know what His friend Moses knew, that "My Presence will go before you."

God's Presence convenes with us in worship, in joy, and in times of trouble. I encourage you to read Psalm 139 where the Psalmist eloquently describes the Omni-Presence of God. He asks the questions,

> *Where shall I go from your Spirit? Or where shall I flee from your presence? If I ascend to heaven, you are there! If I make my bed*

> *in Sheol [Hell or Hades], you are there! If I take the wings of the morning and dwell in the uttermost parts of the sea, even there your hand shall lead me, and your right hand shall hold me… For you formed my inward parts; you knitted me together in my mother's womb. I praise you, for I am fearfully and wonderfully made (Psa. 139:7-14, ESV).*

Praise Strengthens Relationship with God

Have you ever met someone who rarely if ever, laughs or smiles? How many of your friends would you say seldom laugh? The friends with whom I have the strongest attachment are those who possess the gift of laughter or a beautiful smile. Nehemiah 8:10 tells us to *"rejoice for the joy of the Lord is your strength."* The strength that joy produces helps us to overcome, but also strengthens our union with the Living God. Praise is an expression of joy before, during, and after situations that require help and those without consequence. Psalm 28 says, "*The LORD is my strength and my shield; my heart trusts in him, and he helps me. My heart leaps for joy, and with my song I praise him"* (v.7, NIV).

I have discovered, relationships have little chance of survival without joy.

I am thankful to have a family that loves a good 'te-ha.' We love laughter and sharing smiles. On the other hand I have met the families of friends of mine and some of them had the demeanor of dread; as though they hated being around one another.

I believe the absence of joy is why some people refuse to come to Christ. Why would anyone want to come on over to the Lord's side if all they witness is misery and a bunch of dry faces? People would rather risk Hell's fire than to join the sad-sap club and so they choose to keep having, what they believe to be a good time in the world.

To recap: The purposes of praise are for God's good pleasure, to strengthen relationship with God, and because praise is our witness.

Praise Is Our Witness

> *My people, you are my witnesses and my chosen servant. I want you to know me, to trust me, and understand that I alone am God. I have always been God; there can be no others. I promised to save you, and I kept my promise. You are my witnesses that no other god did this. I, the LORD have spoken. (Isa. 43:10, 12 CEV)*

In the above passage, God is speaking to His chosen people Israel. In verses 1-7 God reminds Israel that He is their God and what He had done for them down through the generations; He reminds them of how He had proven Himself by way of miracles, signs and wonders. God is calling on this present generation to make it known to the other nations who He is by their praise.

Often we hear about "favor" or the "season" of blessings for the body of Christ, but this is the season for the body of believers to bless God.

Much of the scripture references for 'witness' have to do with the negative connotation of false witness or accusation. But Jesus came to bear true witness of the Father and glorify Him in His ministry, death, and resurrection. Jesus then entrusted the disciples to go into the world to teach and witness. He proclaimed them to be His witnesses.

We have inherited the assignment of discipleship. We must carry on the work of going into the entire world as witnesses. "*But you will receive power when the Holy Spirit has come upon you, and you will be my witnesses in Jerusalem and in all Judea and Samaria, and to the end of the earth*"(*Acts 1:8, ESV*).

Sometimes you may not actually get the opportunity to say to an individual that Jesus saves, or to talk to them about the plan of salvation, but when they hear you sing or observe you in worship, you are witnessing. Your praise works as a witness of your faithfulness to God. The above passage gives us to know that the Holy Ghost empowers us to be vocal witnesses until the end of the earth.

When we praise God, we are attesting to the truth of who He is, His attributes and His mighty acts. In answer to Pilot's question of whether He was the king, Jesus told Pilot that He had come *bearing witness of the truth.* Note: Jesus did not bear witness of Himself, but of the Father *(John 5:36, 37; 10:25).* Jesus gave praise to the Father, but not to himself.

We are to bear witness by directing our praise vertically rather than drawing attention to ourselves, and in doing so, we become small and insignificant as we enlarge God, which is the will of God.

Summary

There's an old saying that goes something like: "A compliment goes further than a criticism," and another expression that says "you can catch more flies with honey than you can with vinegar." My pastor in Akron used to say, "Sometimes it's just nice to be nice."

American society has been scrutinized in the media for becoming increasingly rude and having little regard for our fellow human beings. The points we can make here is that no one likes to experience criticism, plus good etiquette still demands a "thank you" when someone has performed a noteworthy or courteous act. The same traditions are true of praise.

Again, praise is to speak well of; to make known good deeds or attributes. Praise commends and honors; praise is public proclamation by way of words or acts to express adoration and appreciation. The Hebrew usage for praise means to make a loud, clear sound in admiration of someone (halal). Praise is to rave, to celebrate (tehillah). Praise is unbridled and exuberant. Praise is to sing and to sing spontaneously (tehillah). Praise is to play the instruments and to accompany the voice (zamar). Praise is to laud, to make proclamation, to extol (shabach).

Acts of praise must be unto the Lord.

Also, Praise may be performed alone, corporately or with others without respect to the number in the assembly. Praise should flow from the Pastor as the worship leader, to the people.

A rich corporate praise begins with the daily practice of individual praise. We can and should praise God alone in our secret closets. The secret closet designates a place of naked honesty. Other terms for 'naked' are unprotected, stripped, undisguised, unadorned, and simple. The secret closet offers security to disclose the things we cannot divulge in our public confession. The secret place is where brokenness freely emerges. We can bask in the warmth of the presence and Glory of the living God without the dependency of a particular mood established by worship leaders or musicians. God is omnipresent and seeks to be with anyone who seeks to be with Him.

Developing a passion for praise in our alone time enhances the will to worship when we come together with other believers and seekers. Praise should be in our homes, while we're going about activities, while we are driving or even riding on a bus.

My sisters and I are blessed to have parents who instilled in us the importance of prayer and the Word in our home. Not only did they keep us in church every time the doors were open; but they praised and sang sacred songs – my father with his baritone and sweet whistle and my mother's soprano – while they worked around the house or traveled on family vacations.

Passionate praise is part of establishing and maintaining a relationship with God.

When a relationship has deteriorated, it has first done so on a thought level, and then a communication level. When we don't believe in the other person and when we don't trust the other person, we begin to cultivate not-so-nice thoughts and consequently, the ability to look the person in the eye and speak breaks down. The person can't even *buy* a compliment from us. They could do something spectacular for us and never receive the reward of a 'thank you.'

It is not enough to encounter God. We need to contemplate God and meditate on God.

Think about it. We encounter people all the time. We encounter the dry cleaner, the grocery store clerk, the familiar server at our favorite restaurant – even the folk who sit next to us in the choir stand – but wait! Do we have relationship with those individuals? Most likely, those individuals never cross your mind until your clothes are dirty, or you need food or you attend a rehearsal.

Relationship comes out of a series of encounters, contemplation, communication and shared experiences.

You know the following scenario to be true if you've ever courted someone: There's the initial encounter, then an exchange of phone numbers and extended conversations – which may include just sitting there breathing - frequent outings, meeting each other's families, and sharing key moments in other's lives.

Not praising God evidences a break-down in our thought lives and the lines of communication. Communication with God consists of prayer, praise, prophesy, and worship. David encourages us by vowing to meditate on God's law day and night. Meditation directs our thought processes toward God. Meditation takes time.

Meditation is contemplating about the things of God. Those thoughts become sentiments that emerge in praise. As the praise develops in our spirit and our mouths, we begin to incorporate what God's Word says and how we feel about the goodness of God, which is His Glory. Intimacy results from praising the Living God, but we must allow time for praise to develop.

Developing a passion for praise takes time and effort. We must learn who God is, His attributes, His names and His mighty acts.

When we assemble together in the temple we should be motivated by a desire to experience the Presence of God. We invite His Presence by speaking compliments about God's names, His attributes and His mighty acts.

Praise is more than an ethereal experience. Praise is an integral part of a day to day relationship with God. Praise is our no-strings-attached-no-cost-gift to God.

As believers, we should delight that God has given of Himself so freely and that He wants to come in the space of our praise and dine.

Allow yourself the time to learn how to delight in His Grace and His love. I invite you to put aside this book periodically and apply the principles of praise. You should go ahead and begin to put praise into practice by repeating words and phrases that compliment the aspects of God. It is perfectly all right for you to feel uncomfortable hearing yourself speak. God will hear you even if you speak softly and earnestly in the beginning. I encourage you to begin by reading the Word of God and praying for the Holy Ghost to come upon you as you attempt to glorify and extol Almighty God. Don't forget to tell God how much you love him. You will experience a rebirth in your spirit, along with the assurance of the Presence of God.

Ministry Tip

Take note of how many times you praised God today, and what you said during your time with Him.
Were your words complimentary or commendable?
What did you incorporate into your praise?
Were you audible? Was there motion?
Be honest, did you simply ask God for more stuff?

Chapter 3

Who is God?

The Nature of God
The Nurture of God
The Trinity
The Need for Scientific Proof
Jesus in Scripture
The Holy Spirit in Scripture

> *In the Beginning God created the heavens and the earth. (Gen 1:1)God said to Moses, I WHO I AM; and He said, thus you shall say to the sons of Israel, I AM has sent me you (Ex. 3:14, NASB).*

A person would be short-sighted if he or she said they believed every aspect of the existence of God all the time. As humans, we need compelling evidence over and over to believe something we cannot see, smell, taste, or touch. For instance, we believe carbon monoxide exists and that it is harmful because scientific reports say it is. We believe in the effects or usefulness of natural gas because we can smell it and if we turn the knob on the stove, we expect to see a blue flame appear.

Oftentimes, we fail to see immediate results in our time spent with God and proceed to equate unmet expectations with a perception of the absence of God's presence. You may have prayed and said A-men, but felt as though God had pushed the 'mute' button. You may feel as though you have tried to offer your best praise, with no tangible outcome. Others experience joy in the Spirit but nothing extraordinary happens for you. You feel left out of the move of God.

Thus, we are called on to examine who God is and how we can know Him. Only when we believe God and get to know Him personally can we expect to praise Him effectively.

Take a few minutes to think about these questions, keeping in mind that most of us have been taught that the bible says, "no man has seen God." What do you see when you think of God? When you close your eyes to pray, do you try to visualize God? When you open tear-soaked eyes, do you have a sense that you just got finished doing what you are *supposed* to do, but you have no clue if anyone heard you, or if you will get results?

If we are honest with ourselves, sometimes we feel disconnected. There are days we would rather do anything but try to talk to God or praise, because today we just don't get the point.

Don't be discouraged. Please keep doing what you've been doing, with the understanding that knowing someone takes time. Getting to know someone doesn't happen in a first encounter.

When I was a little girl, I used to have this fantasy about meeting a guy when I grew up and just hitting it off right then and there. We would talk for hours as the sun set over the mountains, until it creased the morning sky of the next day. And then we would say our vows on a cliff above the sudsy shore.

The truth of the matter is that knowing someone takes time, events and – INFORMATION.

So here it is.

We know that God created heaven and earth and everything there is. God established covenant relationship with humankind when He created Adam and Eve. Adam broke the contract, so God initiated a plan to restore the association with Him. This is the God who communed with Noah and instructed Him to build a massive boat to save humankind and the animal kingdom from extinction; the God who talked with Moses; the God throughout the ages who at last, sent His only Son Jesus, to restore communion between Himself and man. The God we praise is the true and living God, who wants us to know Him.

As a child, I watched wide-eyed as folk in church behaved like something was moving them, causing them to cry, to tremble, and to speak words I did not understand. The saints back in those days spoke frequently of heaven, that and the devil. They spoke of these subjects as though Judgment was coming any minute. A little rain or a little thunder was all it took for me to retreat to a closet and repent so I wouldn't get left behind. Even if I hadn't done anything wrong! Those old saints were always saying Jesus was going to "crack" the sky, and the way their eyes glistened and their foreheads creased as they gazed upward put fear in me. On occasion, I can remember calling out for my mother or father in the house, and when they didn't answer I would think, they had been raptured away. This is how I came to believe, for the bible says the "*fear of the LORD is the beginning of knowledge...*" (*Prov.* 1:7, *ESV*).

The old saints drilled into us the verse "*For God so loved the world that He gave His only begotten Son, that whoever believes on Him shall not perish but have eternal life*" (John 3:16, NASB). From these teachings, we were summoned to believe that God is a living being and that His nature is all powerful and all encompassing in every aspect.

Inasmuch as we need no convincing that there is an Earth, we must be sure in the belief that there is a living God; that we will be judged worthy of either an eternal destination of heaven, or the eternal destination in hell.

As kids, the notion of God's existence was played out every chance my sisters and I got in the basement of our house. We would go down there and 'play church.' I always played the part of the preacher – who was my father - and of course, the choir director. Either way, you may not think the sense of God is sinking into your children or those to whom you have witnessed, but trust me, the Word is being worked in their spirit. The truth of God penetrates and plants the seed of faith in our consciences.

To know God is to know His realness and to be in awe of who He is. Who God is has nothing to do with who we are. Who we are has everything to do with who God is.

"Playing church" eventually became the real deal. One day we answered the altar call – not because somebody made us at the yearly revival service, but because the seed of the Word of Truth had taken root in our hearts. We said what we said at the altar because we had come to believe in the Sunday school God, the God the preacher preached about, the God my father fervently prayed about and sung about in those gospel songs. God was no longer relegated to swaddling clothes and the manger in Bethlehem. We began to know for ourselves, that God was real when He said,*"this is my Son in whom I am well pleased.*"

This is the same God who could not look upon his Son as He bore the sins of the world upon the cross. We – I, had to believe that God is not only the Ancient of Days, but the immutable God of the now, who waits to welcome His people to the place He has prepared.

It took time and grace, but my praise developed based on the realization that God is and that He is worth celebrating! The celebration had to begin with me. Faith demonstrated in praise had to begin with me before I could lead others into worship.

> God is not a fictional character, complete with a white beard; deep, echoing voice, blowing strong winds and wreaking havoc all over creation. God is not a caricature or weak figure of an artist's imagination. God is not "Father Time," "Mother Nature," or "Old Man Winter." Nor is He the "Man upstairs."

The reality of God had to be subjective. I had to believe. I had to stop "playing church" and be the church. There needed to be a continuous pursuit of knowing every aspect of God. The good news is that God is faithful and His mercy endures forever to those who have yet to transcend to the place of acknowledging the truth of God. God is still extending grace to those who have difficulty accepting the Word of God as the whole truth. Keep pursuing God, and He'll keep pursuing you.

Signs of Them that Believe

Sometimes I question, *how could people not yearn for the presence of God*? Where are the hunger and thirst? Where is the desperation for the Glory of God? Why would someone who claims to be a follower of Christ limit themselves to portions of truth and miss out on His train filling the temple? Why do we talk about going to heaven and never tiring of singing when we do not sing here on earth? How can we expect to shout all over God's Heaven in golden shoes and long white robes when we do not shout and dance before Him on earth? Why would a believer want to delay entering into that realm of Glory?

Jesus said signs will follow us when we believe (Mark 16:17). The first sign is love and then the works. When we believe God, have an encounter with God and get to know God, there are signs. I'm not talking about the sparkly T-shirts that have the "I am a Christian" message in big, bold letters. I'm not talking about the dove decals or the fish on the Ford. For that matter, tons of people wear the most universal sign of all around their necks: the cross. Some of those cross-wearing folk wear the cross like a charm for good luck or some other reason.

Jesus said, people honor Him with their lips, but their hearts are far from Him. They have grown accustomed to cultivating a form of godliness, but *"deny the power therein..."* (2 Tim.3:5). Not everyone who wears a sign, believes.

Be encouraged for God does not give up on us, and He gives us time to grow in the knowledge of Him and the allotted measure of faith. As we grow in knowledge, we grow in love for the things of God.

Growing in the things of God means we are setting our affections on things above. These steps may not be pleasant and will take patience, but the will of God demonstrated in us is worth the work.

Let us examine how we develop in the knowledge of the things of God by looking at how we grow in the natural.

After birth, we eat and then become more mobile, then more vocal. In becoming more vocal, we form words that make up language that conveys how we feel, what we think, what we know, and what we want.

Getting to know God and appreciate God is crucial to our advancement as believers in an effort to have relationship above ritual, and power beyond religion. Growth in the natural is determined by physical development and maturity in aptitude, along with the ability to express emotions. The same is true with knowing God. As we seek to know God, our passion for praise increases as does our will to worship Him. Praising is a means of seeking out God. When we praise, God is well pleased with those who seek after Him. The Word says, "*And ye shall seek me, and find me, when ye shall search for me with all your heart"* (Jer. 29:13). Continuing in your pursuit of God is a strong sign that you believe.

The Nature of God

> *You are my witness, declares the LORD, and my servant who I have chosen, that you may know and believe me and understand that I am he. Before me no God was formed, nor shall there be any after me. (Isa. 43:10, ESV)*

The theologian and teacher, Saint Thomas Aquinas believed that the existence of God is neither obvious nor improvable. In the *Summa Theologica*, he considered in great detail five reasons for the existence of God. These are widely known as the *Quinque Viae*, or the "Five Ways. Concerning the nature of God, Aquinas argued an approach, commonly called the *Via Negativa*, to consider what God is not. This led him to propose five statements about the divine qualities:

1. God is simple, without composition of parts, such as body and soul, or matter and form.
2. God is perfect, lacking nothing. That is, God is distinguished from other beings on account of God's complete actuality.
3. God is infinite. That is, God is not infinite in the ways that created beings are physically, intellectually, and emotionally limited, this infinity is to be distinguished from infinity of size and infinity of number.
4. God is immutable, incapable of change on the levels of God's essence and character.
5. God is one, without diversification within God's self. The unity of God is such that God's essence is the same as God's existence..."[10]

The Nurture of God

Aquinas had little to say in his "*Five Ways*" about the attributes of God. True, God is characterized by His perfection, His infinity, and that He remains the same, but God is also characterized by the seemingly intangible characteristics of light, love, grace, mercy and strength. God uses His attributes to nurture His children. God cares for us and applies grace, mercy and righteous judgment to provide, protect and punish (correct) us.

When I think about my father, these same characteristics describe him. My father is an 'old- school' dad who was industrious and providing all week long. My sisters and I could count on my dad for safety, but if we messed up and ignored the existence of his rules, we could count on him for punishment. My dad's nature meant that he loved us enough to care, counsel and correct. So here it is: the peanut butter cookie story.

When I was 4 years old, my parents bought a new house at 929 Hartford Avenue, in Akron. I loved that house with its cozy fire place and big kitchen. At least it seemed big back then. My father is somewhat of a perfectionist and apt to place a premium on functionality and being handy with several crafts, he added a dining room and 'glammed up' the place. There were two bedrooms downstairs on the main floor, but upstairs was this massive room in which he built walls to make two additional rooms. Before he added those features, the room was lined with the beds of his four daughters, army barracks style.

I remember the incident like it was yesterday.

On the Friday before Father's Day of that year, my oldest sister came home from school, elated that she had made a cookie for my father. We all looked on greedily as she showed off the cookie she had made in Home-Economics class. The cookie was huge and thick; but best of all it was peanut butter – my favorite flavor of all time. I heard my mother say,

"Take the cookie upstairs until your daddy gets home," she said, gleaming.

I watched my sister take that cookie upstairs and then there is a blank in time.

The next thing I knew I was at the foot of my sister's bed, with warm peanut butter aroma ascending up my nostrils.

I looked to the left and to the right. And then the cookie was gone. Before I could clear the last mouthful from my tongue, I felt like Adam and Eve. I needed some leaves.

I gaped at the crumbs on the paper towel.

I looked to the left and to the right.

Slowly and carefully, I slid my hand under the paper towel and lifted it like a waiter would a loaded tray, tip-toed over and placed the paper Towel of crumbs at the foot of another sister's bed I didn't look to the left or the right, I dashed out to play.

And then it happened.

My father came home.

As usual, when my dad came home all of us would 'bum-rush' him and my mom would give him a report of how we all had behaved – or not behaved that day. To be honest, I didn't participate in the family ritual that day. Instead, I stayed clear out doors.

And then it happened. The most agonizing, distressing weeping and wailing pierced the atmosphere of the house that neighbors blocks away had to have heard. And then above the weeping and wailing, my father's baritone boomed.

"Who ate that cookie!!!"

I was in trouble. He called us all into the hallway between the living room and the kitchen for a group interrogation. One by one, we denied, denied, denied – even the sister that made the cookie, denied.

Now, one of us was sort of known not to tell the truth on occasion, so the finger-pointing quickly aimed at her. Nothing was going to save her now. Not a bible study; not "Nearer My God to Thee." She already had a 'rep' and we deduced that she had taken the cookie. On the other hand, my father, determined to get to the truth, ordered the four of us to the basement and whooped us all.

After two more rounds of that scene my three sisters went through a process of elimination. The theft couldn't have been committed by my oldest sister because she made the cookie as a gift for our dad. Why would she eat it? My other two sisters couldn't have done it because they were together (as usual) the whole time, since the cookie's arrival. Bam!

The nurture of God is demonstrated in the infinite love He shows toward His children.

One way for us to see God is as our Heavenly Father.

You have to know that God is taking care of you through dangers seen and unseen, and through rights and wrongs. You have to know deep down, that your ability to wake up every morning – or even throughout the night – has nothing to do with science. You have to know that our ability to live and move and have being, is attributable to the will of our Heavenly Father.

I learned the lesson of the peanut butter cookie incident some time later.

Sometime after the peanut butter cookie incident, a bunch of us kids went to the corner store after school for snacks and candy. I was the youngest in the bunch that included my two middle sisters, whom everyone called the 'Bopsy Twins.' We went into the store, milled around, and then at first chance, took fists-full of candy and barreled out of the store down the brick street of Hartford Avenue. I watched the others became smaller as I slowed and then came to a halt. I turned back, went inside the store and looked up to the corner store guy behind the counter. I heard myself say,

"Mister, I'm sorry I took your candy," and opened my little fists to him.

The nurture of my father had worked.

I don't know about you, but I have been through some serious hard times, and I know if it wasn't for my Heavenly Father, I would never have made it out. I know that it was the unconditional love of my Heavenly Father that ushered me out of depression and persistent suicidal thoughts. I know the eyes of my Father were on me the whole while my eyes were not on Him.

I need to tell you that getting to know the nurturing side of God may entail some challenges and pain in order for Him to show you His love or to show Himself strong and mighty. Just keep in mind that all of the events of your life work together for your good so that you will glorify your Father God and give Him praise.

The Trinity

Aquinas argued that, "God, while perfectly united, also is perfectly described by three interrelated persons. These three persons (Father, Son, and Holy Spirit) are constituted by their relations within the essence of God."[11] Throughout the entire scripture, the Father, Son and Holy Spirit are at work on earth. The first verse of the bible says "*in the beginning God...*" John 1:1 says *"In the beginning was the Word, and the Word was with God, and the Word was God."* Jesus, the Living Word was with the Father.

Fast-forward to Genesis 1:26 God says "*let **us** make man in **our** image and after **our** likeness*" (NKJV,KJV, ESV, NIV, NASB). God refers to Himself in the plural. There are many interpretations of the truth of the nature of God, some of which propagate division and strife. One thing we know is that *"every spirit that confesses that Jesus Christ has come in the flesh is of God, and every spirit that does not confess Jesus Christ has come in the flesh, is not of God*" also, *"... everyone who loves is born of God and knows God, He who does not love does not know God, for God is love" (I John 4:7, 8, NKJV).* These passages ought to work to settle all disputes and direct the focus on the Glory of God and His love.

We should be passionate about our praise, but never argumentative. We are witnesses, not wardens. Arguments invite wrath, for James 1:20 says, *"A man's* [or wo-man's] *anger does not allow him to be right with God"* (NLV). I consider it a disservice to get involved with settling the score on the truth. The longer the debate, the more intense the wrath. The truth of God will always stand.

Need for Scientific Proof

There is a popular principle that God is not a personal God; that some of the events in the bible are true but all could not possibly be true; that the bible is the 'greatest story ever told.'

Albert Einstein and other scientific greats did not believe in a personal God. Instead, they believed that God is not a God who is concerned with the actions of man. This belief system directly opposes the definitive Word of God. The reason Einstein rejected the existence of a personal God was that he "compared the remarkable design and order of the cosmos and could not reconcile those characteristics with the evil and suffering he found in human existence. How could an all-powerful God allow the suffering that exists on earth?"[12]

The answer is that God is Sovereign. God is not a dictator. There is no tyranny with God. God is self-existent and self-governing, yet he is concerned about every aspect of our being. The bible says so! The bible says that God cares about all of creation: the sparrows, the grass and even the ants. He uses the examples of small creatures to illustrate how much He, as the living God, cares for us. No one has anything to do with God and his decisions; He answers to no one, consults with no one, but operates on his own terms and volition.

More and more scientists are coming to believe God and conclude the finite capacity of man to understand Him. In a *Newsweek* article, "Science Finds God" journalist Sharon Begley quotes 1977 Nobel Prize physicist Steven Weinberg of the University of Texas: "the more the universe has become comprehensible through cosmology," he wrote, "the more it seems pointless. But now the very science that 'killed' God is, in the eyes of believers, restoring faith."[13] Victor J. Stenger adds his perspective:

> And here is where some scientists and theologians currently seem to find a common ground – in the idea that ultimate reality is not to be found in the quarks, atoms, rocks, trees, planets, and stars of experience and observation. Rather, reality exists in the mathematical perfection of the symbols and equations of physics. The deity then coexists with these equations in some realm or mathematical perfection beyond human observation. This God is knowable, not by his or her physical appearance before us but by its presence as that Platonic reality. We all exist in the mind of God.

What! *Reality in mathematical perfections? Deity coexisting with equations*? A God knowable by *his* or *her... Platonic reality*? Professor Stenger got part of it right: "In the idea that ultimate reality is not to be found in the quarks, atoms, rocks, trees, planets, and stars of experience and observation."

The truth of the matter is that God is God beyond our comprehension, and mankind is inherently limited in its capacity to supply sufficient explanation beyond what God chooses to reveal.

I promise you, if you will continue to seek out the knowledge of God and incorporate that knowledge in your praise life, your passion for praise will develop because of your faith in what the Word says about God. I seriously urge you to hold fast to your profession of the truth of the Word of God. The Apostle Paul warned believers of the early church :

> *Therefore, as you have received Christ Jesus the Lord, so walk in Him. See to it that no one takes you captive through philosophy and empty deception, according to the tradition of men, according to the elementary principles of the world, rather than according to Christ (Col. 2:6, 8, NASB).*

Jesus in Scripture

Suppose someone approached you on the street and asked, "Who is Jesus?" how would you respond to the question? Would you give a scripted answer or a cliché, or would you answer like Jesus' disciple Peter, that *He is the Christ, the Son of the Living God?*

Jesus asked his disciples that very question: "*who do men say that I am?*" You would think after dropping everything to follow Jesus; the disciples would have had a clue.

Think about it. Suppose you are hanging out on the beach, and just as you are about to drop your terry cloth towel and dash to the waves, a shadow blocks your view. You squint past the makeshift visor of your hand and hear a voice say, *stop. Follow me.*

How many of you reading this book would abandon your holiday at the beach, your job, your family, and follow a stranger? And then as the two of you proceed to walk along the beach the stranger says to some guy chasing a volleyball: *follow me.*

Afterward the stranger says to a guy smacking sauce on the barbecue 'de choix,' *follow me.*

Everyone who knew you would think you were crazy, and in need of some kind of urgent help. Surely if you followed the stranger, your wife would think you had lost your mind, and she would demand that you make a decision. The enigmatic entourage, or her. Even if you chose the stranger over the wife, a week of not having a place to stay, and eating fish and bread three times a day would send you back home begging for bacon, an omelet and, some potato hash.

Finally, after the whole lot of you had been following this character for two and a half year, and witnessing him doing all sorts of strange things - like spitting on men's eyes, commanding crippled men to carry their beds and walk, sticking up for 'unsavory' women and (ugh!!) raising the dead - he has the nerve to ask, *who do you say I am*?

Jesus knew the villages were abuzz with people conjecturing about him because that's just what people do. He was a household name, but He wanted to know if His followers knew *who* He was.

The most critical knowledge that we can have is to know who Jesus is. Jesus is the Christ, the Son of the Living God. Without Jesus there is no access to God the Father.

I told you the first bible verse that I ever memorized was John 3:16,*"for God so loved the world that He gave His only begotten Son that whosoever believeth on Him should not parish but have everlasting life.*" "Who is Jesus?" is the question that every Christian must be able to answer quickly, passionately and without hesitation.

Knowing Jesus is more than a quote. You need to be convinced that without Jesus there is no connection to God, no life and no hope. Jesus declared in John 14:6 *"... I am the Way and the Truth and the Life; no one comes to the Father except by (through) Me."*

First, Jesus is the Son of God, therefore He is God. It has been said in Christian literary circles that to discuss topics like Jesus, repentance, and salvation through the precious shed blood of Jesus is highly didactic. I will never, ever stop talking about Jesus. Without Jesus we have no reason to praise. If Jesus is excluded from discourse, then the point of that discourse is nullified. In my church we recite a statement of faith every week by way of the Apostle's Creed:

> "I believe in God the Father Almighty, maker of heaven and earth and in Jesus Christ, His only Son our Lord, who was conceived by the Holy Ghost, born of the Virgin Mary, suffered under Pontius Pilate, was crucified dead and buried. The third day He arose from the dead and He ascended into heaven and sitteth on the right hand of God the Father Almighty, from thence He shall come to judge the quick and the dead. I believe in the Holy Ghost; the holy catholic (universal) church; the communion of saints; the forgiveness of sins; the resurrection of the body, and life everlasting. AMEN."[14]

You don't have to recite any particular creed, but if anyone asks what you believe, you had better be able to answer them. God is not counting on you to wear a title. He is counting on your witness. You don't have to go through an ordination, you just need to be a living testimony and you need to proclaim who God is.

Secondly, Jesus is the Christ. The term Christ - sometimes used interchangeably as a name - also refers to Jesus' divinity, His position, His place (residence), His office, and His authority. Jesus is the Messiah, and His position is second in the godhead. His place is a seat at the right hand of God the Father; His office is LORD and His authority constitutes all power given to Him in heaven and earth.

How does Jesus identify himself?

Jesus personifies himself as 'the Light' 'the Way,' 'the door,' 'the Living Water,' 'the Bread of life,' 'the Solid Rock' and 'the True Vine.' He is also called various names: 'Son of man,' Alpha and Omega,' 'Lamb of God,' 'Savior,' 'the Good Shepherd' and 'Lord.' In the process of getting to know Jesus we ought to memorize His names and the specific application. For example, if you are referring to Jesus as 'Lord,' you need to know the implication of the name 'Lord.' The Hebrew term for 'Lord' is 'Adonai,' which means 'master' while the Greek term is 'kurios,' which is also interpreted as 'Lord' or 'master' and has to do with Jesus' **supremacy** [Strong's 2962].

Thus, knowing the significance of Jesus' names implants meaning in your heart when you invoke His names in praise; otherwise you are just speaking words.

What does it mean to you to praise Jesus as the precious 'Lamb of God?' When I say precious Lamb of God, it is a term of endearment because I am grateful that Jesus humbly submitted to the will of the Father and allowed His blood to be shed for our sins by way of crucifixion on a cruel cross. When I say 'Alpha and Omega' I am paying tribute to Jesus' infinite nature. When I call Jesus 'Son of Man,' I say it with the understanding that Jesus came to earth in the form of a man and resigned himself to serve mankind, yet He is God.

The Word of God says Jesus was conceived of the Holy Ghost and born of a Virgin Mary. Jesus' existence had nothing to do with a man, but Mary was used by God to bring the Son to earth. The Sovereign God chose the manner of Jesus advent and we must accept it for what it is. At times the word 'virgin' is omitted or discounted as unlikely. The omission of the virgin birth should instantly alert the believer that the truth has been compromised.

> *Beloved, do not believe every spirit, but test the spirits to see whether they are from God, for many false prophets have gone out into the world. By this you know the Spirit of God: every spirit that confesses that Jesus Christ has come in the flesh is from God, and every spirit that does not confess Jesus, is not from God. This is the spirit of the antichrist, which you heard was coming and now is in the world already (I John 4:1-4, ESV).*

The "flesh" referenced in I John 4:1-4, is Mary. The genealogy of Matthew 1:1-16 excludes Mary's husband, Joseph and instead says, "*and Jacob the father of Joseph, the husband of* ***Mary, of whom Jesus was born,*** *who is called the Christ*" (ESV). Everyone else in the genealogy is born of the father. Jesus Christ was conceived by the Holy Ghost and born of Mary. God used Mary to transport His Son to earth.

The old King James Version underscores the relevance of Jesus' coming in the flesh by stating, *And **every spirit that confesseth not that Jesus Christ is come in the flesh is not of God**: and this is that spirit of antichrist, whereof ye have heard that it should come; and even now already is it in the world (v.3).*

We must not neglect the truth that Jesus came in the flesh of the Holy Ghost. How Jesus was born and how He died is directly linked to His divinity and His resurrection; while his resurrection resulted in His reign. All of these factors are reasons why we praise. We confess His Divinity, the miracle of His humanity, and worship Him as Lord.

> *The angel said unto her, Fear not, Mary: for thou hast found favour with God.*
> *And, behold, thou shalt conceive in thy womb, and bring forth a son, and shalt call his name JESUS.*
> *He shall be great, and shall be called the Son of the Highest: and the Lord God shall give unto him the throne of his father David:*
> *And he shall reign over the house of Jacob for ever; and of his kingdom there shall be no end.*
> *Then said Mary unto the angel, How shall this be, seeing I know not a man?*
> *And the angel answered and said unto her, The Holy Ghost shall come upon thee, and the power of the Highest shall overshadow thee: therefore also that holy thing which shall be born of thee shall be called the Son of God (Luke 1:28-30).*

The Holy Spirit in Scripture

The Holy Spirit, also called the Holy Ghost, the Comforter and the Spirit of Truth, is the third person in the godhead. The Spirit of God is referenced throughout scripture but makes His entry to earth after Jesus' ascension, according to promise.

As His earthly ministry came to a conclusion, Jesus promised the disciples that He would send another comforter. The Comforter would fulfill many functions: abide, teach, remind believers of Jesus' words, empower, make witnesses of believers, pour out of Himself, and cause gifts to be in operation, etc.

The disciples had become dependent on the works that Jesus had performed, yet the time approached for them to assume the responsibility of ministry on earth with the help of the Holy Ghost. Acts chapter 2 details the account of the disciples' encounter with the Holy Ghost:

> *And when the day of Pentecost was fully come, they were all with one accord in one place.*
> *And suddenly there came a sound from heaven as of a rushing mighty wind, and it filled the whole house where they were sitting.*
> *And there appeared unto them, divided tongues as of fire, and one sat upon each of them.*
> *And they were all filled with the Holy Spirit, and began to speak with other tongues, as the Spirit gave them utterance (*Acts 2:1 – 4, NKJV*).*

Therefore the Holy Spirit will,

- Abide,
  And I will pray the Father, and he shall give you another Comforter, that he may abide with you for ever; (John 14:16.)
- Teach and Remind,
  But the Comforter, which is the Holy Ghost, whom the Father will send in my name, he shall teach you all things, and bring all things to your remembrance, whatsoever I have said unto you (John 14:26).
- Empower, Make Witnesses of,
  But you will receive power when the Holy Spirit comes on you; and you will be my witnesses in Jerusalem, and in all Judea and Samaria, and to the ends of the earth
  (Acts 1:8, NIV).
- Pour Out of Himself
  And in the last days it shall be, God declares, that I will pour out my Spirit on all flesh, and your sons and your daughters shall prophesy, and your young men shall see visions, and you old men shall dream

> *dreams; even on my male servants and female servants in those days I will pour out my Spirit, and they shall prophesy (Acts 2:14-18, ESV).*

The Holy Ghost proceeded to make a grand entry into the earth and began to fulfill the promises which were prophesied by the prophet Joel. When we become the recipients of the outpouring of the Holy Spirit, we will witness in prayer, in prophesy, and in proclamation.

Attributes of the Holy Spirit

The English language offers one of the most excellent words to describe God: All. Everything that has to do with God is 'All,' meaning complete, including the Holy Spirit.

The HOLY Spirit is,

- Omnipresent: Have you ever heard the silly expression, *here, there and everywhere*?
  Whoever came up with that saying was trying to cover all bases just as David did in the verses below. He is saying, "There's no sense in me trying to hide from an everywhere God."

> *Where can I go from Your Spirit? Or where can I flee from Your presence?*
> *If I ascend into heaven, You are there; If I make my bed in hell, behold, You are there. If I take the wings of the morning, And dwell in the uttermost parts of the sea,*
> *Even there* Your *hand shall lead me, And Your right hand shall hold me.*
> *If I say, 'Surely the darkness shall fall on me,' Even the night shall be light about me; (Psa. 139:7-12, NKJV).*

- Omniscient: The Holy Spirit knows all things and reveals all things pertaining to the heart of God, the Father.

 Yet to us God has unveiled and revealed them by and through His Spirit, for the Holy Spirit searches diligently, exploring and examining everything even sounding the profound and bottomless things of God [the divine counsels and things hidden beyond man's scrutiny] (I Cor. 2:10, AMP).

- Omnipotent: Jesus said, all power is given to Him. David recognized the matchless power of Almighty God thusly, *God has spoken once, twice have I heard this: that [all] power belongs to God (Psalm 62:11, NASB).*

- Supernatural Abilities. Who would have a hard time believing that some occurrences are outside of human control? Weather events and natural phenomenon such as volcanoes and earthquakes are the most likely prime examples that come to mind. But there are other occurrences that exceed normal expectations. Astonishing events happen and we know it could only happen by the hand of Almighty God. The sun rises, and the earth appears - not because of an act of '*mother nature*,' but by the will of God, El-ohim.

 And these signs will accompany those who believe: In my name they will drive out demons; they will speak in new tongues; they will pick up snakes with their hands; and when they drink deadly poison, it will not hurt them at all; they will place their hands on sick people, and they will get well (Mark 16: 17,18).

- Source of Wisdom. The scriptures say God is the origin and giver of wisdom and that if any of us needs wisdom, He will give it to anyone just for the asking.

 But if any of you lacks wisdom, let him ask of God, who gives to all generously and without reproach, and it will be given him (James 1:5, NASB).

And the[S]pirit of the LORD shall rest upon him, the [S]pirit of wisdom and understanding, the [S]pirit of counsel and might, the [S]pirit of knowledge and of the fear of the LORD (Isa. 11:2).

- Helper, Reminder

But the Helper, the Holy Spirit, whom the Father will send in my name, he will teach you all things and bring to your remembrance all that I have said to you (John 14:26, ESV).

- Power Over devils. If you have received Christ and the gift of the Holy Ghost, then the Holy Spirit has given you power over demonic forces. Satan nor demons can cast out demons.

Jesus summoned his twelve disciples and gave them authority over unclean spirits, to cast them out, and heal every kind of disease and every kind of sickness (Matt.10:1, NASB).

The Work of the Holy Spirit

The Holy Ghost was sent to empower.

Once you are saved, the Holy Ghost will come upon you and empower you to do the work you are called to do. Though Jesus' disciples had followed Him all over Jerusalem, they still had to obey the command to "*wait in Jerusalem*" until they received the promise of the Holy Ghost. The disciples misunderstood Jesus' command as a political prediction, but this was not His intention.

Not even close.

Jesus was talking about readying the disciples for working in the Kingdom of God; not a geographical kingdom. Jesus was not hinting on a political campaign, but a campaign against the prince of the power of the air and the kingdom of darkness.

One thing we must remember is that our journey is a spiritual one, and we cannot fully flourish in our relationship with God until we are filled with the Spirit of God. In Acts 13:2, the Apostle Paul recounts,

"As they ministered to the Lord, and fasted, the Holy Ghost said, Separate me Barnabas and Saul for the work whereunto I have called them" (Acts 13:2, 4).

The Holy Ghost was sent to empower.

The Holy Ghost was sent to comfort.

Have you ever been in the position where you needed the company of a friend or a loved one, so you set up a time to meet him or her, only for them to call with an excuse for pulling a *no-show*? And then they add, "but I was there with you in spirit." (Another favorite is "Charge it to my head, and not my heart.") Somehow, the presence of their spirit did nothing for you. You needed to see them there, alongside you in body.

"The New Testament words for Comforter are 'parakeleo' and 'paraklesis' which come from the verb 'kaleo,' meaning 'to call,' and the preposition, 'alongside of.' The meaning is to call or summon to one's aid, to call for help, to stand alongside of. Further meanings are to comfort, to encourage..."[15] Jesus said, *But I tell you the truth, it is to your advantage that I go away; for if I do not go away, the Helper will not come to you; but if I go, I will send Him to you" (John 16:7, NASB)*. Keep in mind that the Holy Ghost is alongside you and He is near. He is able to comfort you in time of need.

What I'm doing is giving you factors that are relevant to your praise and worship. Knowing God and how He works is what sets in motion development of our praise, and our will to worship. *What a mighty God we serve*! So to recap:

The Holy Ghost was sent to empower.

The Holy Ghost was sent to comfort.

The Holy Spirit corrects.

The Holy Spirit will reprove the world of sin and of righteousness and of judgment. The word, 'reprove' has to do with reprimanding or correcting wrongs. *"And He, when He comes, will convict the world concerning sin, and righteousness and judgment" (v. 8,* NASB*)*. Jesus goes on to foretell that the Spirit of Truth will guide us in the truth (v.13). So, one last point on getting to know the Holy Spirit: The Holy Spirit will guide.

> *"However, when He, the Spirit of truth, has come, He will guide you into all truth; for He will not speak on his own authority; but what ever He hears, that shall He speak;: and He will tell you things to come" (John 16:13).*

More teaching is needed concerning the Holy Spirit. I must warn you that reverencing the Holy Spirit is critical. We have to treat the Holy Spirit with respect and never say anything negative or adjectively common concerning the Holy Spirit. Please pay attention and get what I'm about to say down in your spirit and tell everyone you know. **Blasphemy against the Holy Ghost is the only sin for which you will not be forgiven.**

> *Therefore I tell you, every sin and blasphemy will be forgiven people, but the blasphemy against the Spirit will not be forgiven. [32] And whoever speaks a word against the Son of Man will be forgiven, but whoever speaks against the Holy Spirit will not be forgiven, either in this age or in the age to come (Matt. 12:31,32, ESV).*

Who We Are

As you may know by now, I grew up in the rubber capitol of the world, Akron, Ohio. While living in Akron, I started my education at a little 4-room school house called Maple Valley School. A big brawny former WWII marine named Mr. Taylor was my second and third grade teacher. From Maple Valley all the way through Perkins Junior High, I lived with two conflicting realities; A) we came from apes millions of years ago, and B) we came from God by way of Adam and Eve long, long time ago, but not millions of years. The longer I remained in school I couldn't shake hearing that same old recycled story.

At Maple Valley, Mr. Taylor used long paddles with holes to beat into us every lesson, including the one about those blasted apes. At home, the message was one of love and that God so loved the world; at school I kept wondering how come humans weren't still becoming from apes? *Was I going to become like Godzilla? And what about the Planet of the Apes?"*

In my child's mind, I settled on the account that God created us. Not only had God loved the world, but He made it – and us.

On one of my trips back to Akron I went to my old neighborhood; the brick street of Hartford Avenue, and of course, Maple Valley Road. Maple Valley School was gone, nor did I happen to see any apes limping along the roadside. Only the house of my fondest memories was recognizable by the regal magnolia tree that stretched its arms across the lawn and the bay window.

Who are Humans? Are we animals? Are we self-existent?

According to the Word of God mankind became a living soul, beginning with Adam. God formed Adam and breathed into his nostrils. Afterward, God made the woman from the rib of Adam.

"God formed man out of the dust of the ground, and breathed into his nostrils the breath of life and man became a living soul" (Genesis 2:7).

It is important that believers and seekers know how humankind was created. If we can believe the account of how we came into being, then it follows that we should receive our divine purpose to glorify God in praise. David recognized the craftsmanship of God in this verse: *"I praise you because I am fearfully and wonderfully made; your works are wonderful, I know that full well"(Psa. 139:14, NIV).*

The prophet Isaiah said, *"The beasts of the field will glorify Me, The jackels and the ostriches, because I have given waters in the wilderness and rivers in the desert to drink to My chosen people. This people have I formed for myself, will declare my praise" (Isaiah 43:21, NASB).*

The writers of these passages understood the account of the Word of God and how He fearfully and carefully made the intricacies of man from the dust of the ground. They acknowledged God as the creator of all things.

As a recent graduate with a degree in History, I came to the realization that distance diminishes relevance of events. As a music teacher, the curriculum required fine arts teachers to incorporate a literacy component. To encourage reading, I would always assign to my students a research project involving music history in America. Each pair of students would have to randomly select a genre, write about its origin, the artists, and how that genre influenced other genres.

As I strolled from station to station to work with each group and monitor progress, I found that when a window of time presented itself, short attention spans lead students to venture from the task at hand. Instead of enjoying the space to be creative, my kids would take the opportunity to 'surf the net' and play computer games. I came to the conclusion that they had no interest in history because history was not relevant to them. I had to find ways to expand the project so the students could relate, visually.

The truth of creation is no different.

It's not enough to bang people over the head with the bible and quote scriptures from over 2000 years ago. The world needs to see the reality of God in us or else we are presenting the equivalent of a fairy tale.

First, we must reject all claims that humans came to earth by any other means and see the story of the origin of human-kind as relevant, forever.

We must reject the claim that humans evolved from lower life forms with fewer cells. Our humanity originated with God.

Furthermore, there is no way that non-life gives life to life. It makes little sense to theorize, hypothesize, assert, or assume that non-human life forms inseminate human life. God, the Creator has ordered that each species in life reproduces after its own kind.

Therefore, we can have confidence in the Word of God that there Will be no genetic mutations to transform us into something other than how we were created. Even if scientists, after years of studying and scrutinizing the intrinsic make-up of the human body, including the genetic and molecular compositions, had not finally and thankfully ascertained that the "complexities of the human body's organs are irreducible,"[16] God's Word would stand as absolute truth, AND scientists would have to utilize what God already made.

By now you may be asking, what in the world does all of this have to do with praise? As devotees, we have to certify our faith in who God is and who we are in relation to Him, or else praising God is pointless. Our steadfast faith in God as creator precipitates praise.

If humankind originated by any means other than God's hands, then the rest of the bible is a lie. God not only created humankind in the beginning, He *re*created us by the blood of Jesus. So not only were we made to glorify God, we were made new by the blood of Jesus to show forth His praises. *"But you are a chosen race a royal priesthood, a dedicated nation, [God's own purchased, special people, that you may set forth the wonderful deeds and display the virtues and perfections of Him who called you out of darkness into His marvelous light" (I Peter 2:9, AMP).*

The existence of humankind is not happenstance. Our essence is a mark of the existence of God. All of God's Word has to be true or else if one point is in error, then we all may as well party our way to hell because the rest is a massive fabrication, including the notion of a place called Hell. In his *Table Talks*, Martin Luther spoke of the Greek scholar Cicero's proof of the existence of God:

> The best argument that there is a God – and it often moved me deeply – is this one that he proves from generation of species; a cow always bears a cow, a horse always bears a horse, etc. No cow gives birth to a horse, no horse gives birth to a cow, and no goldfinch produces a siskin. Therefore it is necessary to conclude that there is something that directs everything thus.[17]

Summary

By now you are either rejoicing because you have amassed a greater sense of why praise is so important; or you are asking why is it necessary to discuss the existence of God in order to praise Him?

People are less likely to praise God when they know little about Him.

Knowing God comes by way of reading the Word of God, hearing the Word by a preacher, or by supernatural intervention that produces faith. God is not elusive. He wants us to know Him; for Jeremiah 29:13 says, *"You will seek Me and find Me when you search for Me with all [whole, KJV] your heart* (NASB)"; and "*I love those who love me; And those who diligently seek me will find me (*Prov. 8:17, NASB)." Therefore, God reveals Himself by the Word of God and by the revelation of God through the Holy Spirit.

All that we do as believers is supernaturally connected - beginning and ending with God our creator.

Knowing how God operates ought to spark some praise in us. Believing that God is, removes us from self-sufficiency because the Truth transforms our thinking and our desires, in turn enabling us to direct all that we say and do, toward Him. When our thinking is transformed, we are no longer going through the motions; our lips indicate that we truly believe in God.

There are people who profess to be followers of Christ but still reduce the bible to the 'greatest story ever told,' which explains the absence of a passion to praise and a will to worship. They perhaps, gratuitously repeat something someone has told them to say, but never transcend to the place where praise is contemplated, initiated, and personally activated.

As we spend time digesting the written Word of God, we will come to know God. As we come to know God, we will grow in love and appreciation for Him; we will want to touch Him with our words and to have Him touch us back with the Shekinah Glory. This is not to say we resolve to understand everything about God. But we can bless God by faith. We can bless God with the fruit of our lips because we trust what the Word says about Him, and we know what God can do.

What else can we render unto God other than service and praise? God already has everything. We accept the gift of salvation and then bestow unto Him words of adoration and appreciation.

> *Thy vows are upon me, O God: I will render praises unto thee (Psa. 56:12).*
> *What shall I render unto the LORD for all his benefits toward me? I will take the cup of salvation, and call upon the name of the LORD (Psa. 116:12, 13).*

Thousands of books and journals have been written in an attempt to prove the existence of God. This is where humans error. If we could prove the existence of God, then that proof would negate the very strength of God's character, including His omnipotence. Aristotle attempted to explain the existence of God in this manner: "And life also belongs to God; for the actuality of thought is life, and God is that actuality; and God's self-dependent actuality is life most good and eternal. We say therefore that God is a living being, eternal, most good, so that life and duration continuous and eternal belong to God; for this is God" (*The Metaphysics*, 12.9;1074b28-29).

Humanistic and intellectual thought – not to be mistaken for sound doctrine - can be brilliantly deceptive. Aristotle goes on to refer to God as 'Actuality' and 'the Prime Mover,' 'the Uncaused Cause,' as 'a Being which nothing can be conceived.' (*The Metaphysics,* 12.7; 1072b8-9) The error in these references is the denial of the personality of God, the nature of God, God as beginning and end, the attributes and acts of God and God as Creator and possessor of the universe.

In addition, the description suggested by Aristotle annuls the notion of a personal relationship between God and mankind, plus he repudiates God's involvement with every facet of His creation.

Other thoughts have emerged from this Aristotelian philosophy which may sound good and encouraging such as Human Potential Seminars – EST/The forum, Lifespring, Actualizations, Momentus. These antiquated Aristotelian belief systems focus on the development of the self, in contrast to the principles of praise. These philosophies belittle God and enlarge man. God demands the spotlight of our devotion. God wants us to exalt Him above all else.

On the other hand, thoughts expressed by media mogul, Oprah Winfrey epitomize the new age thinking with respect to Aristotelian and other scientific thought. Denying that Jesus is not the only way to God, she quotes from a book called *Ishmael* by Daniel Quinn:

> One of the mistakes that human beings make, is believing that there is only one way to live, and that we don't accept that there are diverse ways of being in the world, that there are millions of ways to be a human being, and many paths toward what you call God. That there are millions of paths to get to what you call God…. It doesn't matter whether you call it God along the way or not… there can't possibly be only one way. Oprah says, "there couldn't possibly be only one way. Do you think if you are somewhere on the planet and you never hear the name of Jesus, you never hear the name of Jesus but yet you live with a loving heart, you live as Jesus would've had you to live… but you are in some remote part of the earth and you never hear(d) the name of Jesus, you cannot get to heaven you think?" She asks, "Does God care about your heart or does God care about if you call His Son, Jesus?"[18]

God cares enormously whether we recognize [confess] Jesus Christ as the Son of God. We base our belief in God on the truth that Jesus is the way to the Father. Notwithstanding, Jesus said,

> *I am the way, the truth, and the life: no man cometh unto the Father, but by me*
> *(John 14:8).*
> *Truly, truly, I say unto you, He who does not enter by the door into the fold of the sheep, but climbs up some other way, he is a thief and a robber. But he who enters by the door, is a shepherd of the sheep (John 10:2).*

So not only is it paramount that we access God through Jesus but, "*Wherefore God also hath highly exalted him, and given him a name which is above every name: That in (at) the name of Jesus every knee should (must) bow, in heaven and on earth and under the earth, And every tongue frankly and openly] confess and acknowledge that Jesus Christ is Lord, to the glory of God the Father* (*Phil. 9,10, AMP*).

So, who is God? God is a Spirit. The writer of the book of Hebrews gives us this description: *"For God is a consuming fire"* (12:29). In his sermon, *Open Praise and Public Confession* Charles H. Spurgeon said,

> It is a very grievous thing to one who worships the only living and true God, to see others engaged in idolatrous worship. It stirs one's indignation to see a man worship—not his own hands, but what is even worse than that—the thing which He has made with his own hands, and which must therefore be inferior to Himself.[19]

We know God by His spirit nature, His acts, and His attributes. God is not simply nice, or good; nor is He simply a thought (Aristotle), an Actuality, or so-called Unmoved Mover. God is not identified by reason or the righteousness of man. The bible describes our righteousness:

> *For we have all become like one who is unclean [ceremonially, like a leper], and all our righteousness (our best deeds of rightness and justice) is like* ***filthy rags*** *or a polluted garment; we all fade like a leaf, and our iniquities, like the wind, take us away [far from God's favor, hurrying us toward destruction] (Isa.64:6, AMP).*

Knowledge by way of devices or instruments created by mankind to measure, tests, or scientifically conclude, are finite and fallible. When it comes to accepting or believing the existence of things not seen, people have no problem accepting that a few feet or miles can separate weather patterns; we accept the strength of a narrow twister that destroys a vast area. (Even as I write this, the winds of the mighty hand of God are at work outside my window and all of creation is at His command. There is no hiding from the Will of God.)

We can even acknowledge man's ability to create mechanisms intended to access information and each other all over the world - such as the internet and text messaging, faxing or the transmission of information by way of satellites and television. These are mediums subject to scientific principles developed to provide conclusive evidence.

Similarly, we are required to believe God by faith because the truth of His reality depends not on whether we believe, but on the self-existence of God's truth. It is to our benefit to believe and receive the fact of His existence. The truth of God's existence needs no validation or substantiation. Who God is, in the deified Persons of Father, Son and Holy Ghost, make up the reasons why He is worthy to be praised.

Ministry Tip:
Study Psalm 119

Part Two

Praise in Action

Chapter 4

What We Must Do

Obey
Purity
Humility
Tame Tongue
Heart Free of Strife
Truth in Praise
Draw Nigh to God

I don't know if you are old enough – and I'm probably dating myself - but do you remember the days when there were no showers in your bathroom at home? Those were the days when you had to run a tub of hot water and you sat there and soaked for a while, then washed quickly if you were smart. I never really liked baths because the clusters of solidified filth would start swimming around in the water and re-attach itself to my body; which served as a disgusting signal that it was time to get out.

Most of us address the condition of our bodies before proceeding with the day's activities, especially if those activities involve venturing outside the home and convening with other people. I think it's safe to say that no one enjoys being told they don't smell too fresh.

The scriptures reference God's distinction between the holy and the unclean.

Although Psalm 150 states, "let everything that hath breath, praise the Lord," in fact, most of the scriptural texts admonishing us to praise, make little mention of any prerequisite to praise. The bible delineates the condition of repentance to approaching God in prayer, but I believe anyone can praise God as a demonstration that we believe who He is. As we grow in faith, there are some things that will happen in the Spirit realm to advance a deeper level of praise and a deeper relationship. As we acknowledge God in praise, our love becomes perfected, and we begin to show love by obedience, purity of heart, and humility. As a result, we will aim to guard our tongue and submit to the truth in our way of life as we draw nigh to Him.

Obedience

You can be the most passionate praiser, but if you don't obey God, it is for nothing. "Obedience transcends everything."[20] "*So Samuel said: Has the LORD as great delight in burnt offerings and sacrifices, As in obeying the voice of the LORD? Behold, to obey is better than sacrifice, And to heed than the fat of rams" (I Sam. 15:22, NKJV).*

Our first form of praise is in how we live, in reference to obeying God. This is why the Apostle Paul taught in Romans 12:1 that we should present our bodies as living sacrifices: *"appeal to you therefore, brothers, by the mercies of God, to present your bodies as a living sacrifice holy and acceptable to God, which is your spiritual worship" (Romans 12:1, ESV).*

Unmistakably, giving ourselves over to God in obedience is a form of worship. In Romans chapter 13 Paul extends the theme of obedience to include civic leaders and citizens. When we obey authority, we give obeisance to God. So, it is impossible to be a living sacrifice, holy, and acceptable to God if we disobey, for Jesus said, "*If you [really] love Me, you will keep (obey) My commands" (John 14:15, AMP).*

In the next verse Jesus lays out the remainder of the if-you-do-this-I'll-do-this theme by declaring "*And I will ask the Father, and He will give you another Comforter (Counselor, Helper, Intercessor, Advocate, Strengthener, and Standby) that He may remain with you forever"(John 14:16).* We see a repeat of the phrases, *"if you will hear my voice"* and *"if you will obey my voice"* throughout Old Testament scripture in reference to the condition of what God will do, what He will not do, and obedience as our way of staying connected to God and demonstrating love for Him.

The subject of obedience is an exhaustive one, but sin was inaugurated by way of dis-obedience, thus separating mankind from the company and favor of God. Mankind (Adam and Eve) then saw their flesh, was condemned, and sought to hide from (ignore, escape) the voice of God. To be obedient is to listen and adhere to the will of God (John 10:27 NASB). In his teaching on the matter of obeying the Will of God, Pastor John Hagee of Cornerstone Church uses the illustration of the rich, young ruler and He asserts:

> "It's not what you believe, it's what [who] you obey. He [the rich, young ruler] believed He was the Son of God, he just couldn't obey Him. And if all you do is believe, without obedience you really have no more faith than a demon. Demons hear, believe the name of God and tremble… Thy Will be done is the least we can do and it is the most we can do. Nothing takes the place of the absolute surrender to the Will of God"[21]

Accordingly, if you want to be connected to God in your praise, submit your will to the will of God. Hagee further affirms, "Delayed obedience is dis-obedience."[22] Obedience is primary with God. In Deuteronomy 28:58, God said, "*If you are not careful to observe all the words of this law which are written in this book, to fear this honored and awesome name, the Lord your God, then the Lord will bring extraordinary plagues on you and your descendants even severe and lasting plagues, and miserable chronic sicknesses.*" Verse 58 is a part of the blessings/curses outlined in chapters 27 and 28. First God puts forth the promises of blessings for those who are obedient followed by the extensive consequences for those who disobey. These passages remain relevant today because believers under the period of grace (v. the law) are the inheritors of God's promises.

Purity

God was particular in the biblical times about how the people should approach Him. Additionally, God issued detailed instructions to the priests who made sacrifices. By comparison, these were sacrifices offered for transgressions. The point here is that a perfect God wanted no blemishes on the animals. As a matter of fact God is so perfect that one time he instructed to make an altar – without an ax!! Huh? If an axe was used, then the altar was no longer fit to be used for the sacrifices. Check out *Exodus 20:25: "And if thou wilt make me an **altar** of stone, thou shalt not build it of hewn stone: for if thou lift up thy tool upon it, thou hast polluted it."* Read the following passage of the instructions that God gave Moses. Please do not skip the next section:

> *Now the LORD spoke to Moses and to Aaron, saying, "This is the statute of the law that the LORD has commanded: Tell the people of Israel to bring you a red heifer without defect, in which there is no blemish, and on which a yoke has never come. And you shall give it to Eleazar the priest, and it shall be taken outside the camp and slaughtered before him. And Eleazar the priest shall take some of its blood with his finger and sprinkle some of its blood toward the front of the tent of meeting. And the heifer shall be burned in his sight… Then the priest shall wash his clothes and bathe his body in water, and afterward he may come into the camp. But the priest shall be unclean until evening. The one who burns the heifer shall wash his clothes in water and bathe his body in water and shall be unclean until evening. And a man who is clean shall gather up the ashes of the heifer and deposit them outside the camp in a clean place… And the one who gathers the ashes of the heifer shall wash his clothes and be unclean until evening. And this shall be a perpetual statute for the people of Israel, and for the stranger who sojourns among them (Num. 19:1-9, ESV).*

The above account details how important cleanliness is to God. We no longer make animal sacrifices for our sins because Jesus gave Himself up as the last and only perfect sacrifice for all of mankind, for all time.

Purity concerns the condition of the heart rather than the outside appearance. Belief that God sent His only Son Jesus in the flesh and that He rose from the dead cleanses us on the inside (I John 1:7, ESV). If you have not yielded your heart to God and someone has shared this book with you, the plan of salvation may seem over-simplified, but there is good news. The Holy Scriptures state that sin does not have to keep us separated, for grace through faith in the shed blood restores relationship with God. I know there are people who say this discourse is theological, formal or didactic, but the aim is to ignite an on-going transformative praise, rather than assist in going through the motions and omit the foundation. God holds those of us in ministry accountable for people's souls. We cannot simply offer a partial truth.

Obedience, holiness, set-apartness, and cleanliness must be integrated components in our way of life. You may have some challenges along the way, but the bible states these criteria as our "reasonable service" (Romans 12:1). God makes no demands on us which we cannot accomplish. Attaining salvation is not difficult, and for that we should be grateful. Cleanliness is accomplished by simply coming clean before Him. God already knows the ins and outs of the stuff in our closets, and what we do in the dark. Again, confession is for our benefit.

A component of confession is forgiveness. We must forgive those who have committed wrong toward us and appeal to God for them en route to purification. This is important because we want to present ourselves before God with a clean heart so that He receives our sacrifices of praise.

Isaiah 59:1, 2 states,

> *Behold, the Lord's hand is not shortened at all, that it cannot save, nor His ear dull with deafness, that it cannot hear.*
> *But your iniquities have made a separation between you and your God, and your sins have hidden His face from you, so that He will not hear. (AMP)*

King David said,

> *Hide Your face from my sins and blot out all my guilt and iniquities.*
> *Create in me a clean heart, O God and renew a right, persevering, and steadfast sprit within me.*
> *Cast me not away from your presence and take no Your Holy Spirit from me*
> *(Psa. 51: 9-11, AMP).*

The previous entries give us to know that if we are feeling disconnected from God when we praise, we should consider if we are coming before Him with clean hands. How have you occupied your time this week? Were you idle? What was your thought process in that time of indolence? What did your eyes behold, and what did you allow passage into your soul? If you have allowed unclean things to sneak through the portals of your soul, are you burdened with guilt? The *Message Bible* further expounds the passage in Psalm 51:

> Soak me in your laundry and I'll come out clean,
> scrub me and I'll have a snow-white life.
> Tune me in to foot-tapping songs,
> set these once-broken bones to dancing.
> Don't look too close for blemishes,
> give me a clean bill of health.
> God, make a fresh start in me,
> shape a Genesis week from the chaos of my life.
> Don't throw me out with the trash,
> or fail to breathe holiness in me.
> Bring me back from gray exile,
> put a fresh wind in my sails!
> Give me a job teaching rebels your ways
> so the lost can find their way home.
> Commute my death sentence, God, my salvation God,
> and I'll sing anthems to your life-giving ways.
> Unbutton my lips, dear God;
> I'll let loose with your praise (v. 9-15, MSG).

In Psalm, chapters 47 through 50 David praised God and admonished the people to do the same. In chapter 51 he begins by asking God to have mercy on him. After asking God to do A-Z on his heart, the Psalmist ends with a benediction promising to praise. The Reference notes in the Scofield Study system state:

> The 51rst Psalm must ever be, in its successive steps the mold of the experience of a sinning believer. The steps are; 1) sin

> thoroughly judged before God (vv. 1-6); 2) forgiveness and cleansing through the blood (v. 7); 3) cleansing (vv7-10) 4) Spirit-filled for joy and power (vv.11-12) 5) service (v.13) 6) worship (vv.14-17; and 7) and the restored believer in fellowship with God. It was David's pathway to restored communion after his sin with Bath-Sheba by murdering her husband," so he could satisfy his lust for her.[23]

We may also pray Psalm 51: 7,

> *Purge me with hyssop [a shrub used in water to purify] and I shall be clean: wash me, and I shall be whiter than snow.*

Malachi 3:2-4 states,

> *But who can endure the day of His coming? And who can stand when He appears? For He is like a refiner's fire and like fullers' soap.*
>
> *He will sit as a refiner and purifier of silver, and He will purify the priests, the sons of Levi, and refine them like gold and silver, that they may offer to the Lord offerings in righteousness.*
>
> *Then will the offering of Judah and Jerusalem be pleasing to the Lord as in the days of old and as in ancient years. (Mal. 3:2-4, AMP)*

These verses are worthy of note because the sons of Levi or the priestly order of the Levites, were a tribe of Israel appointed to be the praisers. The Levites were set apart to care for the temple, but a major part of their duties was to praise God day and night. The background is that the namesake of the tribe – Levi – was far from honorable. His father Jacob referred to him as an "*instrument of cruelty*" since he and his brother Simeon killed all the people of a certain town and confiscated their stuff because Sechem, who was uncircumcised, slept with their sister Dinah. Yet God did not hang their past over their heads. The God of Abraham, Isaac, and Jacob entrusted them with an inheritance as keepers of the tabernacle including the vessels and the perimeter *(Num. 1:49-53 ESV)*.

God said, "*So the Levites shall be mine.*" The Levites also offered sacrifices for the sins of the people.: "*Is it not enough for you that the God of Israel has separated you from the rest of the congregation of Israel, to bring you near to Himself, to do the service of the tabernacle of the LORD, and to stand before the congregation to minister to them*" *(Numbers 16:9, NASB)*.

God is saying that the praisers needed to offer sacrifices in righteousness. The Levites' sacrifices consisted of praise. Interestingly, the tribe of Judah inherited the name that means praise. Jesus came down through forty-two generations of the tribe of Judah, which also produced the kings of Israel. The prerequisites for the Levites were exceptional because they were also the priests who offered sacrifices for the sins of the people. The Levites had to get themselves right before they could act as mediators for others or operate in their appointed office as praisers.

There are believers who desire a high worship experience; they want God's Spirit to descend into the temple, so they can enter the Holy of holies. God wants to meet us, but there is a degree of praise attainable by first cleansing our hearts. There is a degree of separation required to enter the Holy of holies.

In the days of old the priest had to offer sacrifices for his sins before entering to offer sacrifice for the sins of the people. After offering sacrifices, he had to go through another purification process.

Purification under grace is so much more simplified than under the law because Jesus is the High Priest with the only authority to welcome us to come boldly before the mercy seat. Praise can happen by itself but ultimately, we should want to attain a praise that is pleasing beyond motion and emotion. This is unprompted praise that comes out of Godly relationship.

How to Do it:

1. Confession. We first admit that we are fallible and either knowingly or unknowingly missed the mark in thought, word or deed. This is how we come clean to God and offer unto

Him ourselves as living sacrifices of praise. The admission has to be verbal. For the bible says that we must confess with our mouths. Someone else's prayers on our behalf cannot substitute for personal confession.

Confession purifies and leaves us nowhere to hide. Confession exposes the darkness and the secrecy of sin. Confession weakens the power the devil has to hold your sins over your head. It becomes a done deal; it's out there. Confession is liberating. Confession is for our benefit because an omniscient God already knows. Public confession pleases God. Confession uncovers then allows covering by the blood of Jesus so that God can look upon us and hear us.

2. <u>Believe.</u> Believe that God sent His Son Jesus to be the ultimate sacrifice. We become purified, and we become sanctified by believing on Him and asking Him to forgive us of all our faults and to cover our sins with His shed blood. He is faithful and just to forgive us; unlike the Old Testament where the people or the priests were required to kill animals (depending on the type of sacrifice) and sprinkle blood. After coming in contact with the blood, the priest was deemed unclean until evening.

As a believer, the steps above should be applied daily to keep your spiritual valves clean.

Hebrews 12:24 states,

> *And to Jesus the mediator of the new covenant, and to the blood of sprinkling, that speaketh better things than that of Abel.*

> *My little children, I am writing these things to you so that you may not sin. But if anyone does sin, we have an advocate with the Father, Jesus Christ the righteous. He is the propitiation for our sins, and not for ours only but also for the sins of the whole world. And by this we know that we have come to know him, if we keep his commandments (I John 2:1-3, ESV).*

Apostle Paul used as an example the sacrifices of Abel to illustrate that Jesus was the better, more perfect sacrifice. He taught, "*It was therefore necessary that the patterns of things in the heavens should be purified with these; but the heavenly things themselves with better sacrifices than these" (Heb. 9:23).*

Jesus is the way to the Father by His shed blood on the cross. He made the mercy seat available to all of us by the resurrection. The Book of Hebrews states that He has given us access to the throne that we can come boldly to the throne of grace that we may obtain mercy. Heb. 4:16,

> *Let us therefore come boldly unto the throne of grace, that we may obtain mercy, and find grace to help in time of need.*

> *Hezekiah assigned the priests and Levites to divisions—each of them according to their duties as priests or Levites—to offer burnt offerings and fellowship offerings, to minister, to give thanks and to sing praises at the gates of the LORD's dwelling (II Chron. 31:2).*

II Chr. 29 speaks to how the doors to the temple of the Lord had been closed and there had been no sacrifices made. First, Hezekiah instructed the priests to consecrate themselves and later they purified the temple.

To consecrate means to be committed to a holy purpose; to be dedicated for the purpose of worship. The term consecrate is first mentioned with respect to sanctifying Aaron for the office of priest (Exodus 28:3) as well as his garments. There was nothing day-to-day or common about the priestly garments. The garments and the artifacts were exclusively set apart for a divine purpose. Consecration suggests the farthest distance between the Holy and the unholy. If you want to experience a deeper level of praise, set yourself apart to a holy way of life. Anyone can go through the motion of praise, but we achieve the ultimate goal of a closer relationship with God when our lives are consecrated for a holy purpose, daily.

Later, in Nehemiah Chapter 9 the Israelites return from exile and captivity to rebuild the walls that were in ruin and burning. They did this under the leadership of Nehemiah. Upon completion of the walls, the people began to set themselves back in order with a Holy God. The events surround building the wall for protection, setting in order the genealogy. The people were reminded of the law, and they worshiped (8:6). They were taught the feast of the Tabernacle and they sat in sackcloth and ashes in the booths to confess their sins and the iniquities of their fathers.

Sometimes set-apartness means running to seek the face of God in prayer and praise in the middle of the day. Sometimes we feel a pulling or an urgent need to wait in the presence of God, and we race to the spot where we can commune with Him. This Communing with God may be in the company of others, or you may have to go it alone to pour out your soul to the point where your face becomes saturated with tears. It's all right to weep, to cry out, and to mourn. The Israelites in Nehemiah's day mourned until they became broken before Almighty God. They made themselves insignificant and lamented before God, and God heard them.

God is looking to purify unto Himself a holy people *(Titus 2:14)*. He wants a Holy people as He is Holy (*Peter 1:16).* To be Holy is to be set apart, separated from uncleanness and ungodliness, devoted, and consecrated in our activities, our thoughts, our conversations, and how we occupy our time. This includes our choice of entertainment. It is impractical to think that we can sit in front of the television hour after hour, day in and day out, allowing foolishness and filth to enter our spirit and at the same time be separated unto God: "*For as he thinks within himself, so he is. He says to you, Eat and drink! But his heart is not with you (Prov. 23:7, NASB).*

Remember, nasty, ungodly thoughts will take up residence in your mind like a relative or uninvited visitor that won't leave and surface at a time of prayer, or when you desire to spend time with God. John Wesley's commentary expounds the verse this way, "You are not to judge him by his words, but by the constant temper of his mind." Before we set ourselves to serve in the kingdom, let us purify ourselves as vessels of honor.

Humility

> *Humble yourself in the sight of the Lord and He shall lift you up. (James 4:10)*
>
> *For thus saith the high and lofty One that inhabiteth eternity, whose name is Holy; I dwell in the high and holy place, with him also that is of a contrite and humble spirit, to revive the spirit of the humble, and to revive the heart of the contrite ones (Isa. 57:15).*

There was a time when I did not praise and participate much in the service beyond my duty as a musician because I was concerned that someone would see me praising and have something to say. It took God delivering me from death's door to actually humble me to a place of praise. My praise was activated when I nearly died. I see people all the time who are too busy holding on to their dignity or the traditions in the Temple of the Lord; afraid to become broken. Brokenness requires humility. James 4:10 reads, "*Humble yourselves before the Lord, and he will lift you up in honor*" (NLT).

I would not trade anything for my praise. During that time when the death angel was beckoning, I could not lift my hands, could not raise a praise, nor see to read the Word of God. I had had several strokes and seizures associated with the brain aneurism. According to my family, the doctors stated that if I had lived, I would be blind and paralyzed on my left side; that I would never play the organ again. But the God I serve – who is Jehovah-rapha – delivered me and awakened me. I sent every nay-saying doctor and physical therapist out of my room. With all that I have been through, I am not perfect and still have to pray to God to give me a clean heart. The ordeal taught me that I must remain insignificant in the sight of God but I will never deny God the glory and honor that is due unto Him.

The Amplified version reads: "*Humble yourselves [feeling very insignificant] in the presence of the Lord, and He will exalt you [He will lift you up and make your lives significant]... for God resisteth the proud and giveth grace to the humble" (I Peter 5:5, AMP).*

There is no shame in praising God and no shame in others seeing you praising God without restraint or inhibition. Praise God every moment you can because the next one is not promised to you.

Humility means crucifying the flesh, submissiveness or denying one's self. It takes humility to praise in an unabashed, loud (halal) and public way. Periodically, I ask God to "kill me! Mark me. Take ownership over every aspect of my being." By this I mean commanding my flesh to die – to be crucified and buried so I can become that living epistle or witness, for Him.

In the days of the priests, the Levites cried out with a loud voice (Nehemiah 9:4). They played trumpets and instruments (zamar) ordained by David the King. When we get loud (shabach) in our praise we are bold in our expression. We are not ashamed to praise God. We purpose in our hearts to proclaim Him and declare Jesus as Lord regardless of who hears our praise. The exception to this is when the Word of God is going forth, when the Holy Spirit is at work, and someone is rendering prophecy or revelation. In these situations, we are to be still and silent. God would not have us to override the Holy Spirit or the Word. There is a time for everything.

The weird thing about the notion of humility in praise is that the Word of God also tells us to come boldly before the throne of Grace. Some may pick apart this scripture and say the bible is contradictory. The context of the passage in Hebrews 4 specifically refers to the provision made for forgiveness.

Apostle Paul continues to talk about Jesus, our High Priest who, having come to earth in the form of a man, knows what it's like to be human, yet without sin. So we are to come boldly before God for the purpose of forgiveness, meaning that God, through His Son Jesus is approachable. But the deeper we go into praise and worship we will experience brokenness; humility in the willingness to become vulnerable before the Lord. Humility means becoming small so that He is enlarged and extolled.

I want to encourage you not to shy away from humility.

Honestly? I wish I could be more humble.

I am amazed by the various interpretations of the term humility. Some people equate humility with weakness or being a 'punk' or 'sissified.' Trust me, Jesus was all man and all God and those derogatory characterizations have 'zero' to do with humility. There wasn't a weak bone in Jesus' body. Please understand that humility is brokenness, not broke or broken down. We are abased so that He is exalted.

Exalting God is the purpose of praise. In his sermon, "*Judging Yourself Unworthy*" Pastor Jentezen Franklin of Free Chapel declares, "Humility is not putting yourself down, it is lifting Jesus up. You can debase yourself all day and it will not be a blessing. Praise is not a burden, but a blessing."[24]

Humility may mean setting aside how we appear while we praise God.

In the Old days of the black Pentecostal church a person wasn't considered saved until they had stayed on the altar - for as much as several hours – calling on Jesus, over and over and until there was spit forming at the mouth. This was called "tarrying." Somebody would wipe that spit but usually the saints would encircle the seeker and shout out cheers, urging us to call Jesus and to say thank you Jesus, etc. and to do it really fast until it sounded like you were speaking in tongues.

This was that old method of the churches that came out of the Azusa Street revivals but as it relates to praise, those old saints didn't care about perspiration, saliva, or if clothes came off, wigs fell off, and teeth may have come out, but they were serious about salvation and serious about glorifying God. They praised God without respect to their condition.

Churches had yet to reach a comfort level in terms of the aesthetic. The pews were hard, and if people danced too much, those ol' creaky floors took on a rhythm of their own. Many years ago you didn't see forests of opulent flowers lining the altar. There was no air conditioning in the sweltering heat; nor was the heat perfect for the bitter cold. The drummer may have had only one stick and the guitarist three strings while the piano sounded like it had been sitting in a damp basement. But with all of these conditions lavish praises were dispatched to the heavens with joy and trembling. People went through hard times back then. There was a 'mourners' bench, but people didn't exactly mourn there; they praised. The people loved God, and they praised God with passion in spite of their troubles and their circumstances.

Humility suggests submissiveness, brokenness, and a contrite heart. This is not something we need to force but something God appreciates as a result of our attitude and heart that fears Him. "*The sacrifices of God are a broken spirit; a broken and contrite heart, O God, you will not despise" (Psa.51:17, ESV).*

We should never be embarrassed about our public confession regardless of the emotional response. The world is passionate and vocal about whom they love and so should believers. Jesus said if we are ashamed to own Him, He will be shamed to own us before His Father in heaven. So take ownership in praising God. Boldly proclaim Him as your own in a way that becomes known to others.

Tame Tongue

I am a witness that one of the most difficult things to do is to control the tongue.

As a child - other than the occasional prank - I was a somewhat quiet kid. I don't know why, but for some unknown reason kids who don't bother anybody, get picked on by everybody. I was one of those kids. I was picked on because I was ugly, my outfit was ugly, my shoes were ugly, I was told I had a hooknose - AND I had the "cooties," besides, I was too skinny and too fat (all at once).

One day, and without warning I became less passive, and it took microscopic provocation for my temper to kick in and knock somebody down. Over and over my Dad would tell me, "ease your head out of the lion's mouth." The bottom line was that I couldn't get a grip on my mouth because I was not humble. I came to the conclusion I would no longer be a victim – but the method was all wrong.

Humility precedes a tame tongue.

The Apostle James held nothing back in addressing untamed tongues:

> *For every kind of beast, and of birds, and of serpents, and of things in the sea, is tamed and hath been tamed of mankind: but the tongue can no man tame; it is an unruly evil, full of deadly poison. Therewith we bless God, even the Father; and therewith curse we men, which are made after the similitude of God. Out*

> *of the same mouth proceedeth blessings and cursing. My brethren these things ought not so to be (James 5:7).*

The above passage conveys that the believer's mouth has to become utilitarian. Our mouths should function for the purpose of honoring God with blessings.

There is a reason why the Word says study to live a quiet and peaceful life. The reason is that untamed tongues are a set-up for so many other things that can go wrong and that could have been avoided. James also says the tongue cannot be tamed and that it is an "unruly evil." (Verse 8)

A helpful exercise is to make a written note of your conversations for one week. In doing so, you will discover that much of our conversations are about other people or about events that are negative, such as the news headlines, or complaining, or murmuring. Some individuals are well meaning in discussing others, on the other hand, people are intentionally damaging another person with gossip or criticisms.

An uncontrolled mouth also involves complaining and negativity.

Blessings never come out of murmuring and complaining.

Believers can benefit better from filling their mouths with praise and having a heart of thanksgiving or just not talking. Utilize talk time with reading the Word. The more you read the Word of God, the more you will come to know God. And the more you know, the more your heart becomes filled with the things of God, which you will then release from your mouth. Another exercise that I practice is, I have friends hold up a hand and say, 'stop L.' This exercise helps me to bridle my tongue from speaking negative words or griping and complaining. I also return the favor, so we help keep each other in check. Also, limit casual phone conversations to a brief, infrequent exchange concluded with a prayer.

You may feel honesty and outspokenness is within your personality, and you just can't help it. If you possess this trait, you need to seek the wisdom of God as in James 3:17, and also pray that God will help you to "*be swift to hear, slow to speak, and slow* to wrath (James 1:19)." Ask God to help you not to be critical or judgmental of others. This is an area of weakness for many Christians, including myself. One verse that I try to speak over my life on a daily basis is James 1:19, "*Wherefore my beloved brethren, let every man be slow to speak and swift to hear and slow to wrath, for the wrath of man worketh not the righteousness of God."*

James links wrath to the tongue. Many disputes can be quenched long before the destructive stage if somebody would elect to be quiet and keep a zipped lip! David said "*Set a watch, O LORD, before my mouth; keep the door of my lips. Incline not my heart to any evil thing, to practice wicked works with men that work iniquity: and let me not eat of their dainties" (Psa.141:3, 4).*

As children of God we should never feel reluctant to solicit the help of the Holy Spirit in keeping our mouths shut about things that are impractical and unproductive to spiritual growth in building the kingdom and bringing us closer to God.

Here's what you can do:

- Pray: "*God tame my tongue,*" "*keep a watch over the door to my mouth.*"
  Continuously pray the Word over yourself in this area.
- Ask God to help you not to gossip, to have self–control, and not to be the receptacle for people's garbage. GET OUT OF THE LOOP! When someone approaches you venting or presenting FYI's, stop them that instant so they'll know you're not the one to collect their garbage.
- Ask God to help you not to respond to people and situations in anger where you have to issue a retort and the last word. This is an area where you will most likely be tested without warning, but with God's help you can be swift to hear and slow to wrath.
- Ask the Lord to help you not to criticize or complain.

Corrupt communication should never leave the mouth of a believer.

A believer's conversation should reflect a pure heart. Expressly, believers should not utter any negative words about another person, and believers should refrain from engaging in profanity. I have heard believers cuss better than unconfessed sinners – and not just to express anger. If you practice the traits of negative words, explicit and cheap sexual or flirtatious conversations, curse words or derogatory language, bear in mind the spirit under which you are operating is the same spirit that operates as you go through the motion of praise and worship in public and most-likely someone has witnessed a very different private you. Here a few passages to remember:

> *Be not deceived: evil communications corrupt good manners (I Cor. 15:32).*
> *Don't use foul or abusive language. Let everything you say be good and helpful, so that your words will be an encouragement to those who hear them (Eph. 4:29, NLT).*
> *And so blessing and cursing come pouring out of the same mouth. Surely, my brothers and sisters, this is not right! (James 3:10, NLT)*

Untamed tongues are tearing churches apart in unprecedented fashion to the degree that people don't even fear God concerning how damaging their actions are to the cause of Christ. Untamed tongues discourage sinners and saints from attending church because of the stereotype associated with 'church folk' as phonies (imposters).

People in the congregation tend to treat each other in the fellowship worse than unconfessed sinners. There are those within the church who have been offended and hurt because of someone's tongue. Reputations are assassinated all the time because another believer could not control his or her tongue either by revealing a truth, embellishing a truth, or telling an outright lie. Moreover, an untamed tongue is a blemish against an offering of praise. God will not receive an offering of praise that is blemished by an untamed tongue. "*The tongue deviseth mischiefs; like a sharp razor, working deceitfully. God shall likewise destroy thee forever, he shall take thee away, and pluck thee out of thy dwelling place, and root thee out of the land of the living. Selah" (Psa. 52: 1, 5).*

On the off-chance that you praise God after lying, contributing to chaos or instigating 'mess,' you have done the equivalent of jumping jacks, push-ups or blowing hot air. All you did was bodily exercise. We must put holiness into practice and into perspective. We needn't speak everything we think. Ephesians 5:4 states, "*Neither filthiness nor foolish talking, nor jesting but rather giving of thanks."*

This verse signifies that engaging in explicit sexual jokes and conversation is unbecoming and impractical for moving forward in a holy life, for our God is Holy.

Ministry Tip

Track your conversation for a day, then a week in a calendar or in a journal.

Life Free of Strife

The tongue is clearly linked to whether the believer's life is peaceful or full of strife. Often strife can be averted if people would be quiet. Strife can be deflected if someone who is spiritually minded would pray or praise rather than get involved. Apostle Paul pluralizes the conditions in II Corinthians 12:20. He declares, *"there are many debates, many strifes, many backbitings, many whisperings, many swellings, many tumults."* Later in the letter to the Galatians, the Apostle places strife alongside witchcraft, seditions, and emulations – the worst kind of spiritual wickedness. The same problems we witness today were happening back in Apostle Paul's day.

Finally, the solution is found in Philippians 2:3: esteem others better than yourself.

This takes us back to humility. It takes humility to back down in the face of confrontation. It takes humility to keep your mouth shut, or as the cliché goes: bite your tongue.

Can you accept the proposition that developing a life of praise and worship will transform your stinking thinking? Can I testify? I know for a fact that if you will make God LORD over your mind, your mouth and your manner, the Comforter will do the work. The work of the Comforter, who is the Holy Ghost, is to destroy habits that bind and restrict your praise and worship.

Again,

> *Do nothing from factional motives [through contentiousness, strife, selfishness, or for unworthy ends] or prompted by conceit and empty arrogance. Instead, in the true spirit of humility (lowliness of mind) let each regard the others as better than and superior to himself [thinking more highly of one another than you do of yourselves] (Phi. 2:3 AMP).*

Address God as Jehovah-shalom and say, "Lord you are my peace." Say, "God let my feet be shod with the preparation of peace" and "God help me to have the fruit of the Spirit in my heart which is love, joy, peace, longsuffering..."

Free yourself of situational debris! The strife of life is weighing people down. We manage to barely praise God in the temple before returning to a house filled with exhausting chaos, arguments, and anguish. A synonym for argument is "trickery" or "deceit." Strife is just a tool of satan. On a daily basis people put on a 'saint' face in the presence of other Christians and return to instigate craziness in the home or to be at the receiving end. Freeing yourself of situational debris may mean giving your social life a good pruning. There are people who simply do not belong in your life. Every other word from their mouths at any moment is discord. Discord is bait. Discord is a distraction that causes discouragement and unbelief. Remember that distractions and unbelief are tools of the devil to blur our focus on God. The scenario progresses like this: The 5 D's:

> **Distractions → discouragement → disbelief → disobedience → destroy**.

There is a process to destruction and it begins with distraction. For that reason we must remain spiritually alert. Know that when you praise, demonic forces will begin to launch an assault against you. Instead be:

> **Discerning → a deterrent → dedicated → determined → durable (unbreakable)**

Proverbs 17:1 states, "*Better is a dry morsel, and quietness therewith, than an house full of sacrifices with strife.*"Apostle Paul addressed the issue of strife in his letter to the Colossians:

> *And let the peace of God rule in your hearts, to the which also ye are called in one body; and be ye thankful.*
>
> *Let the word of Christ dwell in you richly in all wisdom; teaching and admonishing one another in Psalm and hymns and spiritual songs, singing with grace in your hearts to the Lord.*

> *And whatsoever ye do in word or deed, do all in the name of the Lord Jesus, giving thanks to God and the Father by him (Col. 3:15–17).*

> You can pray, "LORD over take me, run me down; let my cup overflow with your love. Press it down and complete your love in me exceedingly."

From these passages we see plainly that the peace of God, oneness, thankfulness, and the Word of God are components which work to eradicate strife. The most prominent part mentioned in each of the above verses is praise, as a result of the knowledge of God. You've got to put praise in your mouth, in your manner, and on your mind so you can keep the enemy in flight.

The Love Factor

The bible says, *Charity [love- NIV, NASB, AMP] doth not behave itself unseemly, seeketh not her own, is not easily provoked, thinketh no evil: (I Cor. 13: 5)*

Love, peace, and joy are the fruit of the Spirit. A heart of love is poised to govern how believers behave. If someone is problematic all the time, that person does not possess the love of God. If that person is provoking strife, that person does not possess the love of God. Summon the courage to sever unloving relationships that diminish your spirit. If you love God, do not settle for associations with people who do not love and respect you as a person or your place in God; gauge the situation by the Word: 1 John 4:20, 21 says, "*how can they love God whom they have not seen?*" You can be a witness by your praise in these situations. Agitators won't like it - and it may provoke that spirit in them to rise even more - but it's about God and you!

In his book, *Exploring Worship* Bob Sorge addresses the subject of love as it relates to worship:

> The Bible makes it clear that our love for God and our love for our fellow believers are inextricably linked: "*If anyone says* I *love God, yet hates his* brother, *whom he has seen, cannot*

> *love God, whom he has not seen* (I John 4:20)." Sorge goes on, The principle is this: our love for God can never transcend our love for one another. Put another way, we can never enjoy a measure of worship that exceeds the quality of relationship we have with our brethren. It is not possible to have a dynamic, personal relationship with God and be at odds with other Christians. If we are growing in loving worship of God, we will inevitably grow in our love for others, for worship causes us to grow in love and unity within the body of Christ.[25]

In order to express our love for God, we must love one another.

Truth to Our Praise

John 8:32 identifies one of Jesus' names as "Truth." The noun is personified*: "ye shall know the truth and the truth shall make you free."*Jesus is the Living Word and the Word is Truth.

The bible says in Romans 3:4, "*God forbid: yea, let God be true, but every man a liar; as it is written, that thou mightest be justified in thy sayings, and mightest overcome when thou art judged.*"

Consequently, when there is 'truth' or 'Truth' to our praise, Jesus is the center because He is the focal point of our confidence and our trust. God trusts us with knowing Him. He has no problem revealing who He is. Also, Truth in praise yields the best results. Jesus is the truth for our life.

Draw Nigh to God

Praising God is within our capacity to move closer to God. Praising God is simple and painless. Our praise to God should surpass our expectations of what we may receive from God. This book began by directing your attention to the importance of praise and worship as conduits to a deeper relationship with God. Drawing near to God invites Him to draw near to you, which defines relationship. The Amplified version reads:

> *Come close to God and He will come close to you. [Recognize that you are] sinners, get your soiled hands clean; [realize that you have been disloyal] wavering individuals with divided interests, and purify your hearts [of your spiritual adultery]. [As you draw near to God] be deeply penitent and grieve, even weep [over your disloyalty]. Let your laughter be turned to grief and your mirth to dejection and heartfelt shame [for your sins].*

Earlier we dealt with the attitude of praise. Our attitude in approaching God should be a broken spirit and a contrite (not contrived) heart.

> *The LORD is nigh unto them that are of a broken heart; and saveth such as be of a contrite spirit. (Psa. 34:18)*
> *My sacrifice [the sacrifice acceptable] to God is a broken spirit; a broken and a contrite heart [broken down with sorrow for sin and humbly and thoroughly penitent], such, O God You will not despise (Psa. 51:17, AMP).*

Drawing near to God involves:

- The attitude of praise. The **attitude** of praise determines the **altitude** of praise, which results in the **proximity** of praise.
- Feelings of brokenness as a condition of the heart.
- Purposeful and deliberate use of time. Drawing nigh calls for a sense of time management to minimize the amount of time wasted in our spiritual walk in order to put God at the highest point of our daily agendas.
- Prioritizing God in our agendas means awakening and immediately directing your thoughts to God so He will preside over your day and direct your path.

Consider this example of a typical weekly schedule:

5:30 a.m.	Rise	**or**	6:00	rise
7:30	leave for work		7:30	arr. school
8:00	arrive at work		3:00	arr. home
5:00	leave for home		3:15	snack
5:30	arrive at home		3:30 - 4	homework
6:00	supper		4:00 -	
6:20 -11:00	T.V.		- 10:00 +	T.V., games,
12:00 midnight	bed			phone

Do you have a passion for drawing nigh to God? How much time do you spend doing something that is unproductive? What is your involvement? How much of your time is sedentary? Are you running and ripping, and engaging in insignificant business? Are you acknowledging God in all that you do according to the divine purpose? What are the first words out of your mouth as a new day and new mercies dawn?

It would be unlikely to expect a person to spend 24/7 in praise and spiritual pursuit. We have to function in the world system: obtain an education, work, grocery shop, brush our teeth, and groom ourselves, etc. But with all of these day to day survival functions, setting aside a block of time as an investment in our relationship with God – not just a few minutes but throughout the day – is essential.

Our motive in drawing nigh to God through praise is to express love, obedience and appreciation to Him; praising God helps keep our mind and our affections on things above. Too many times we are told that if we learn to praise God we will have a book deal, the business, a house, or the Benz. Consequently, we are conditioned to equate blessings with things. We send up praises with the incentive to receive something back from God or to get a harvest.

I do believe that when we "draw nigh to God, He will draw nigh" to us; that He will grace us with His presence. So instead of praising to get 'stuff,' we, should take time to praise God because of who He is; because we desire to know Him and have an intimate relationship with Him.

Again, we should aim for a deeper relationship. I'm not talking about calling on God like those people who call a friend only when they need something.

Honestly, I don't know about you, but eventually, I avoid those people. If a person who calls himself my friend has difficulty calling to simply see how I'm doing – minus a request – then, I'm smart enough to know, we do not have a relationship.

Regrettably, Christians have less of a relationship with the True and Living God than people who worship idols. Pagans, Goths, and atheists are more passionate about their belief than are Christians. I know this is a radical saying, but the truth of the matter is that believers of Jesus Christ make excuses about not knowing the Word of God; not having time to study, to pray, to witness, or even to serve. Saints go into the worship service tired and worn out; barely able to lift up a 'thank you Jesus.' Churches fill calendars with more and more services, annual events, banquets, revivals, and endless conferences and civic obligations, and still people are no closer to a viable relationship with the living God. (In fact, some of these activities lend themselves to bondage and not worship or the saving of souls.) We can correct these issues by prioritizing drawing nigh to God individually and corporately.

I challenge every believer to love God simply for God and make time for Him beginning and throughout every day. The schedule below is a guide to assist you in structuring your day.

Revised Schedule:

6:00 a.m.	Rise
6:10	Prayer/worship (4 p's penance, praise, petition, Praise)
6:45	prepare for work
7:30	Leave for work
12:00	lunch and meditation in the Word
5:00 – 6:00	errands
6:10	supper
7:00	chores, family prayer/bible study
10:00	Prayer, prepare for bed

An intimate relationship begins with the individual and God. When we love God, something is missing in the absence of alone time with the Father, Son and Holy Ghost. When we love God, we seek hard after Him; we pant after Him as the deer pants for the water. When we love God, we must praise and be in His presence; we must sup with Him, and He with us. When we love God, we will commit to making time for Him and we will put Him first according to the first commandment that "Thou shall have no other gods before me" (Exodus 20:3). When we love God, no other presence will suffice; no other voices will do, and the presence of another is an invasion of our peace. Agitation is appropriate until we have our moment with Him.

The kingdom of God will grow as we press forward in our individual relationships with God. Growth is accomplished by way of redeeming the time in prayer, praise, fasting and reading the Word of God, which results in an effective, meaningful life of praise and worship.

Summary

There are people who want to minimize the importance of a discussion on how we come before God. I too grew up on the hymn, "Just as I Am" and though that theme is appropriate for those seeking salvation, as believers we want to experience a deeper dimension when we come before our Maker. We must come before Him with obedience, a pure heart, humility, a tamed tongue, a heart free of strife, and drawing near to Him.

Addressing the issues of obedience, a pure heart, humility, a tamed tongue, a heart free of strife, prepares our hearts for praise that invites the Presence of God.

Hebrews Chapter 12, verse 22 reads "*Let us draw near with a true heart in full assurance of faith, having our hearts sprinkled from an evil conscience, and our bodies washed with pure water.*" In this verse, we see the requirements intermingled. As Christians we must remember that God knows our hearts and our intentions. To attain purity, we may have to let some things – and some people - go. Purity and being holy or separated unto God means guarding our minds and our bodies from unclean things. For example, sitting and watching people fornicating on T.V. or entertaining ourselves with violence and horror does not lend itself to a pure heart. Plainly, that unclean stuff remains in the mind and will resurface at any moment.

Do not think that you are so deep in God that you are exempt from temptation. And do not undermine temptations that can become habitual. The information and tech age have made things that satisfy curiosity, accessible with little accountability. The Word of God says, "*But every person is tempted when he is drawn away, enticed and baited by his own evil desire (lust, passions)" (James 1:14, AMP)*. As we mature in Christ, we demonstrate love through obedience to the precepts and commandments of God (Psalm 119) and then praise God for who He is.

After reading this summary, purpose in yourself to work on your relationship with God. Begin by taking inventory of the deficit areas. Are you obeying the Word of God? Sometimes we are waiting to hear from God by the Spirit of God while neglecting the truth that the Father, the Word and Holy Ghost agree (I John 5:7). Are you drawing near to God or are you distracted with strife and talking about things that have no relevance to your spiritual relationship?

Developing your relationship begins with studying the Word of God consistently on a weekly basis. Close this book for a while and study the Word of God on your own. Meditate on God and sing sacred songs in your secret closet.

Your secret closet may be your head beneath a pillow or the powder room or as you are en route somewhere. We can avoid the pitfalls of the devil simply by immersing ourselves in praise and thinking about the goodness of the Lord! All it takes is a few consecutive days where we neglect to take the time or make the time, and temptation will blindside us. Jesus told the disciples; pray that you enter not into temptation. Do not take your spiritual life for granted, nor should you be in denial about the power of the flesh in the absence of spending time with God. Spending time with God is key to drawing near to God and preparing our hearts before Him.

A few more points.

Drawing near to God must be willful and habitual.

Do not think that you will stand just because you accepted Christ.

I am a witness that spending time in the Word has increased my love for God and revealed how I should praise Him. Personally, this came as a result of praying for God's help in this area. I prayed that God would give me a hunger and thirst for His Word and that He would cause me to remember His Word in praise.

We are compelled to do all that it takes continually and perpetually, that is: Humility, taming the tongue, living a life free of strife, abiding in Truth, and drawing near to Him. The reality of the situation is that we are humans, subject to what our eyes see and what our bodies feel. Our faith is vulnerable. No matter what your position in the church, you could fall. Our faith must be proactive as evidenced by the efforts we make to increase and enhance our relationship with God. Spend time with God. Spend time in prayer and praise unto God!

I encourage you to trust God. He knows we have bills and that we get caught up worrying about how we're going to make it in this world. If we were to be honest, we would have to admit to believing that a million dollars would solve all our problems. Some of you have been waiting a long time for a miracle in your body.

Don't just sit there! Be active in your time waiting. Open your mouth and release the delicious 'pineapples and oranges' of your mouth to Jehovah-rapha, your healer. We love God not as an ATM card or as though we expect *Publisher's Clearing House* to show up, but just because He is God. We should have a no-strings-attached-no-give-and-no-take agape love that invigorates our praise. When we pray or praise, we seek to bless God rather than for God to bless us, which is a hard saying. Show that you trust God by placing a greater weight on blessing God, exalting God, rehearsing His names and His goodness.

Praising God is not a proverbial Simon says. Praising God becomes a natural response to the supernatural, to His light, His holiness and to His absolute goodness. We praise God voluntarily and automatically as though it was autonomic, but we are in control. Our desire is to please God and to express love and appreciation. For example, consider the word autonomic.

Autonomic has to do with the autonomic nervous system. The autonomic nervous system regulates key functions of the body, including the heart, digestive system, and glands. These systems work without any prompting from us. In contrast, our praise is completely conscious and voluntary. As we grow spiritually, praise becomes more auto-matic. 'Drawing near' is absent of being pushed, shoved, coerced or compelled. Drawing near suggest of one's will or volition. Remember: "*Let us draw near with a true heart in full assurance of faith, having our hearts sprinkled from an evil conscience, and our bodies washed with pure water" (Heb.10:22).*

Finally, the water in verse 22 is Jesus Christ, the Living Water. Jesus refers to himself as these most basic elements indispensable to sustaining life. Interestingly, at other times He referred to Himself as 'bread,' and as 'light.' All of these components are needed for growth; hence a healthy life. The application is that Jesus the Living Water is our everlasting supply. Water serves to quench the thirst, to cleanse, to assist in growing, and for medicinal purposes, etc. The writer of Hebrew uses a recurring natural element to describe a spiritual state: washing with water. When we partake of the Living Water we are clean and we will never thirst, which means we will live.

Chapter 5

Forms of Praise

Lifting of Eyes
Singing
Dance
Shout!
Noise
The Banner
Whisper

Are you a person who bores easily? Do you get frustrated with monotony, and sameness? The good news is that you don't have to get bored with praise. God accepts various forms of praise. You can lift your hands (towdah), or sing (tehillah), or you can clap and bang on a tambourine (zamar), you can dance or shout (shabach). God receives our praise when it is done unto the Lord.

God has people who love him all over the world. We all have different cultural experiences, even within America, but we are united by our praise **unto the Lord**. Unless you have a physical limitation, you can do it all! Praise is the fruit of our lips, lifting our hands, clapping the hands, dancing, shouting, making a joyful noise, waving banners, crying out, and whispering. You can begin praising God in your own way right now.

Lifting of Hands (Yadah)

During the 1990's, there was a phrase popularized by the rap/hip-hop movement that went like this: "Wave your hands in the air! Wave'em like you just don't care!" I'm sure you've seen televised performances with the rapper cavorting and shouting for the people to do this, and they do it, with no problem and no shame. Also, I have seen this extending of the hands in succession around the stadium at football games. Sections of fans take turns standing and waving uplifted hands in an uninhibited fashion to urge their team and celebrate each score.

When it comes to the church, people are reluctant to raise their hands or yadah God. Raising the hands denotes surrender, victory or honor. In lifting the hands the person's most-vital organ – the heart, is exposed. They're out there for all to see – chest, armpits, and all! The person is making a statement that he/she is unashamed. Boxers, track stars and other athletes, as well as politicians raise both hands high to declare a victory.

Lifting the hands is a high form of praise throughout the Word of God. Lifting the hands serves as a vertical sign of blessing the Lord and honoring His Holiness; it conveys a message to God of your willingness to become insignificant and vulnerable in His presence and give Him reverence.

David invites the people to bless the Lord with uplifted hands:

> *Come, bless the Lord, all you servants of the Lord, who stand by night in the house of the Lord!*
> *Lift up your hands to the holy place and bless the Lord!*
> *(Psalm 134: 1-2, ESV)*

The Amplified Version adds the phrase "affectionately and gratefully praise" (AMP).

I believe David addressed the tribe of the Levites because they were explicitly assigned the task of praising God at the gate of the temple day and night. They were the watchmen who guarded the temple with praise.

> This Psalm instructs us concerning a two-fold blessing:—I. Our blessing God, that is, speaking well of him, which here we are taught to do, v. 1, v. 2. It is a call to the *Levites* to do

> it. They were *the servants of the Lord* by office, appointed to minister in holy things; they attended the sanctuary, and kept the charge of the house of the Lord, Num. 3:6, etc. Some of them did *by night stand in the house of the Lord,* to guard the holy things of the temple, that they might not be profaned, and the rich things of the temple, that they might not be plundered..."[26]

Yadah has little relevance to our situations. For example, you may have to tithe from an unemployment check, welfare check or another source of fixed income but continue to speak well of God for the little that you do have. Even if you no longer have an address to call home, God's Word is true, and you can praise Him for the abundant life and God being an ever-present help in the time of trouble. Praise because you believe Jehovah-jireh will provide, and that you should take no thought for your life.

I have been in the unfortunate situation where I had to trust God in the midst of homelessness, no job, and lack. I have slept consecutive nights in brutal -5° weather. One of those times in my vehicle, I awakened to find that someone had tried to break in by prying the driver door open; another time after I had finally fallen asleep, I was awakened by voices beckoning,

"Hey, what are you doing in there? Why sleep alone? Come sleep with us."

I opened my eyes to find my vehicle surrounded by people in animal costumes doing unseemly things. What God has brought me through falls under the category of His Mighty Acts as well as attributable to His mercy and His loving-protection.

Sometimes we see people in church and we have no clue how survival mode gnaws at their sanity or tenacity every moment of every day. We can never know what people are going through. Sure, lifting hands in praise is easy when we see His benefits, or when we have all the stuff that we need and no worries. It takes faith to keep on blessing God when your pockets, your hands, and your bank account are empty and when you've lost all your possessions.

I know what it's like to lose everything except the clothes on my back and the possessions I could carry. Recently I lost all my creative works: including every song I'd written, every poem, every short story, every CD, a library of 100's of books including my bibles, every painting, and all but three manuscripts. There were clothing and other irreplaceable items too, but I felt I could never live without my writings. Can you imagine what living with no physical evidence of years of existence?

The good that came from the situation was that I had to come out of self-sufficiency and rely solely on God. I learned to trust God, to contemplate Him more and continue to trust and to live a life focused on glorifying Him.

I continued to show up for rehearsals and church services, despite not knowing where I would go after the benediction. Somehow I managed to get dressed and cleaned up and give God the tenth and an offering. There were times, while sitting in that vehicle in someone else's parking lot, or I would be sick on the floor of a public bathroom - that I felt like I couldn't make it another day. Somewhere and somehow a blessed song or Word from the Lord would make its way into my hearing and into my Spirit and once again I would lift up praises because the good and the not-so-good things were being worked out for my good.

I want to encourage you that God has given us the garment of praise for the spirit of heaviness (Isaiah 61:3); He has clothed us with song and adoration. He has promised to take care of you. Begin to learn of His promises and to proclaim them over your life. He said he would *"keep us in perfect peace whose mind is stayed on Him" (Isaiah 26:3)*. The catch is trusting in Him. These are words that stay with me: that I must trust Him. Trusting Him is directing our thoughts toward Him. To direct your thoughts means to will. To willfully and persistently direct your thoughts is to allow passion to develop in you.

Throughout scripture lifting hands signifies praise, worship, blessing God, or swearing an oath. Lifting your hands is quite often equivalent to what is known in Hebrew as a *yadah*; especially when listening to music. Chronicles 20:19-20 is the yadah type of praise. Also, lifting the hands in combination with another form of praise - is a celebration to express excitement about God, as in towdah: *"And Ezra blessed the LORD, the great God. And all the people answered Amen, Amen, With lifting up their hands: and they bowed their heads, and worshiped the LORD with their faces to the ground"* (Neh. 8:6).

Notice in the above passage the people combined praise and worship with uplifted hands and bowing their heads and faces to the ground.

Lifting the Eyes

Lifting the eyes can have a double meaning: one implication is to be prideful and uplifted; the other directs our praise heavenward. David said, *"I will lift up mine eyes unto the hills, from whence cometh my help"* (Psa. 121:1-3). Though David starts off by saying he is looking to the hills, in the very next verse he exclaims where his help actually comes from and why: "*My help cometh from the LORD, which made heaven and earth.*" The scriptures distinguish lifting the eyes unto the true and living God in sharp contrast to idols. Anything we lift up must be reserved for God. There is no fault in opening your eyes and directing your gaze heavenward in praise, such as the psalmist: "*Unto thee lift I up mine eyes, O thou that dwellest in the heavens" (Psa. 123:2).*

As you praise God, open your eyes from time to time. Lift up your eyes as unto the Lord on occasion. Direct your attention away from your surroundings as though you are peering into the heavens. Envision God sitting on the throne and His only begotten Son on His right hand with the heavenly hosts crying Holy, Holy, Holy, in your spiritual imagination. Yearn to experience ecstasy in the presence of God.

Singing (Tehillah)

Singing is easy. God does not require us to sound like professionals, to have taken voice lessons, or to sing in pitch! For every form of praise, God requires only that we do it unto the Lord and with all our might. In the verses below, the Psalmist directs us to, "*Sing praises to God, sing praises: sing praises unto our King, sing praises.(Psa.47:6) and Sing forth the honour of his name: make his praise glorious"(Psa. 66:2).*

Many people are uncomfortable when it comes to singing in public. After all these years I still hear individuals in the choir saying, 'I'm really not a singer,' and I'm left wondering, why did they come to choir rehearsal, and why are they in the choir stand?

As a musician, choir director and music educator, I have always believed everyone can sing; that everyone possesses a measure of musical ability, even if it means just emulating sound. I still believe there is inherently a song within all of us; in spite of the fact that there are different levels and special abilities in a select few.

The Psalmist directs us to sing. You are not asked to be a singer, but to sing. You can ask the Holy Ghost to help you in your desire to sing and to give you songs that are complimentary, melodious and filled with jubilation. I have heard people who clearly had trouble identifying their pitch and holding their vocal part, who are often the folk who sing the loudest and in earnest. Their hearts are in it even if their ears are not. I didn't mock these individuals; I began to pray for Supernatural intervention and that God would honor their heart's desire to sing for Him, in part because I had exhausted what I could otherwise do.

Over time, what happened was that God heard and answered my prayer to the extent that the improvement surprised me. So if you are reading this or you know someone who makes a noise that's not so joyful when they are supposed to be making a sweet, sweet sound in His ears, do not mock them. Pray for Holy Ghost intervention and see what God will do.

The songs that we sing should have less to do with the human experience and more to do with celebrating the source of our triumph. Also, true praise has little to do with preaching to others or listing the problems of the week. Praise God that gospel music has transcended its roots in the Blues and come to feature the 'good news.'

It bears mentioning that many of the hymns to which the church clings were written before the 20th century and too few give the believer joy or hope for victory. Too many of the old hymns lack jubilation. Over and over the bible states '*sing unto the Lord* a *new song*.' God wants us to sing joyfully and with gladness in our hearts. There are some great hymns of the church that encourage, buildup, and lift up the human spirit, despite vernacular which falls short of providing a voice beyond the 19th century. God wants us to encourage each other in psalms and in hymns that edify.

C.S. Lewis said "the Psalm are poems and must interpret as such."[27] Believers are supposed to offer up praises to God with intent to give glory and honor. The songs of the church should evoke delight, gladness, and the beauty of holiness. The songs and hymns are not supposed to be sorrowful, slow-dragging, and burdensome.

Songs of praise should reach the heart of the unbeliever and cause the believer to celebrate, march, dance, raise their hands, laugh, and experience the joy in loving God. Hymns such as *"We have heard the Joyful Sound, Jesus Saves" and "Victory in Jesus," or* my favorite," *Oh How I Love Jesus."*

Dance

Not everyone possesses the physical capacity to dance and not all of us share equal ability to sing or play an instrument. I can remember the last time I danced before the Lord was not long after high school. I remember singing and then the whole church was going at it, jumping and rejoicing so much so the floor and everything attached, was shaking. I got up and started bucking around and next thing I knew I saw stars. I had slammed my head into the cement wall. That was the last time I danced. Now I only wish I could dance on occasion.

But wait! Don't let this story deter you.

Dancing expresses happiness and joy. You would be hard-pressed to find someone dancing because they were miserable. People dance because they want to escape misery. Dancing is an extraordinary outlet for pent up frustrations. Luke 6:23 urges us to leap for joy and Nehemiah 8:10 says "*...do not be grieved for the joy of the Lord is your strength.*" The bible says that God will give us "*the oil of joy instead of mourning and a garment of praise for the spirit of despair" (Isa. 61:3, NIV*). This is how to do it. Get the body moving, dispose of stress, release the happy chemicals (endorphins), get the heart pumping, and perspire a little.

Not long ago the church began experiencing an aversion to dance; more specifically, choreographed dance was becoming a controversial and divisive topic. Consider three scenarios: I have observed children, dressed in their beautiful flowing attire enter the sanctuary in a manner which should not have been offensive to anyone, only to be 'snubbed' by some in the assembly. A popular praise song was cued and some stood and received the presentation while others sat in judgment. This ought not to have been. The young people were dressed decently and their movements were modest. There was no reason for anyone to judge whether the dance was unto the Lord.

Secondly, I have seen young people enter the sanctuary to pumping music that sounded like the club, their clothing was skin tight, body parts were exposed and gyrating; the dance steps emulated the stuff one would see on BET or VH1. In some circles this whole routine would be referred to as 'booty' shakin' to put it nicely. That day I discerned that the dance was not of God and left immediately.

The third situation is in reference to dance in the church which is spontaneous and un-choreographed, without 'form or fashion.' In this example people do whatever suits them, whether it entails jumping or bucking around, a cute little dance with a one-leg skip. The question is, what is the difference?

The Bible has the first and last word on which of the above circumstances is acceptable. The first criterion that the church should understand is that dance is a form of praise – whether spontaneous or choreographed - and is a ministry unto God and for the people of God.

Next, praise in the form of dance must be unto the Lord. Thirdly, dance should be of one's free will. In reference to dance, people who defend dance always say, "Well, David danced out of his clothes." Well, the people who say that omit the scriptural fact that *"David* ***danced*** ***<u>before the LORD with all his might</u>****; and David was girded with a linen ephod."* (II Sam. 6:14) So according to the Word of the LORD, there is nothing wrong with dancing when we do it unto the Lord and of our free will.

In the first passage, David was demonstrating that he was exceedingly glad to see the Ark of the Covenant marched into the city that day. Now the Ark of the Covenant was the most important piece of architecture at that time prior to the first Temple built by Solomon. The Ark of the Covenant of the Lord was really a large chest-like box made of acacia wood and covered with gold inside and out. It had four large rings for the poles which allowed the priests (Levites) to carry it. The Ark of the Covenant carried just that – the covenant or tablet of commandments that God gave to Moses. Inside was also a mercy seat which was covered with gold and two large winged Cherubims. The Ark was specifically designed by God and built to last because later it would be housed in the temple. The mercy seat is where the priest would sprinkle blood and offer sacrifice for their sins and the Israelites.

The Ark of the Covenant represented the Presence of God – or the Shekinah Glory - and would go before the Israelites as they traveled or went into battle. Only the Levites who were set apart by God for the purpose of carrying the Ark of the Covenant of the Lord of the earth could do so. Everyone else was instructed not to touch it and to keep a distance of sometimes as much as 2000 cubits, or risk the consequence of death.

The Presence and the power of God were closely connected to the Ark of the Covenant. For instance, when the great high priest Eli heard that the Ark of the Covenant of the Lord had been taken, he fell back off his chair, broke his neck and died; his daughter-in-law heard the same news and gave birth prematurely. She called her newborn son 'Ichabod' and said, "*for the Glory of the Lord is departed*" and she then died.

The Ark of the Covenant corresponded to the power of God and David continued to rejoice and offer sacrifices unto the Lord and bless all the people including his house. But when he returned to his house his wife Michal criticized him with scathing sarcasm (v. 20). What I get in the verse is that she was embarrassed by David's jubilance. David wasn't behaving in a very kingly manner. David simply responded to her "*It was before the Lord,*" in v. 21. Because Michal mocked something that was unto the Lord, she was cursed with barrenness for the rest of her days. Therefore it is critical that we not issue criticisms when people are offering praise unto the Lord or before the Lord.

Please hear me on this point. We need to 'get over' the business of minding other people's praise business. For your own safety, DO NOT JUDGE ANOTHER PERSON'S PRAISE.

Conversely, on this point, we need to judge ourselves on the appropriateness of what we do in God's house. There is no room in God's holy temple for dances resembling 'twerking' or 'getting your eagle on' or the 'wave' or "sciatica" or 'crumping,' or 'clown walk' "Detroit jit," or whatever the current dance trends. Look at the titles of the dances mentioned.

The titles of the dances of the world bear out the devil's job to seduce and entice the senses. People who are involved in this are victims of deceit but I am convinced they know better but just do not fear God. We've used restraint in mentioning some of the disgusting dances of the world but the point is God wants us to come out from among them and be separated unto Him. We want God to be pleased with all that we do unto Him and bring no glory to ourselves. For this reason, it is critical that we know what the Word says is acceptable to God and we are taught that **proper praise can still be passionate praise**. Proper praise enlarges God and minimizes attention directed to the praiser.

We must not compromise in order to attract young people to a congregation.

People needn't get delivered from the club, only to be reminded of the club atmosphere in the church. Why should people get delivered from the habits of sin, join the church, and get to learn hip-hop dances and perform them in worship services? The Devil is a liar and a deceiver! For that matter, music genres come and go along with their extended dance expressions, but the unchangeable God will always desire a church which is set apart. To be set apart means to be outside of, to be different, and to be holy. There must be distance between the holy and the unholy. There's nothing wrong with being on the perimeter of what is hip. God's standard may not be hip, or happening, but it is heavenward.

Shout! Why are you so quiet?

As an avid football fan I am amazed at how many people fill 50 – 90,000 plus seat stadiums to watch or get a glimpse at guys in uniform running around and essentially playing keep away with a football. With each ten-yard down the fans – dressed in their team's attire – wave towels, stand and shout even before the team scores, wins, or loses.

Why are believers compelled to be quiet about our devotion to our Lord and Savior when the rest of the world is loud and passionate? How is quietness blessed if "joy is flowing like a river since the Comforter has come?"[28] For that matter, I never got the point of the introit "*The Lord is in His Holy Temple*" (let all the earth keep silent before Him)[29] followed by a call to worship exhorting people to make a joyful noise unto the Lord and serve Him with gladness. Truthfully, the two directives seem contradictory. [The scripture for this hymn is Habakkuk 2:20 which is in reference to the people being quiet in order to hear the voice of a Living God, in contrast to idols (vs. 18, 19) which cannot respond.] If a believer thinks of the goodness of Jesus and all He has done, why is there no urge to shout? Clearly, whether a person is quiet natured or more extraverted, he or she will holler when and if the situation arises. For some reason when roof-raisin' people come over to the Lord's side they get bashful.

Throughout scripture shouting was a good thing. Shouts were used to declare war, as weapons, to exclaim victory, and to demonstrate joy. Shouts allow us to release. A good shout sets free those who are experiencing bondage in an area. Even the Lord shouts: *For the Lord himself shall descend from heaven with a shout, with the voice of the archangel, and with the trump of God: and the dead in Christ shall rise first" (I Thess. 4:16).*

Shouts of praise are weapons of warfare against the devil to the pulling down of strongholds. A shout of praise is like an ADT® alarm system screaming to alert the authorities, and release the power of the Lord Mighty in Battle against the intrusion of demons dispatched by the devil. If only God's people would simply begin to shout, we could put the enemy to flight.

Shouts put the devil and his army of demons on notice.

Shouts signify a spiritual declaration of war.

Once on a rare Sunday off I had the opportunity to visit another church. Upon arrival, I heard some people singing praise songs. The singers and musicians didn't seem too inspired, but I noticed that there were an inordinate amount of people in the congregation responding by shoving their fingers in their ear canals. The little old lady on the pew in front of me was brazenly distributing packets of ear plugs to the people on her row - who in turn ripped opened the packets and stuffed the plugs in their ears. Another time, I had visited the same church and it was vibrant, full of life and praise – and people. The people rejoiced with shouting so much that I remember thinking, *maybe they ought to slow it down a bit.* Not long after, I remember talking with the minister of music who told me the people wanted a change in the music, and he was fighting to stay. It was a shame to see what had become of that church. The congregation had dwindled to a fraction of its former numbers. Without praise, it was fundamentally dying.

Consider the verses below as they relate to the shout in praise:

> *And when the ark of the covenant of the Lord came into the camp, all Israel shouted with a great shout, so that the earth resounded (I Sam.4:5, AMP).*
>
> *And when the Philistines heard the noise of the shout, they said, What meaneth the noise of this great shout in the camp of the Hebrews? And they understood that the ark of the LORD was come into the camp (I Sam. 4:6).*
>
> *O clap your hands, all you peoples! Shout to God with the voice of triumph and songs of joy! And songs of joy! (Psa. 47:1, AMP)*

Shouting yields results, such as power in the shout, along with joy and victory released in the shout. Something happens when we shout unto the Lord. Not only does God hear the shout, but the enemies of God take notice when we shout.

Noise

Noise is very much like the shout, except that noise is inanimate. Noise can be made with objects such as instruments. Noise is devoid of speech, melody, rhythm or varying elements of music that make sound pleasant, ordinarily. Again, we turn to God's expert on praise, the psalmist David:

> *Make a joyful noise unto God, all the earth; Sing forth the honor and glory of His name; make His praise glorious (Psa. 66:1, 2)!*
>
> *O come, let us sing unto the LORD: let us make a joyful noise to the rock of our salvation.*
> *(Psa. 95:1)*

In Nehemiah's day, the function of noise was to avert the enemy without the exchange of violent battle. The natural ear is subject to sensibilities which fluctuate and most people, if asked, would find noise objectionable. We would prefer pitch, bass lines walking on a driving beat. Popular culture has raised expectations high for singers and musicians, but the awesome thing is that God receives noise.

I was once affiliated with another church as a member and Minister of Music. The church was lively and fiery. During the worship service, the praise leaders would urge the people to get involved. One day after the Word of God had come forth the people were invited to make noise. They began to march around the walls like Joshua and the Israelites. Before the next service later that afternoon, it was a tradition to provide a meal for people who remained. The afternoon service began as usual to call the people to worship. There were a few more songs when suddenly I heard "rackety–rack–clackety-clack!" and "ping, ping, ping, ping" and "cha, cha, cha, cha, cha." People had brought from the dining hall and their homes – pots and pans, hangers, wash boards, wooden spoons and anything metallic from a kitchen. The people danced and marched around the walls with their home made instruments. This clamor went on for several Sundays.

To the first time observer, those people most likely appeared unsophisticated and the sound of the clanging was deafening as it drowned out the band. But on the faces of the people was joy spoken of in the Word of God.

A similar event happened in Samuel's day. First, you should know that God's chosen people the Israelites, were a noisy bunch. As they were ordered to make noise or the occasion presented itself, their noise level raised to a frightening pitch. I Samuel 4 gives the account of how the Israelites made noise with the shout so much so that the Philistines surmised that God Himself was in the camp, and went on the defensive, taking the Ark of the Covenant and killing 30,000 foot soldiers along with the sons of Eli the Priest.

I told you, you will become a target of demonic forces when you praise and give God Glory.

Back to the church.

So as the weeks went on with all the noise-making, the number of people in attendance grew until there was barely standing room.

Does God require only melody in praise? Is praise defined by melody? Rhythm? Perfectly blended harmonies? Perfectly enunciated words?

What do we need to praise God? Do we need the latest tech gear in keyboards and workstations to praise God? Does a person need vocal training or an understanding of the anatomic mechanisms that cause us to produce and project sound from our voices? Do we need to spend rehearsals delving into music theory and musicology or how sacred music evolved? Does the Minister of Music need a degree from Oberlin or the University of Miami or Berkelee? Does a song have to have AABCD form?

The answer to all of these questions is none of the above. When it comes to praise, the above credentials or features are inconsequential. The important matter is having a passion for praise and a will to worship God. Do not worry about others judging you, talking about you, looking down on you, saying, "it doesn't take all of that," or "that you're doing too much."

Noise is indicative of victory, of declaring war (Ex. 32:17); of celebration (I Sam.4:6); noise is musical in God's ears. And yes, making noise means you feel good about praising your God. Having all the musical elements in place certainly helps our appreciation, but the most important thing is to make a *joyful* noise or praise in our own way, unto the Lord. "*O come, let us sing unto the LORD: let us make a joyful noise to the rock of our salvation. Let us come before his presence with thanksgiving, and make a joyful noise unto him with Psalm" (Psa. 95:1, 2).*

Noise demonstrates,

- The Greatness of God:
  Thou shalt be visited of the Lord of Hosts with thunder, and with earthquake, and great noise, with storm and tempest, and the flame of devouring fire (Isa.29:6).

- The Judgment of God:
  But the day of the Lord will come like a thief, and then the heavens will vanish (pass away) with a thunderous crash [noise KJV], and the [material] elements [of the universe] will be dissolved with fire, and the earth and the works that are upon it will be burned up (II Peter 3:10, AMP).

- Rejoicing:
  Make a joyful noise unto the Lord, all ye lands (Psa. 100:1).

The secular knowledge of the term noise is a lot of racket or sounds that are unpleasant, and therefore undesirable. But I get the sense from the command, *make a joyful noise unto the Lord,* that noise sounds anything but unpleasant to God. There is peace within Godly noise.

The Banner

Banners are signs, flags, or a piece of cloth to display or advertise something of note.

In biblical times, banners were related to war and used as a display of victory. Banners convey for whom or what one stands. Today, we see banners in parades, at rallies or protests to affirm a belief. I was so moved when I witnessed the sacred dancers dance and then raise the banner with an inscription: "*Jesus is Lord*." Tears began to flow at beholding a precious affirmation for all to see.

Again, check out a football game sometime. A sea of fans wave towels in unanimity signifying support of their team. Reportedly, the Pittsburg Steelers started what is now a tradition in football, hockey, and basketball involving waving white towels. The towels – called 'terrible towels' - cost as much as $26,000 for 30,000 towels, were distributed for free and used to rally the team and pump up the energy.[30] The towels add frenetic energy to a stadium, especially when accompanied by a chorus of cheers.

Waving of Banners displays, Victory,

The Hebrew term for the "Lord my banner" is Yaweh-nissi or Jehovah-nissi; such as the passage in Exodus 17. This is the same God of Psalm 24 who is strong and mighty in battle. In Isaiah 13, the banner (in this case a hand) was used as a signal of war. God bids us to call on Jehovah-nissi, our banner and to praise Him when He gives you the victory. You can add impact to that praise by waving a handkerchief or scarf and marching around your house or apartment. "*Lift up a banner upon the high mountain, raise your voice to them, wave your hand, that they may go into the gates of the nobles"(Isa. 13:2, NKJV).* Waving of Banners displays,

> *Put this on your wall!*
> ***Address God as Jehovah-nissi and speak "Lord you are my banner. Please go before me in the time of battle. You are my victory." Now take a handkerchief and go into exuberant praise.- Wave it as though you have already won! Now wave that banner and add a shout.***

- The Promises of God
  Then the LORD said to Moses, 'Write this for a memorial in the book and recount it in the hearing of Joshua, that I will utterly blot out the remembrance of Amalek from under heaven.' And Moses built an altar

and called its name, The-LORD-Is-My-Banner; for he said, 'Because the LORD has sworn: the LORD will have war with Amalek from generation to generation" (Ex. 17:14).

- Truth
  You have set up a banner to them that fear You, that they may flee to it because of the bow [truth]. Selah. (Psa. 60:4, ESV).

- Display of Love
  He brought me to the banqueting house, and his banner over me was love (Song of Sol. 2:4).

- Advertisement
  We will rejoice in thy salvation, and in the name of our God we will set up our banners: the LORD fulfill all thy petitions (Psa. 20:5).

Soldiers and Olympians display flags of allegiance from the country for which they fight or represent. I was mesmerized by the incredible pageantry created around banners at the 2008 Olympics in Beijing. The athletes marched proudly and waved their country's flags as the masses of spectators cheered them on. As each heat of the track and field competition was complete, the winner ran an extra lap around the track, draped in their country's flag.

T-shirts are another type of banner. Additional types of banners are bumper stickers, signs, billboards, the Steeler's 'terrible towels.' With all of these types of banners, a statement is made declaring the person's passion. We can voice our values, but the written word emphasizes a particular belief with a different dynamic and permanence.

Whisper

Sometimes in our brokenness before God, we barely manage to utter a whisper. For instance, just listening to the words of "*Great is thy Faithfulness*" may cause us to whisper gentle phrases unto God in appreciation of the fact that He is faithful.

Many of the biblical references on the word whisper have a negative connotation; for instance contention, tale bearing, defamation, factions, jealousy, gossip, and arrogance (II Cor. 12:20). Earlier, we discussed noise and the shout. You should know that God also hears the whisper – especially the small uttering of those who are weak and vulnerable.

There will be times in our lives when our strength or circumstances will allow only a whisper to our Lord God. Perhaps you are close to someone who is planting the seed of discord or inciting an argument. A praise or prayer whispered in the time of need is enough for God to act on our behalf. We approach Him ever so gently and quietly; yet audibly so that our words enter the atmosphere. There are times when our lives are storm-filled and we are powerless to calm the upheaval. God responds to the slightest plea and the slightest praise. "*He hushes the storm to a calm and to a gentle whisper, so that the waves of the sea are still" (Psa. 107:29).*

God brings peace in the midst of the storm and reduces the boisterous effects of it to a whisper.

Perhaps you are in a court room or a meeting on your job where the devil is raging. That is not the time to start making a noise – joyful or otherwise - or to begin singing and waving around a banner. It would be inappropriate to launch a halal praise or a tehillah praise at that time. People would think you were fanatical, to say the least. The volume of your voice in these circumstances has nothing to do with God's ear and His ability to hear, or the effectiveness of your words.

The next time someone starts up with you, just begin to procclaim His name based on what God can perform at that time. Begin to praise Jehovah-shalom, the God of peace. Thank Him that His name is a Strong Tower and a place of safety for the righteous. Thank God that He is keeping a watch over the door to your mouth that you would otherwise use to retaliate and fire back.

The Instruments (Zamar)

David the son of Jesse was a man of war. Throughout his life he acclimated to fighting, and conquering, beginning with his triumph over Goliath. The bible records that as King David killed tens of thousands of God's enemies, he placed equal value on the importance of Zamar praise in battle. He knew that it was God who was mighty in battle. During the time of this passage in I Chronicles, David reprimanded the Levites for taking shortcuts on protocol. The Levites had slipped in their duty to consult God, bear the Ark of God, and to offer zamar praise to God. David said since they hadn't done it right the first time (resulting in God's anger), he would instruct them again on God's expectations for their office as the appointed praisers, beginning with sanctification.

The nature of the office of the singers and musicians was serious. They were not just a bunch of 'hacks jammin' out. Their services were needed in times of battle and as keepers of the gates of the temple. The Levites were musicians entrusted with carrying the Ark of the Covenant of God.

Consider the magnitude of the musical aspect of their office: "*And, said David, 4,000 shall be gatekeepers and 4,000 are to praise the Lord with the instruments which I made for praise" (I Chron.23:5).*

Huh! Four thousand instruments? This was a great volume of work that amounted to a brigade of skilled musicians. The task of Zamar praise takes time, thought, care and contemplation. David made time in the midst of all his other activities: ruling over Israel, running from enemies, fighting enemies, pleasing all of his wives, writing songs and Psalm and yet crafting a body of instruments solely for the purpose of praising God.

It is no wonder that John Wesley wrote the song, "O for A Thousand Tongues to Sing/O for my great redeemer's praise/the glories of my God and King/The triumphs of His grace."[31] We may not be able to sing, but we can praise God on a range of instruments, some of which are mentioned in Psalm 150.

At the time of the passage in I Chronicles 23, David was old and it was time to transition Solomon to the role of king. The transition involved conducting the census and assigning everyone to their respective offices, including the duty of offering sacrifices of praise and assisting the priests. The Levites were a tribe of Israel separated for the purpose of caring for the temple and praising God day and night. The bible says that God himself was the inheritance of the Levites.

> *And to stand every morning to thank and praise the LORD, and likewise at even:*
> *And to offer all burnt sacrifices unto the LORD in the Sabbaths, in the new moons, and on the set feasts, by number, according to the order commanded unto them, continually before the LORD:*
>
> *And that they should keep the charge of the tabernacle of the congregation, and the charge of the holy place, and the charge of the sons of Aaron their brethren, in the service of the house of the LORD (I Chron. 23:30 – 32).*

The Levites were charged with praising God on the instruments and singing every morning and every evening. Their charge was to do it well, in unison and to do it loudly while 'looking the part:'

> *And all the Levites who were singers--all of those of Asaph, Heman, and Jeduthun, with their sons and kinsmen, arrayed in fine linen, having cymbals, harps, and lyres--stood at the east end of the altar, and with them 120 priests blowing trumpets;*
>
> *And when the trumpeters and singers were joined in unison, making one sound to be heard in praising and thanking the Lord, and when they lifted up their voice with the trumpets and cymbals and other instruments for song and praised the Lord, saying, For He is good, for His mercy and loving-kindness endure forever, then the house of the Lord was filled with a cloud,*
>
> *So that the priests could not stand to minister because of the cloud, for the glory of the Lord filled the house of God (II Chron.5:12 – 14).*

These are amazing passages.

First, imagine hearing 120 trumpets in unison. To put the impact in perspective, a modern day full size orchestra has various classes of instruments with typically over eighty musicians on its roster. In some cases an orchestra may exceed over a hundred - but the actual number of musicians employed in a particular performance could vary according to the work being played and the size of the venue. A leading chamber orchestra might employ as many as fifty musicians; some are much smaller.

Also, marching bands are known for their musicianship as well as incorporating choreography, moving formations, banners, and drum majors. The Fightin' Texas Aggie Band has over 400 members.[32] The power that emanates from marching bands heralds their presence in such exhilarating fashion that leaves audiences pumped up long after the event.

In David's day there was no sound reinforcement for the vocals, no amps for the other instruments – just sounds created with breath and body unto the Lord. The praise was so awesome and powerful that God responded by filling the house with His Glory. What a mighty God we serve! Just referencing verse 14 ought to move somebody. A visit from the Holy Spirit covered by a cloud! This phenomenon was no ordinary cloud, but one that was dense and encompassed the house of God from ceiling to floor, wall to wall.

The occurrence epitomizes the verse in Psalm 22:3 which reads: *"Yet you are holy, O You who are enthroned on the praises of Israel."* This verse is popularly translated as *God inhabits the praises of His people.*

I firmly believe in the omnipresence of God, and that His Spirit resides where His people render praises unto Him in various forms. The context of Psalm 22:2 is one of desperation, of feeling forsaken, or abandoned by God during times of tribulation. Verse 3 reassures us that God's presence is with us when we direct our thoughts to Him. When we begin to extol and compliment God, His wonderful presence will be in the room.

So be encouraged. God is the same today as He was yesterday. The difference is in our praise, our actions in the House of God and the lack of oneness. Go back to II Chronicles 5. Oneness was indicated by the words *unison* and *one* sound. Notice, they all had one voice – not voices.

Earlier we talked about corporate praise and how important it is to be on one accord. Fast-forward to the Day of Pentecost when the people were in one place and on one accord. The people were in one place, of one mind, one spirit and one purpose - not doing their own thing. I believe there was oneness in Love, oneness in prayer, oneness in praise, and oneness in expectation. Again, look at the occasion where there were 4000 – that's 4000 players assigned to the office of praising God continually (I Chron. 23). The passage embodies persistence and dedication to the daunting task of praising God on the instruments.

God responds with power when we are on one accord. When the church is on one accord, everyone in the assembly has a mind to reach heaven. The events of the Day of Pentecost are prime examples of what happens when people come together with one mind and one purpose. As with the Levites, the oneness of the people who gathered in the upper room set the atmosphere for the presence of the Holy Ghost.

The Holy Spirit made an entry on the Day of Pentecost in spectacular proportion. The noise was so powerful it was like a rushing mighty wind. The explosive power of the Holy Ghost (dunamis, Strong's Greek: 1411) is what I long for as I play on the organ and sing the songs of Zion. I want to extend an invitation for the manifestation of the Holy Ghost to descend and fill the house.

The Holy Spirit answers words of exhortation, joyful songs, and music with a chain of supernatural responses. When the Holy Spirit counters our praise with His presence, our reaction should be to let Him have His way; to take our hands off the process, for the Holy Spirit operates singularly, without our help. There is no need to fan worshipers, call in the ushers to help hold people back or restrain them when the anointing is at work.

Instruments were also used to communicate messages between the tribes since they did not have fast and instant technology. Instruments were used as effective weapons to scare off the enemy, and to express triumph or celebration.

We know there will be instruments in heaven such as harps and the psaltery and trumpets, but The Word of God also states that there will come a time when instruments will be no more (Ezek. 26:13, Rev. 18:22) on earth. After the new heaven and the new earth, there is no mention of instruments on earth. The instruments were created to accompany our praise but not to take the place of praise with the mouth.

While you have a chance, praise God upon the instruments, even if it's a tambourine. Find a way to maximize your praise with the Zamar.

Laughter

Who doesn't love to laugh? Who isn't drawn to people who will laugh until they lose their breath and collapse on the floor?

Most likely you are drawn to someone who has a nice smile or a great laugh. Laughing is popular and deliberate. There is even an tech-acronym or shortcut in text messaging: LOL – or laugh out loud. There are endless comedies that come and go and comedians make a fortune trying to make people laugh out loud. In fact, every day I like to get my laugh fix with an old *Seinfeld* or *Honeymooners* episode to end the day on a positive note. (I confess I've cut back from 5 episodes to 3).

Under normal conditions, laughter expresses joy and gladness. Why wear a frown when it comes to praising? I have seen people singing the praises of God with all their might, but their expression contradicts their song. People sing about the joy of the Lord being their strength but their body language suggests the complete opposite. A smile or laugh added to our praise edifies the saints and sends a message to unconfessed sinners that we are happy to have made Jesus our choice. A pleasant demeanor in praise is beautiful and infectious.

Laughter is the biological reaction humans have to moments or occasions of humor. Laughter is an outward expression of amusement. "Laughter is sub-categorized into various groupings depending upon the extent and pitch of the laughter: giggles, clicks (hat is virtually silent) chortles, chuckles, hoots, cackles, sniggers and guffaws are all types of laughter. Smiling may be considered a mild, silent form of laughter. Some studies indicate that laughter differs depending upon the gender of the laughing person: women tend to laugh in a more "sing-song" way, while men more often grunt or snort."[33] The Word of God has this to say about laughter as it pertains to praise: "B*ehold God will not cast away a perfect man; neither will He help the evil doers; Till he fill thy mouth with laughing, and thy lips with rejoicing" (Job 8:20, 21).*

Laughter is connected to the Lord. Smiling is a gift of God. Demonstrate that you enjoy God. Add smiles to your praise! Demonstrate that you feel good about praising. Smiles are loving and pleasant. Minister a smile to God and those around you.

Crying

In contrast to laughter, generally, crying is not something people aim to do in public. A range of theories suggests the function of crying as a nonverbal response to communicate emotions. "Recent psychological theories of crying emphasize its relationship to the experience of perceived helplessness. An underlying experience of helplessness can usually explain the reason people cry from this perception. For example, a person may cry after receiving surprisingly happy news, ostensibly because the person feels powerless or unable to influence what is happening."[34]

My theory about crying in praise is that tears convey earnestness like no other emotion. People don't take into consideration chemical build up or workings in the body and then consciously decide to cry. Crying expresses a deep emotional response. Some people cry easily and frequently; while others may be considered tough because they rarely – if ever – respond by crying. Words are just words but when someone expresses thoughts or feelings with tears, it seems more authentic or convincing. Sincere tears invoke action.

Often times the phrase, *"and they cried out to the Lord,"* or *"he cried out to the Lord,"* in the Word of God was followed by the, *"and He heard him/them"* or *"and he helped them."* The same was true of Jehoshaphat, the servant of the Lord, in heat of battle:

> *When the chariot commanders saw Jehoshaphat, they thought, "This is the king of Israel. So they turned to attack him, but Jehoshaphat cried out, and the Lord helped him. God drew them away from him…" (II Chron.18:31).*

Crying may speak sorrowfulness as in guilt: "*They cried out to the Lord and said, We have sinned; we have forsaken the Lord and served the Baal and the Ashtoreths. But now deliver us from the hands of our enemies, and we will serve you" (I Sam. 12:10).*

Jesus wept concerning the death of His friend Lazarus even though He had the power to raise him and would ultimately do so. He also cried out to His Father during His crucifixion because of the agony and suffering He would endure on behalf of the world. Jesus' crying did not amount to a pity-party, but a natural reaction to the events surrounding His sacrificial death, including the disconnect from His Father, the humiliation of the accusations, plus physical pain (John 11:35). Jesus wept on the cross to express agony and feelings of abandonment: "*About the ninth hour Jesus cried out in a loud voice, "Eloi, Eloi, lama sabachthani?"—which means, 'My God, my God, why have you forsaken me?"(Matt. 27:46, NIV).*

Society has propagated the idea that crying denotes weakness. I believe God created humans with a range of emotions which are activated to restore good health.

Earlier, I wrote concerning humility. Crying exposes our vulnerability. Sometimes we are seen at our best or worst when we cry. God sees and appreciates it all. Jesus' empathy for those who cry is shown in the eminent account of the woman who washed His feet with her tears:

> *And there was a woman in the city who was a sinner; and when she learned that He was reclining at the table in the Pharisee's house, she brought an alabaster vial of perfume, and standing behind Him at His feet, weeping, she began to wet His feet with her tears, and kept wiping them with the hair of her head, and kissing His feet and anointing them with the perfume. Now when the Pharisee who had invited Him saw this, he said to himself, "If this man were a prophet He would know who and what sort of person this woman is who is touching Him, that she is a sinner" (Luke 7:37-39, NASB).*

Every time I read this passage I envision the woman standing there, behind Jesus, her slight shoulders shuddering, her posture slumped. I get a sense of her weakness, and her shame.

We don't know whether or not she was crying as a consequence of some problem – only that she wept and that she worshiped. The bible does not characterize her as poor or in pain – only that she wept. She had in her possession a very exquisite alabaster container (KJV says box) of expensive oil. Alabaster is gypsum-calcite or onyx marble. By today's standard onyx-marble is considered a high-end material (at about $100-500/sq. meter) so the woman - who is nameless – was of significant means despite how she came by it, and most likely was not weeping because she was broke. More than likely she wept because she was in the presence of the promised King, Jesus the Christ.

> *Turning toward the woman, He said to Simon, "Do you see this woman? I entered your house; you gave Me no water for My feet, but she has wet My feet with her tears and wiped them with her hair. You gave Me no kiss; but she, since the time I came in, has not ceased to kiss My feet. You did not anoint My head with oil, but she anointed My feet with perfume. For this reason I say to you, her sins, which are many, have been forgiven, for she loved much; but he who is forgiven little, loves little." Then He said to her, "Your sins have been forgiven." (Luke 7:37-39, 44-48 NASB)*

There is no record that this woman, who invited herself into Jesus' personal space, spoke any words; only that she wept or cried. Her tears, along with the act of anointing Jesus' feet with special perfume, were physical ministrations (praise) of her love and devotion (worship) to Jesus, irrespective of her past sins. She was silent but, her tears were indicative of her praise and worship. Crying touched Jesus' heart; wiping Jesus feet with her tears gave her part with Him. Later, In John chapter 11, we learn that this 'woman' is Mary, Lazarus' and Martha's sister. She is the same Mary who chose to sit at Jesus' feet while her sister Martha busied herself cooking. Jesus said Mary had made the better choice of worship over service. The story reinforces the notion that 'works' falls short of true worship.

Crying is not something we have to force, but God has compassion on tears and not only that, the Holy Scriptures state that *"if we sow in tears we will reap in joy" (Psa.126:5).* Praise God and let the tears flow! Have no fear in humility, in brokenness. As the tears come you may say "Lord, I surrender," "Lord, I give myself over to you," "Lord, I deny myself," "Lord, I die right now that you might live in me, and I offer myself to you a living sacrifice of praise."

Embrace the emotions that come with the visitation of the Presence of God as you exalt Him. Visualize God. Begin to sense His holiness, His greatness, His vastness, His goodness, His perfection. Take no thought to wipe the tears. As the tears flow and cleanse, continue to esteem God and Glorify Him.

A Loud Voice

I have written at length on the volume of praise (e.g. noise, shout). The world is succeeding in quieting the saints to the extent of praising God in the public square. Presently, our time on earth is critical, both spiritually and morally, and believers should be lifting up the name of our God boldly. Our voices should be heard above all others; particularly in America where everyone but Christians seem to be protected by the first Amendment to say anything, hold a sign up about anything, have a parade and lobby legislation for anything. Christians are not only supposed to be tolerant of those ideas, but accepting and embracing.

There was nothing hidden about Jesus nor His acts. In fact, Jesus said, *"Think not that I am come to send peace on earth: I came not to send peace but a sword."* Did you know that we are to be forceful in our stance for Christ? Our position includes praise as a witness.

John, chapter 11 illustrates the effectiveness of a loud voice. Jesus used a loud voice to call forth the dead. He called forth Lazarus specifically by name so other dead folk would not come forth. Jesus called out Lazarus for the purpose of glorifying God the Father, and so people would believe in the resurrection power. Mary, the mother of Jesus, saluted Elisabeth with a loud voice to the extent that the babe inside Elisabeth leaped, and she was filled with the Holy Ghost. During their meeting, both women exclaimed the praises of God, and to the yet to be born Savior in loud voices:

> *… and she exclaimed with a loud cry Blessed are you among women, and blessed is the fruit of your womb! And why is this granted to me that the mother of my Lord should come to me? For behold, when the sound of your greeting came to my ears, the baby in my womb leaped for joy. And blessed is she who believed that there would be a fulfillment of what was spoken to her from the Lord.* (Luke 1:42-45, ESV)

Present day laws quiet believers, and the bible says there will come a time when believers in America will be persecuted for the sake of Christ. Organizations like the American Civil Liberties Union (ACLU) have championed the rights of every leftist anti-Christ cause but have worked vehemently to deny Christians the same right to express their beliefs in the public square. The time to resist the efforts of the enemies of God is now. Our praise and our witness should be visible, vigilant and audible. We must shout and we must cry out with a loud voice unto the glory of God.

I admit that my first impression of seeing someone hollering and waving a bible in hand on a busy downtown street corner was that there was possibly something clinically wrong. In retrospect, that person was doing precisely what John the Baptist did, what Peter did, and what Apostle Paul did: loudly proclaim the good news. Believers should get to the place where we lose a little of that dignity or pride that holds us back from proclaiming the name of Jesus and the things of God publicly.

The Bible states:

> *And when he was come nigh, even now at the descent of the mount of Olives, the whole multitude of the disciples began to rejoice and praise God with a loud voice for all the mighty works that they had seen; (Luke 19:37)*

> *Saying with a loud voice, Fear God, and give glory to him; for the hour of his judgment is come: and worship him that made heaven, and earth, and the sea, and the fountains of waters. (Rev. 14:7)*

There were a few occasions in the bible where people cried with a loud voice because they had unclean spirits seeking the attention of Jesus or the disciples [read Mark 1:25-27, Mark 5: 6 -8, Acts 7:56 – 58], but the saints had no shame in those days about proclaiming the great things of God loudly and publicly. We should get ready because there will be a lot of loud praises going on in heaven for eternity:

> *Then I looked, and I heard the voice of many angels around the throne and the living creatures and the elders; and the number of them was myriads of myriads, and thousands of thousands, saying with a loud voice, "Worthy is the Lamb that was slain to receive power and riches and wisdom and might and honor and glory and blessing" (Rev. 5:10-12, NASB).*

There is no shame or offense in having a loud voice for God. To halal praise is to express praise clamorously and foolishly. That is, praise in such a way that you may get on people's nerves and they'll have to loosen up, join in or go away.

One of my favorite sermons is, "*There's* a *Story behind my Praise*" by Pastor Sheryl Brady. In this sermon, Pastor Brady talks about the same woman with the alabaster box who ministered to Jesus by pouring expensive oil on His feet, anointing them with her tears and wiping them with hair. In the sermon, Pastor Brady says the woman was criticized for ministering to Jesus or worshiping Him. Everybody else wanted something from Jesus; but the woman wanted Jesus. She was desperate, not distracted. The people who were criticizing and judging did not see that there was a story behind her praise. As praisers, sometimes we will have to get past crazy, hateful, lyin', backbitin', trifling folk to get to Jesus. She had come to see Jesus. True worshipers don't need an organ or a praise team; true worshipers only need a flashback to launch into a 'you don't know like I know' praise. She was a sinner but she acknowledged the Lordship of Jesus. She reverenced. She gave her best, earnestly.[35]

Instead of utilizing the voice to complain and fuss, lifting the voice in praise is more advantageous to a godly relationship. Try marking where you are in this book and just begin to say out loud, "blessings and honor, glory and power be unto Him. Worthy is the Lamb who was slain; He is the Alpha and Omega, the First and the Last." Praise God as though you remember what He has done and like you owe Him. Don't concern yourself with what others think. Incorporate the praise phrases in the verses below by first reading and then repeating them.

> *And I beheld, and I heard the voice of many angels round about the throne and the beasts and the elders: and the number of them was ten thousand times ten thousand, and thousands, of thousands; Saying with a loud voice,* ***Worthy is the*** *Lamb that was slain to receive power, and riches, and wisdom, and strength, and honour, and glory, and blessing.*
>
> *And every creature which is in heaven, and on the earth, and under the earth, and such as are in the sea, and all that are in them, heard I saying Blessing, and honour, and glory, and power, be unto him that sitteth upon the throne, and unto the Lamb for every and ever (Rev. 5:11-13).*

Loud voices are powerful. Loud voices command attention.

Returning to the example of Jesus, when He cried out with a loud voice one last time before giving up His spirit, a chain of events occurred: "*at once the curtain of the sanctuary of the temple was torn in two from top to bottom; the earth shook and the rocks were split, The tombs were opened and many bodies of the saints who had fallen asleep in death were raised [to life]" (Matt.27:51-53, AMP*); and after the dead came out of the tombs, they went into the holy city and appeared to many people.

In Revelations 5, we see that the voices were loud, magnified, thunderous, even deafening. When we get to heaven, there will be no need to concern ourselves with whether our voices will be too loud for God. There was hollering going on throughout the book of

Revelations to the delight of God that sits on the throne. No one rose up and said "hey, everybody be quiet! It's too noisy in here!" There are no 'quiet zones' in heaven. Heaven is not a library. So it's time to start practicing what you hope to do for eternity. Praise God with a loud, thunderous voice. OPEN YOUR MOUTH AND SAY AHHH!

Clapping

Clapping is to strike together two hard surfaces such as the palms. Clapping is a manner of making a joyful noise. Clapping also signifies assent, such as when someone is making a speech and there is agreement and encouragement. With clapping, we can urge someone on. Clapping is a universal expression of approval, joyfulness or gladness (I Kings 11:12). Clapping commands attention and can be used as a command: "*O clap your hands, all ye people; shout unto God with the voice of triumph" (Psa. 47:2)*.

Not long ago I happened to turn on the international news, and there were well dressed people poised behind a podium of the NYSE clapping to help signal the start of trading. No doubt, few of us get the point of that custom, but it regularly happens, Monday through Friday without fail - whether the points are up or down. Perhaps clapping in that instance is a way of promoting a positive outlook or it could represent nostalgia.

You may not have thought of it in such a way, but clapping is a self-contained percussion instrument. You can make a lot of musical sounds with your body.

Inanimate objects also clap: "*Let the floods clap their hands: let the hills be joyful together"(Psa. 98:8)*. The verses in Psalm 98 declare that inanimate objects such as trees, glorify God. They may not literally clap but a flood certainly slaps and swooshes and does its thing all as a testament to who God is.

I trust you attend a place of worship where these forms of praise are not prohibited or inhibited and that there is liberty where you worship. However, you needn't wait until you are in a formal worship service to clap or engage in these forms of praise. You can crank up music that is favorable and complimentary towards God and have a good time, clapping, making melody and making noise, singing and dancing in the Spirit at home. Praising at the start of the day is akin to clapping at the ringing of the bell at Wall Street's NYSE; it prepares you for whatever tasks are ahead. People may look at you and wonder why you are so happy and why you have so much energy, but do it anyway. Make it infectious. Pass it on to someone else!

Ministry Tip

Memorize the six forms of praise
Along with the Hebrew names and
Definitions for each.
Next, analyze your praise life.
Which of forms of praise do you
Engage?

Summary

This chapter outlined seven forms of praise: 1) Yadah –to up Lift hands to Him; 2) tehillah – means to sing; 3) Barak- To kneel or to bow; 4) halal - to make a show, to boast; 5) towdah-To give worship by the extension of the hand; 6) zamar - striking with the fingers, to touch the strings or parts of a musical, i.e. to make music; 7) shabach - to address in a loud tone, a loud adoration, a shout! Proclaim with a loud voice. However, SIX are actual forms of praise – with 'Barak' specifically being a form of worship because it involves bowing down. Also crying, laughter and waving the banner are acts of praise (Psa. 20:5).

Indeed, there are a host of issues Christians can be sad-sap about. It takes time to be miserable and depressed. We can choose to sit and dwell on issues, or elect to have experiences that are counter-productive to spiritual growth, or we can give it over to God and focus our attention on Him.

I know first-hand about the time it takes to be depressed and how cultivating negative thoughts makes the devil's job easier. I must confess that even during the time of these writings the weight of my life came down on me and instead of yearning for God I found myself wanting death and asking God to take me. Since beginning this project the enemy had come against me like a flood and instead of applying the principles of the Word, I lay listless for many days listening to sad bluesy songs; allowing the devil to make me think life was not worth living and that I was a constant failure.

Instead of wasting time with negative thinking, we need to concentrate our energy on contemplating the praises of God. We have to be exuberant and glad about life and our relationship with God on purpose. We can 'yadah' or 'towdah' God. We can lift our hands unto God. We favorably express ourselves to God in these many forms because He is worthy and because praising Him invigorates our passion for God.

It is an awesome thing to be afforded a personal relationship with a God that is alive and abiding in our praise. God is pleased when His people praise with the dance, clapping, loud voices, and making noise unto Him. I believe to praise God in these manners, we seek the heart of God as opposed to His hand. We praise in these various forms out of pure love for Him.

Praise is no longer limited to an elite section of the believing population (Levites) as it was in the Old Testament. God expects everything that has breath to praise Him. Praise is our witness to the world that we know the one, the only, true and Living God. If this message is going up before God and to the world, it also notifies the enemy that God alone is worthy of honor and praise. So begin immediately to put the enemy into flight by practicing lifting up hands, shouting, crying, raising loud voices, dancing, making a joyful noise, and waving banners. Let us praise God continually.

Chapter 6

The Character and Attributes of God

Holiness
God is Light
God is Love
God is Perfect

Character is a blend of inner qualities that factors in a person's moral decisions; while attributes (characteristics) elicit the manner in which a person is depicted, identified, or recognized physically. Character is the set of noticeable values that distinguish our behavioral patterns, as determined by conscious traits such as love, kindness, gentleness, peacefulness, etc. Physical features are superficial aspects that are readily branded to a person, whereas character determines whether there is the propensity to habitually lie, steal, punch someone in the face, criticize, speak unkind words, or even cheat on our taxes. Other terms synonymous with character are nature, temperament, personality, spirit, makeup, and moral fiber.

The terms 'attribute' and 'character' are often used interchangeably; with attribute having to do with one's positive traits. A person's character enables that person to act according to his or her relative moral makeup. A more common way of identifying these terms is within the context of how a person is inclined to behave or 'carry' him or herself in a manner. Likewise, character is associated with judgment or decisions in behavior. Again, character will determine the choices we make; such as to steal or not to steal; lie or tell the truth; sleep around with people or keep ourselves clean.

Character is what guides actions and is internal while attributes may be visible or the strong point of personality. Character is a person's inner make up. It is not only what determines our judgment, but how we are judged and known.

The character and attributes of God are more profound than imagery. Antithetical thought personifies God in a box; it seeks to depict God as a character in a manner of caricature. But the essence of God is so much more complex than the limitations of our imagination, or our intellect. We believe what the infallible Word of God says: that no man has seen God at any time and that no man can see God and live. Therefore, our faith prohibits any attempt to reduce God to the confines of physical form. I think of God as exceedingly vast, encompassing, absolute, and brilliant in the brightness of His glory.

Incorporating descriptions of God's character and attributes is relevant to complimenting God and saying, God I know this to be true about you. I know you are holy. God I recognize that you are righteous. God I acknowledge that you are Mighty.

As you read the Word of God, keep a running list of attributes or references to the character of God. Periodically read over the list until those truths are implanted in your spirit and come out of your mouth automatically in praise. As you draw into the presence of God, speak what you have learned about Him; whisper it to Him, cry unto Him, shout it unto to Him.

Holiness, the Primary Aspect of God's Character

The Holiness of God pertains to His supremacy in all aspects of His being, His perfection in character, the sovereignty of His acts and principally, His absolute purity manifested in the brightness of His Glory.

God made other things holy as well: the seventh day was to be regarded as holy; the ground on which Moses stood was holy and therefore not to be contaminated by his shoes. There were dwellings that were holy; garments that were holy; musical instruments and vessels were holy; nations were holy, but moreover holiness signified set apartness unto the Lord God.

R.A. Torrey defines holiness as being "free from all defilement, pure. "God is holy means God is absolutely pure."[36] "The adjectives expressive of the idea of Holiness or 'hieros,' found in

I Corinthians 9:13, has to do with things that are set apart unto God; hosios occurs more frequently and appears in Acts 2:27, I Timothy 2:8 and Hebrews 7:26. This term applies not only to things but to God and to Christ. It describes a person or thing as free from defilement or wickedness or more actively (of persons) as religiously fulfilling every obligation."[37] Also, there is the term 'hagios,' or the Greek 'hagiazo' which means sanctified or separation, consecration and devotion to the service of God.[38]

From these Hebrew terms we get a definitive confirmation that one must be separated unto God to be like God. We are separated from darkness, separated from wrong doing, separated from wrong beliefs and things not pleasing to God and ungodly behavior on the whole.

Moreover, holiness is about what we are separated **unto**: purity, light, loveliness, honesty, and all that is good as defined by God. Holiness means not only that there is no darkness but there is no gray, and no beige. The lines and limitations are clearly and absolutely defined. Too many Christians verbalize – with a shrug of the shoulders - the attitude that everyone sins and nobody's perfect, no matter what. Yes, beyond falling short of the glory of God, if we say that we have no sin, we deceive ourselves, and the truth is not in us. The fact that we all sin does not negate the fact that holiness is required to see the LORD. "*If we confess our sins, he is faithful and just to forgive us our sins, and to cleanse us from all unrighteousness. If we say that we have not sinned, we make him a liar, and his word is not in us" (I John 1:8 – 10).*

We must make every effort to meet God's expectation of holiness. *Therefore, since we have these promises, dear friends, let us purify ourselves from everything that contaminates body and spirit, perfecting holiness out of reverence for God" (II Cor. 7:1, NIV).*

God, in His absoluteness has always required holiness.

In the beginning God created mankind in His own likeness and in His image. When Adam and Eve disobeyed they essentially died to God; they became separated from God, from His grace and His favor and separated from His light.

The only thing we still have with God when we sin is His unconditional love that provides a way back to Him where He can look upon us and receive us into His presence. He has required no less of us in our living. He stipulates set-apartness and separation unto Him. God said, "*Because it is written, be ye holy; for I am holy" (I Peter 1:16).*

Conditions of holiness are 1) set apartness 2) separation unto God, 3) not having fellowship with darkness, and 4) keeping one's self unspotted from the world and unclean things. "*Therefore, come out from their midst and be separate, says the lord, And do not touch what is unclean; and I will welcome you" (II Cor. 6:17 NASB).*

Praising God and recognizing His holiness elevates our level of praise. When we acknowledge that He is light and that in Him is no darkness; that He is the hope that sustains us in this world and the world beyond gives us reason to praise God. *But ye are a chosen generation, a royal priesthood, an holy nation, a peculiar people; that ye should shew forth the praises of him who hath called you out of darkness into his marvelous light (I Peter 2:9).*

And,

> *I appeal to you therefore, brethren, and beg of you in view of [all] the mercies of God, to make a decisive dedication of your bodies [presenting all your members and faculties] as a living sacrifice, holy (devoted, consecrated) and well pleasing to God, which is your reasonable (rational, intelligent) service and spiritual worship (Rom. 12:1, AMP).*

The above passage gives us to know that we can live holy, walk in the light, and live undefiled. The scriptures state that presenting our bodies as a living and holy sacrifice is our *reasonable* service. This means God would not say do it or be it, if it was unattainable or impossible. It is thoroughly possible - and punishable if we do not.

God's holiness concerns being set apart unto Himself since there is no higher standard (Heb. 6:13). Theologian and author, Stephen Charlock declares:

> The holiness of God negatively is a perfect and unpolluted freedom from all evil. As we call gold pure that is not marked [by] any dross, and that garment clean that is free from any spot, so the nature of God is estranged from all shadow of evil, all imaginable contagion. Positively, it is the rectitude or integrity of the divine nature..."[39]

God is distinct and transcendent with regard to creation in all of His attributes. His "apartness" involves all of His being (Ex. 15:11; I Sam. 2:2; Is. 57:15). Louis Berkhof describes this as the "majestic-holiness" of God, which is His comprehensive, all-inclusive holiness. In this sense God's holiness includes His exalted spirituality, righteousness, sovereignty, wisdom, wrath, grace, etc., so that man as a mere creature is overwhelmed with His awesome, unique presence; resulting in creature abasement. Berkhof goes on to contend that "It could be claimed that God's moral holiness is at the heart of His majestic holiness since it permeates every aspect of His being."[40]

> THE HOLINESS OF GOD (2) With regard to God Himself: (a) He is His own, consistent, unchanging, morally pure standard, and never has any need to be compared with another standard outside of Himself (Ex. 15:11; Is. 6:3; Heb. 6:13). God is independently sufficient in His own moral being. This aspect declares who God essentially is. (b) He is set apart from all that is alien to His purity. There is not a speck of defilement, not the faintest stain of impurity in His person, "no darkness at all" (I John 1:5). This aspect declares who God actively is. He is set apart unto all that is in harmony with His moral excellence, His utterly righteous...[41]

The holiness of God is manifested in that God will not look upon sin. In fact, Jesus who knew no sin, died and therefore, His Father could not look upon Him. In Mark 15:34 and Matthew 27:46 Jesus cried out "*My God, my God, why hast thou forsaken me?*" This agonizing plea expressed the abandonment and separation Jesus experienced as He transitioned from life to death on behalf of the world.

> *And at the ninth hour Jesus cried with a loud voice, Eloi, Eloi, lama sabachthani?—which means, My God, My God, why have You forsaken Me [deserting Me and leaving Me helpless and abandoned]? (Mark 15:34, AMP)*

In our case, death is the result of disobeying God or turning away from God; but our Lord's death was to expedite our stay of execution, so we could have eternal life in the place called heaven which God prepared. Church, take a moment to think about the dynamics of the last sentence. The blood of Jesus effectively nullified the charges against us. Jesus is the best news of our lives when we deserve nothing less than death row. So why would anyone choose to sabotage the opportunity for eternal life when God's way is so easy?

So if you are unclear about where to begin in praise, begin with the holiness of God. Acknowledge the light of God, the love of God, and God's unmerited favor. I tell you, if nothing else evokes praise in the church, God's amazing grace should make you praise. If nothing else stirs up praise in the church, thoughts of what our blessed Savior suffered on our behalf, should make us praise.

A word about holiness. The world has transmitted the idea that being holy is a social status or acting 'better' than someone else. Holiness is the subject of ill-mannered jokes like 'holy roller' and 'holy cow.'

The notion of holiness deserves reverence rather than being paired with common terminology. I trust that as a believer, you will not make light of holiness, as holiness belongs to God. In some religions sin is not an issue. But to make light of the holiness of God is sacrilege. Please do not do it, nor should you tolerate the misappropriation of what belongs to Almighty God.

God is Light

The second aspect of God's character is light. The verse below is note worthy considering that in the beginning of time God said let there be light and there was light. The first things God created were the heavens and the earth which were without form. Some would disagree, but the heavens and the earth were actually water. God did not have to create darkness because the absence of light rendered the earth (water) dark. For the sake of argument consider the verse(s) in Genesis Chapter 1:

> *In the beginning God created the heaven and the earth.*
> *And the earth was without form, and void; and darkness was upon the face of the deep [water]. And the Spirit of God moved upon the face of the waters.*
> *And God said, Let there be light: and there was light. (Verses 1 – 3)*

God spoke into being a physical, visible light that was an extension of Himself upon the waters. Without getting into the breakdown of the various scientific theories, according to the definitions used in physics, light – or visible light, is electromagnetic radiation of all wavelengths, whether visible or not. Electromagnetic radiation can have both waves and particles.[42] This discussion does not further necessitate reasoning on photons, measurement of brightness, and all the other elements, but it is sufficient to note that without light nothing can be substantiated or sustained. Before the inception of any life-form, light was instated – not created but deposited in its proper place on earth because God was already light. Therefore, the aspect of God that is light is fundamental to the creation and survival of all living things.

Although scientists have developed instruments to measure and determine light, the light of God is immeasurable, uncontainable, and unbearable. The Word of God records how the children of Israel could not look upon Moses' face after the Lord's Glory (absolute Goodness/ purity/holiness) shined upon it. After being in the presence of God the attribute of light was transferred to Moses face, he had to cover with a veil to face the people (Gen. 34:29 – 35).

The bible states that Jesus is the light of the world and that,

> *In the beginning was the Word, and the Word was with God, and the Word was God (John 1:1).*
>
> *Then spake Jesus again unto them, saying, I am the light of the world: he that followeth me shall not walk in darkness, but shall have the light of life (John 8:12).*
>
> *I am come a light into the world, that whosoever believeth on me should not abide in darkness (John 12:46).*

Jesus is the light of the world for He is the moral, spiritual, and intellectual illumination. One day Jesus will also be the light of Heaven because the Word says,

> *And the city has no need of the sun nor of the moon to give light to it, for the splendor and radiance (glory) of God illuminate it, and the Lamb is its lamp.*
> *The nations shall walk by its light and the rulers and leaders of the earth shall bring into it their glory (Rev. 22:23-25 AMP).*

If you truly want to visualize something to praise God about, read Revelations 21. You don't have to wonder about heaven, the description is there and you can begin praising God for the home that is prepared and that your name is written in the Lamb's Book of Life. You can praise God that we won't have to deal with this nasty, polluted earth because there will be a new heaven and a new earth. Our Great God will dwell among us and wipe away our tears. There will be no more sickness and no more death. Is praise what you do?

God is Love

The scriptures state that we cannot say we love God and hate others. If love is both an attribute and a characteristic of God, it follows that we must possess the same characteristic, for the bible says, "*Behold, what manner of love the Father hath bestowed upon us, that we should be called the sons of God: therefore the world knoweth us not, because it knew him not"(I John 3:2).*

God demonstrated the finest act of love when "*He so loved the world that he gave His only begotten son that whosoever believeth on Him should not perish but have everlasting life*" (John 3:16). This is the apex of our faith and the reason we praise. God loved us enough to provide a way so that we don't have to perish! God provided a way to restore relationship with humankind, and if we accept His plan of restoration we will reside with the Father, the Son, and the heavenly hosts in a place that is even better than Eden!

God's infinite love is manifested in the love we have toward each other: "*He that loveth not, knoweth not God; for God is love"(I John 4:8).* God says people will know that we follow Him by the love we have for one another. This is a love that is not in reserve, but a Godly love evidenced in kindness, gentleness, and compassion continually.

Picture this: It's Sunday Morning. The sun is bright against a sharp blue sky. No Sunday brunch drivers to frustrate your press and - for once - you arrive on time for worship service. Upon your arrival, the atmosphere is right for the Presence of God. The music is good and the Word is delivered with a fervor that sets the church on fire. The fellowship is warm.

And then it happens.

You decide to forgo supper at home and head to the restaurant buffet where many saints gather for fried chicken and greens. You order your meal and get to eating.

All of a sudden, there is a commotion.

(Now this hypothetical commotion is unusual because my experience has been chatter ceases when people commence to eating.)

You look over and it's 'sho' nuff' Sistah So-and-So making demands on the server. And this 'ain't' the first time. Another time she was fussin' and causing a scene in the grocery store.

Lord have mercy.

"Wasn't she just shouting and carrying on with the praise team?"

"Where is the love?"

The saints of God ought to be so grounded in love that love follows everywhere we go. We should exemplify the love of God in and outside the realm of praise, for the scriptures say people will know us by our love. Our love for God is illuminated in the love we have for believers and the world.

The Greek word for love 'Agapao' is a verb and calls for action in relationship; Agapao speaks of a love "in a social or moral sense; while 'agape' is affection or benevolence; a love feast: (feast of) of charity…"[43]

So we not only love God affectionately as He loves us, but we love one another (agapao) as we embody this prominent attribute of God to which there is no end.

Love in our Thought Life

Hiding inside our thoughts and our imaginations may give a false sense of security, but actually, God knows our thoughts afar off and He knows if we exemplify love in our thought life. Zachariah 8:17 states, *that we should not imagine evil in our heart against our neighbors.*" I Corinthians 13:5 says, *It [love] does not dishonor others, it is not self-seeking, it is not easily angered, it keeps no record of wrongs (*NIV).

Ultimately we become what we think. If this is an area where you are having difficulty, be sure to address it in prayer, soliciting God's help and He will do it. Psalm 139*:2* says, *Thou knowest my down sitting and mine uprising, thou understandeth my thoughts afar off.*

Our emotions are a part of our thought life. Do you have to like everybody? Is everyone going to like you? If you dislike someone to the point of hatred, you must be cleansed of this evil. Begin by coming clean about your feelings. Be honest with the Lord. As Christians, it is entirely possible to harbor a dislike for someone. Even if the person has given you good reason to dislike them – if they've lied on you, conjured up a false witness against you, back-stabbed and scandalized your name, you must filter out all of this unrighteousness with love so you are true in your praise. "*Finally, brothers, whatever is **true**, whatever is honorable, whatever is just, whatever is pure, whatever is lovely, whatever is commendable, if there is any excellence, if there is anything worthy of praise, think about these things"(Phil. 4:8, ESV).*

God is Perfect in His Character

People say all the time, *God is perfect and He can never make a mistake.* To say God is perfect is not to say He is perfect according to our limited understanding of perfect. In our sense of perfect there is room for error, but if there is even a microscopic imperfection in God, then there's no point to anything, and all truth is void.

The preacher and scholar A.W. Tozer said, "If there were a point when God stopped, then God would be imperfect."[44] God's infinity is a part of His perfection.

God is self-existent, eternal, faithful, and omnipresent which means He is everywhere; He is omnipotent, which is to say, all powerful; He is omniscient, meaning all knowing, and God is sovereign. Sovereign means God answers to no one. He is autonomous, self-sufficient [an attribute He does not desire in us] and self-directed.[45] These qualities are also a part of what makes God perfect, for perfection is completion [i.e. perfect in all your ways].

Our praises need to be inclusive of the fact that God is perfect, meaning there is nobody like Him or equal to Him. God is perfect in His goodness, His Love, His wisdom, His strength and might, alongside His mercy, His grace and His justice. He is the epitome of Honor, majesty, glory, beauty, and righteousness. God is faithful and immutable. "God's power and might is not exercised in a self-centered, self-seeking or narcissistic way. [Sic]To be sure, we are to give thanks and praise to God in all circumstances…"[46] In "*A Journey into the Father's Heart*" Tozer wrote:

> Without doubt the mightiest thought the mind can entertain is the thought of God, and the weightiest word in any language is the word for God" and "it is my opinion that the Christian conception of God current in these middle years of the 20th century is so decadent as to be utterly beneath the dignity of the Most High God and actually to constitute for professing believers something amounting to moral calamity."[47]

As Christians we needn't conceptualize God. God has already revealed Himself; therefore we praise and honor Him with the best expression out of our mouths. We acknowledge and compliment the character, attributes, and manifestations of God. Believers should take pleasure in speaking words concerning the aspects of God, for in doing so, He is well pleased.

Psalm 103

[1]Bless the LORD, O my soul: and all that is within me,
bless his holy name.
[2]Bless the LORD, O my soul, and forget not all his
benefits:
[3]Who forgiveth all thine iniquities; who healeth all
thy diseases;
[4]Who redeemeth thy life from destruction; who
crowneth thee with loving kindness and tender
mercies;
[5]Who satisfieth thy mouth with good things; so that
thy youth is renewed like the eagle's.
[6]The LORD executeth righteousness and judgment for
all that are oppressed.
[7]He made known his ways unto Moses, his acts unto
the children of Israel.
[8]The LORD is merciful and gracious, slow to anger,
and plenteous in mercy.
[9]He will not always chide: neither will he keep his
anger for ever.
[10]He hath not dealt with us after our sins; nor rewarded
us according to our iniquities.
[11]For as the heaven is high above the earth, so great is
his mercy toward them that fear him.
[12]As far as the east is from the west, so far hath he
removed our transgressions from us.
[13]Like as a father pitieth his children, so the LORD
pitieth them that fear him.
[14]For he knoweth our frame; he remembereth that we
are dust.
[15]As for man, his days are as grass: as a flower of the
field, so he flourisheth.
[16]For the wind passeth over it, and it is gone; and the
place thereof shall know it no more.
[17]But the mercy of the LORD is from everlasting
to everlasting upon them that fear him, and his
righteousness unto children's children;
[18]To such as keep his covenant, and to those that
remember his commandments to do them.
[19]The LORD hath prepared his throne in the heavens;
and his kingdom ruleth over all.
[20]Bless the LORD, ye his angels, that excel in strength,
that do his commandments, hearkening unto the voice
of his word.
[21]Bless ye the LORD, all ye his hosts; ye ministers of
his, that do his pleasure.
[22]Bless the LORD, all his works in all places of his
dominion: bless the LORD, O my soul.

Ministry Tip:

Activity:
Underline the attributes in the verses of Psalm 103.
List the underlined words in descriptive form. Example: Loving-kindness, knowing, merciful and gracious.
Begin memorizing theses words and incorporating them into your prayers and creating daily praise.

Summary

Incorporating language about the character and attributes of God is another way to elevate our praise. Knowing the character and attributes of God is vital to knowing God. It follows that we can speak well of, commend, laud God when we know His intrinsic make-up and what is good about Him. These facts are not hidden but plainly revealed by God and recorded in scripture.

The scriptures give us to know who God is in terms of His character and his attributes. God reveals His holiness, His incomprehensible love, and His light, throughout the Word. For that reason, we must immerse ourselves in the Word to become intimately aware of God's attributes and character, beyond intellectual knowledge.

We need to attain a level in the Spirit where God is on our minds all the time and we pursue Him. We know this is possible because Isaiah *26:3* states, *"Thou wilt keep him in perfect peace whose mind is stayed on thee because he trusteth in thee."* So there is no point during the day when our minds our devoid of God-thoughts on some level. If we are to attain any godly pleasure, we must exalt the attributes, character, and Spirit personality of ever-present God.

To have no thought of the attributes of God is indeed beneath the privilege afforded us that other beliefs do not have: of having a personal relationship with a living God. In order to develop relationship and appreciation, we must know the attributes and character of God. We must consciously divest ourselves of negative thoughts, sarcasm and cynicism, and instead pursue His justice, purity, loveliness, and goodness according to Philippians 4. We are to think on these things in order to have a life full of passionate praise.

When you praise, say out loud what you know to be true about God. Let the Lord God know He has found grace in your heart. Talk to God honestly as you would a friend. Your words need not be packaged beautifully with a bow. Just be real with God; speak His attributes and His character. We can expect that at times our righteousness will be less holy than at other times. We mess up but we praise Him anyway.

Acknowledgement of God has little to do with our worthiness. God gives us access to Him through His Son Jesus. There is no weight of condemnation as we enter the realm of praise. This means we are no longer immobilized by the bondage of the past because it is now buried beneath the blood.

To acknowledge God is to pay tribute to His holiness, His perfection and His all-encompassing character and attributes, including His infinity.

In the Old Testament and even in some cultures today, the shoes are removed indicating respect of place and space. Personally, I have a thing about people walking indoors with street shoes because they are likely dragging substances into the house on their shoes, making the living space unsanitary. Moses knew God to be so holy that he had to remove his shoes in reverence of the holy ground upon which he stood. For the record, removing shoes does not make us holy under grace. Maintaining a repentant heart and abandoning ungodliness makes us holy.

Do not allow condemnation to prevent you from praising. Simply tell God He is good and that He is righteous, that He is Light and in Him is no darkness at all. Build upon these truths and increase your fervor for the Lord God. No one – I mean NO one - can tell you that praising God will eradicate the tendency for error. Just know that there is no condemnation in Christ Jesus if you will set your heart toward Him, walk after the Spirit and keep a repentant heart as you continue to increase in praise.

Chapter 7

Speaking the Names of God

What's in a Name?
Familiarity
Glorifying His Name
The Name of the Lord
YWVH
Other Names

"If ye will not hear and if ye will not lay it to heart, to give glory unto my name, saith the Lord of host, I will even send a curse upon you and I will curse your blessings, yea I have Cursed them already, because ye do not lay it to heart" (Mal. 2:2).

What's In a Name?

An early lesson in our lives is that names serve to identify. Identification connotes distinction from another person, thing or entity. The first question strangers ask when they meet is, "*What's your name?*"

To refer to someone by name demonstrates regard, respect and responsibility to a relationship. For example, it would be inaccurate to claim someone as a good friend if you could barely recall the person's name. The importance of names is illustrated by the common practice of expectant mothers who comb through books in search of a name for an expected new born, based not just on the meaning, but culture and uniqueness. Others change their name to fit their profession.

Matthew Henry is popularly quoted as saying, "The better God is known, the more He is trusted, the more He is trusted, the more He is sought... [48] The scriptures state, "*And they that know* thy name *will put their trust in thee...*" *(Psa.9:10)*.

The names of God derive from the actions of God. He is thusly named based on what he does at that time. Now, I am careful to add, mankind did not name God; rather individuals of the bible memorialized events and places of Divine intervention with an identifier (and an altar) that permanently marked the moment for generations to come,

God had no reservations about identifying Himself. The names attributed to Him served to credit Him with specific actions, e.g. the name Jehovah-shalom, which Gideon called Him ('God of peace') or Jehovah-jireh, which Abraham called him in reference to the ram which was provided in place of Isaac.

Another function of biblical names was the foretelling of the character, attributes, and foibles of a person before they were born.

The angel Gabriel was sent by God to Elizabeth and to Mary. Mary was told that she would call her son Jesus, meaning, "Son of the Highest," Savior (Luke 1:31, 32); and Emmanuel, meaning "God with us" (Matt. 1:23). Nearly 2,000 years before the birth of Jesus, Jacob's (meaning 'sub planter') destiny as a deceiver/achiever was already in motion before he was born. As the twins Jacob and Esau struggled inside Rebekah's womb, she inquired of the Lord, and the Lord told her that two nations and two peoples were inside of her. Jacob came out holding onto his brother's heel. (Gen. 25: 21 – 26). Therefore the name (Yaqub in Arabic, Ja'akov in Hebrew, Jake in English) also means 'heel grabber.' These are examples of how names factor a particular persona.

Interestingly, throughout the Bible people were known during their lives as 'the son of so-and-so' and it became a part of their name, e.g. 'David the son of Jesse,' 'Joshua the son of Nun,' or 'Hosea the son of Beeri.' Likewise the name(s) of God work within the linguistic limitations of mankind to identify the encompassing personality of God.

In her defining book "*Praying the Names of God*" Ann Spangler declares "This ancient name Elohim... is the one that began it all, creating heaven and the earth... this ancient name for God contains the idea of God's creative power as well as authority and love."[49]

How well do you remember a person, thing, or occurrence without a name? Absence of a name makes lasting connections most strenuous. In modern times, fame is based on repetitious promotion of a name – the name along with images. Names on posters are placed on people's lawns, on stickers, on the windows of people's cars and on t-shirts so that the masses will remember the name of a particular candidate for political office. Congruently, having a name is important to who a person or entity is. Speaking that name should evoke pleasing thoughts and feelings of the goodness of a person, the good the individual has done.

God identified Himself first. During the period of creation, God was known as El or Elohim, Creator. Adam came to know God by his footsteps and by his voice calling out. Noah knew God in an intimate manner sufficient to following verbal instructions for the building of the ark. God said to Abram, *"I am the Almighty God; walk before me and be thou perfect" (Genesis 17:1).* Abram fell on his face before God and obeyed God's command to get from among his kindred, then continued on until his name was changed to Abraham (father of many nations).

Abraham obeyed God and went to the mount to offer up his son Isaac for sacrifice. God honored Abraham's obedience and willingness, but instead reserved that particular sacrifice for Himself in the person of the only begotten Son, Jesus. God provided a substitute sacrifice, therefore, the name of the place was called Jehovah-jireh or "it shall be seen" (Gen. 22:14) and "The Lord will provide." The place was to be remembered for how God miraculously intervened so that Abraham would not have to sacrifice Isaac. To Moses (drawn out of the water) God identified himself as "I AM, that I AM." (Exodus 3) Moses knew and talked to God the same as we speak to each other today:

> *Moses said to God, 'Suppose I go to the Israelites and say to them, "the God of your fathers has sent me to you," and they ask me, "What is his name?" Then what shall I tell them?" God said to Moses, "I AM WHO I AM. This is what you are to say to the Israelites: I AM has sent me to you." God also said to Moses,"*

> *Say to the Israelites, "The LORD the God of your fathers-the God of Abraham, the God of Isaac and the God of Jacob-has sent me to you. "This is my name forever... (Ex. 3:13-15, NIV)*

In these passages, God exercises sovereign right to 'name drop.' He references Abraham, Isaac, and Jacob because the people were always looking for proof or some sign and wonder to authenticate the truth of what God said. The people of Israel were good for meticulous observance and the keeping of their history and so God included recognizable, revered names so they would take Him at His word.

Names speak to what family a person belongs. A person may be entitled to privileges in life solely on the basis of his or her name. On the other hand, the connection of a name may say to people that someone is bad news. It is difficult to get ahead in life if your name is ruined either because somebody said something negative about you, or because of your own doing. There is an old cliché that "it's not *what* you know but, *who* you know." Proverbs 22:1 says, "*A good name is rather to be chosen than great riches, and loving favour rather than silver and gold.*" Ecclesiastes says "*A good name is better than precious ointment...*"

We must become familiar with the contextual significance of the names attributed to God based on events at that time.

It is powerful to call the names of God out in praise as a tribute to what an immutable God can do. For examples, you may thank Jehovah-nissi for giving you the victory over an oppositional situation; you may express your trust in God by saying '*the name of the Lord is a Strong Tower, the righteous run into and they are safe*'; or praise Jehovah-rapha for healing your body even before the miracle is done.

I have mentioned calling out the names of God as a tribute. Note the close resemblance of the word 'tribute' to the word 'attribute.' To call the names of God is a mark of respect for His attributes; which means to esteem or pay tribute to Him.

Declaring His Names and Glorifying His Name

To declare something is to state emphatically as if to certify it as law. To glorify the names of God as Jesus glorified the Father in John 17:1 makes His names famous and writes them in our hearts.

> *These words spake Jesus, and lifted up His eyes to heaven and said Father the hour is come; glorify thy son, that thy son also may glorify thee.*
>
> *And now, Oh Father, glorify thou me with thine own self with the glory which I had with thee before the world was.*

The passages in the Gospel of John are a poignant illustration that true worship begins with our obedience. Jesus was not exempt from obeying or glorifying the Father, even though all power was given to Him, and that by His name – the name of Jesus - we have access to the Father. Jesus the Son of God honored the Father by glorifying His name.

We must always reverence the name of the Most High God.

The opening passage of this chapter is a stern warning from God concerning desecrating or profaning His name in sacrifice. The Message Bible expounds the passage in the following manner,

> *And now this indictment you priests! If you refuse to obediently listen, and you refuse to honour me, God-of-the-Angel-Armies, in worship, then I will put you under a curse. I'll exchange your blessings for curses. In fact, the curses are already at work because you are not serious about honouring me. Yes, and the curses will extend to your children. I'm going to plaster your faces with rotting garbage, garbage thrown out from your feasts. That's what you have to look forward to (Mal. 2:2-3, MSG).*

The most alarming words in the passage are "*In fact, the curses are already at work because you are not serious about honouring me.*" The scriptures indicate that God's people, the nation of Israel, were cursed and the inheritance of honoring God's name was passed on to the Gentiles. God said "*shall*" meaning, He commanded the people to honor His name and make it great or famous. This inheritance was made possible by the name of Jesus.

> *For from the rising of the sun until the going down of the same my name shall be great among the Gentiles: and in every place incense shall be offered unto my name, and a pure offering: for my name shall be great among the heathen saith the Lord of hosts (Mal.1:11).*

The passage in Malachi was talking about priests who profane the name of God with the sacrifices, and who sought wives among idol worshipers. The priests were supposed to be in God's service. They were the mediators (in proxy) until God's plan worked to bring about a more excellent priest, Jesus Christ. Yet they turned from God. God's name (I AM that I AM, LORD God, etc) had no place or significance in their hearts. They were prideful and self-sufficient. Eventually the God of our salvation unveiled a new name for all people, in particular the Gentiles. Jesus Christ, Son of the living God was a name the Jews did not receive, but is given by God for all of man-kind to be saved by calling out the name.

The verses give us to know our inherent purpose of glorifying God and that if we don't, we too will be cursed. A whole heart is not limited to our attitude in the corporate worship setting. A whole heart is a heart for God all the time and a reverence for God all of the time: *"I will praise thee, oh Lord my God, with all my heart: And I will glorify thy name forever more" (Psa. 86:12).*

The Name of the Lord

The term 'Lord' is used regularly in worship, in prayer, and in praise by Christians. The term 'Lord' means that He is Lord but not in a tyrannical sense. He reigns more than He rules. He is Lord because we desire Him to be Lord. There is no negative connotation in referring to God as Lord as in enslavement. I have actually heard unbelievers criticize Christians for calling God 'Lord' or when Christians make a statement that they will 'serve' him. They lack the spiritual understanding of the relationship's composition and so they belittle or judge.

'Lord' is sometimes used in the context of Master or an attempt to esteem another person higher in an aristocratic manner. Though Gideon refers to an angel that visited him as Lord, the angel credits the real Lord: "*fear not the Lord is with thee, thou mighty man of valour"(Judges 6:12).* The angel was not referring to himself, but his Master, the Most High God (El Elyon) by whom he was sent. "The Greek term for Lord is 'despotes,' 'kurios,' or 'kurieu' for lord over." [Strong's 2960, 2962] We acknowledge God for being both Lord and lord over all the earth.

The reference of Lord is to state a title or position.

The Lord was 'over' others; he had more possessions, more power, more control, and the ability to bless or punish. Subordinate creatures submit and surrender their will to the Lord God.

At the time of Judges 6 chapter, the people of Israel were hiding out in caves for fear of the Mideanites. Israel did not have the protection nor provision of God because they acknowledged other gods at that time. They had no food or substance at all – not sheep, ox, nor ass the bible says. And so they cried out to God and God heard them. Gideon the son of Joash was hiding wheat from the Midianites. He had this conversation with the angel of the Lord:

> *And he said to him, "Please LORD how can I save Israel? Behold, my clan is the weakest in Manasseh, and I am the least in my father's house." And the LORD said to him,"But I will be with you, and you shall strike the Midianites as one man." And Gideon said, "Alas O Lord GOD! For now I have seen the angel of the LORD face to face." But the LORD said to him, "Peace be to you. Do not fear; you shall not die." Then Gideon built an altar there to the LORD and called it, The LORD Is Peace. [Jehovah-shalom]* (Judges *6:12-1, 23-25 ESV)*

In the passage in Judges, Gideon had to have his pity-party as did many of the great leaders of Israel down through the years. In spite of Gideon's admitted weakness, The angel of the Lord called Gideon a 'mighty man of valour' in reference to his capabilities as a warrior; but not only did Gideon not sound like a mighty man, he probably wasn't feeling very courageous at that time. He needed a lot of hand-holding and reassurance so that when the sign was given, Gideon believed on the sent Word of the Lord. The result of the dialogue with the angel was a name – to mark the place and the moment. Gideon called the place 'Jehovah-shalom" or God is our peace. Thus, in this scenario the name was ascribed to memorialize fulfillment of the promise of peace.

YWVH – The Tetragrammaton

The most important and most often written name of God in Judaism is the Tetragrammaton, the four-letter name of God, pronounced 'Yahweh' in modern times. This name is first mentioned in the book of Genesis 2:4 and is traditionally translated in English as 'The LORD.'[50] "It stems from the Hebrew conception of monotheism that God exits by himself for himself and is the uncreated Creator who is independent of any concept, force, or entity; therefore "I AM that I AM."[51]

El, Elohim, Elyon

El is used in both the singular and plural for the God of Israel. Other examples of its use with some attribute or epithet are: El Elyon ("Most High God") El Shaddai (God Almighty) El Olam (Everlasting God) El Hai (Living God) El Ro'I (God of Seeing) El Elohe Israel (God the God of Israel).

A common name of God in the Hebrew Bible is Elohim. Eloah, Elohim means, 'He who is the object of fear or reverence,' or 'He with whom one who is afraid takes refuge.' Another theory is that the name is derived from the Semitic root 'uhl' meaning 'to be strong.' Elohim then would mean 'the all powerful One,' based on the usage of the word 'El' in certain verses to denote power or might.

The name 'Elyon' occurs in combination with El, YHWH or Elohim, and also alone, It appears chiefly in poetic and later Bilblical passages. The modern Hebrew adjective 'Elyon' means 'supreme'...or

'Most High.' 'El-Elyon' has been traditionally translated into English as 'God, Most High.'[52]

Shaddai

"According to Exodus 6:2-3, Shaddai is the name by which God was known to Abraham, Isaac, and Jacob. The name Shaddai is ascribed to God later in the Book of Job. In the Septuagint and other early translations, Shaddai was translated with words meaning "Almighty." The root word "shadad" means to overpower or to destroy. This gives the name Shaddai the meaning of destroyer as one of the aspects of God. We say All Mighty God or God Almighty, or All powerful to describe Him.

Shekinah

Shekinah is the "presence or manifestation of God which has descended to 'dwell' among humanity. It is said that Rabbis used the word when speaking of God dwelling either in the Tabernacle or among the people of Israel. The root of the word means 'dwelling' and of the principle names of God, it is the only one that does. The word is also used in the context of 'security' and is derived from the root sa-ka-na which also means to dwell. We will discuss the subject of the Presence of God later."[53]

A-men

Many times we hear the name 'Amen' being used as a term to express consensus or agreement to something we believe to be the truth. Preachers urge congregations to chime in 'amen' to their sermons effectually as a means of saying 'it is so.' A-men is not just a term to be taken lightly. A-men is a name attributed to the Lord and should be reverenced as such. A-men means 'tantamount to an oath.' II Corinthians 1:20 says, "*For all the promises of God in Him are yea, and in*

Him Amen unto the glory of God by us" while Revelations 3:14 personifies 'Amen:' "*...These things saith the Amen, the faithful and true witness the beginning of the creation of God.*"

Thus the term 'Amen' is attributed to Jesus as a name, based on Him being the keeper of promises. Also there is 'finality' in the name of Jesus in that after Him there is nothing, and before Him there was nothing. Amen is found primarily at the end of a phrase, sentence, chapter or book.

Other Names of God:

Adonai, Gen 15:2

Amen

Almighty God, Gen 17:1

Ancient of Days
El Elyon, Gen 14:18 Most High God
El Olan, Gen 21:33
El Shaddai, Gen 17:1
Strengthener and Satisfier
Elohim, Gen 1:1
Eternal God, Gen 21:33
Father of the Heavenly Lights, Jamess 1:17
God, Isa 26:4
God of Heaven, Ezra 5:11; Neh 1:4..
God of Spendor
Holy One, Job 6:10; Ps. 16:10; Is 10:17...
Holy One of Israel
I AM THAT I AM
Jealous, Exodus 34:14
Jehovah, Ex 34:6
Jehovah Sabaoth, I Sam 1:3

Jehovah-shalom, God my peace, Judges 6:2
Jehovha-shammah, The Lord is there, Ex. 34:6
Jehovah-tsidkenu, The Lord our righteousness Jeremiah 33:16

Lord God, Genesis 15:2
Mighty God, Ps. 50:1. Isa 9:6

Most High, Gen. 14:18
Jehovah-rapha, God who heals
Jehovah, everlasting strength Is.26:4
Strong Tower, Prov. 18:10

Ministry Tip

These names represent a partial list of names attributed to God based on His acts, His character and His attributes. You will undoubtedly discover other names as you continue to study scripture and contemplate the events surrounding the application. Acknowledge God by speaking these names "God, You are Jehovah__________" etc. before you petition God and at the conclusion of your prayers.

Summary

Speaking the names of God in praise will result in your praise becoming more meaningful. Remember that God identified Himself early on and ultimately names came to be attributed to God based on His actions at that time, such as Jehovah-jireh given by Abraham when God provided the ram sacrifice in place of his son, Isaac (Gen 21:1-13).

Throughout the book of Leviticus, the book of the laws, God refers to Himself as "I AM the Lord (Adonai – Heb)" or I AM the Lord God." The reference to Lordship, first used in Genesis 2:5-7, established His authority. Thus, to refer to God as 'Lord' is to acknowledge the authority of God: maker of all things, giver of all things, governor all things.

Overall, names serve to identify or distinguish one person, thing, or entity from another. To refer to someone by name demonstrates regard, respect, and responsibility to a relationship. Names speak to things like lineage and heritage or to whom or what we are inextricably linked. For instance, a person may be entitled to privileges in life solely on the basis of his or her name. Proverbs 22:1 says, "A *good name is rather to be chosen than great riches, and loving for rather than silver and gold."* Ecclesiastes says, *"A good name is better than precious ointment."*

To recall someone's name shows recognition and respect. Periodically you may hear someone use the old excuse, "I'm good with faces but I'm so terrible with names." When we form acquaintances personally or in business, it is complimentary to speak the person's name. I believe omitting someone's name disclaims that person. Knowing a person's name acknowledges an individual's existence.

God's names are more precious than any other name. To commend, laud, extol, God by His names is to reverence Him and invite intimacy with Him.

How awesome is the name of Jesus!

There is power in His name. There is salvation in His name. There is healing in His name. There is deliverance and victory in His name. We know the bible says, *at the mention of the name of Jesus, demons tremble.* At the same time, we are to do everything in the name of Jesus. We go in His name, we fast in His name, we pray in his name. By Him and through Him is everything done and only by His name may we obtain salvation. We have access to the Father by use of Jesus' name.

Jesus said, *"I am the way, the truth, and the life. No man cometh to the Father except by me" (John 12:6).* Apostle Paul said, "*Neither is there salvation in any other: for there is no other name under heaven given among men, whereby we must be saved" (Acts 4:12).*

We are privileged to speak the names attributed to God. When you take a moment to think about it, God has made the processes of knowing and having access to Him, simple. Our connection to God begins with confessing that He is Lord. The time to make the confession is now rather than later. In the Day of Judgment every knee shall bow and every tongue shall confess that 'Jesus' is Lord; but if you did not confess to the name of Jesus before the judgment, your confession will too late.

I encourage you to fall in love with the name of Jesus and to let it be in your mouth as often as you think of Him. Also, speak the names of the Father, Son, and Holy Ghost, in praise. I strongly recommend Ann Spangler's classic book "*Praying the Names of God.*" Make the effort to memorize a name of God on a weekly basis. This is not easy, but becomes easier with repetition and use. You must make the effort to deposit the meaning of the names into your understanding as they relate to what God has done in your life, and those close to you.

Chapter 8

The Acts of God

His Hand
His Spirit
His Word
His Will

> *Give thanks unto the LORD, call upon his name, make known his deeds among the people (I Chron. 16:8).*

We have heard the term 'Act of God,' particularly when there has been an incident or natural disaster for which no one wants to assume responsibility and to which we assign blame. 'Act of God' is considered a legal or business phrase as - opposed to a simple cliché - for events outside of human control. In my experience this is especially the case in insurance matters. People say 'act of God' when there is an inexplicable natural occurrence that causes a lot of havoc and damage and no person can be held liable.

To act is to perform a deed voluntarily or willfully.

The Acts of God pertains to what God does. He performs acts in four ways: 1) with His hand, 2) by His Spirit, 3) by His Word and 4) by His Will.

God Performs by His Hand

One time my vehicle was stolen which resulted in me having to commute to work by bus. Taking public transportation in the city can be quite humbling, or keep you tip-toeing on the edge.

My coping mechanism was to fix my eyes on the outside scenery and avoid eye contact and conversation.

One day, during one of those commutes I was well-deep in my routine of living the moment in the theater of my 'anywhere-but-here' imagination, when the bus came to a halt for a pick-up. My gaze shifted to the shuffling feet of new passengers boarding, when two feet sat across from me. I was drawn out of the tunnel of my thoughts by the sight of the person taking his shoes off. I became captivated by a young man with no arms. He reached inside a book bag and took out a wallet, then from the wallet he fetched a bus pass between his toes. He stretched his leg around so the bus driver could take the pass, pay the fare and return it to him.

What an amazing young man.

I have had occasion to smash a finger or twist a finger back and have the nerve to feel incapacitated. Yet, I witnessed that young man eat a sandwich using his feet, drink an ice coffee, turn pages in his notebook – and smoke! Would you say the young man was performing by his hand?

I cannot envision what God's hand looks like, but I can tell you His hand is mighty and it is outstretched:

> *And I will stretch out my hand and smite Egypt with all my wonders which I will do in the midst thereof: and after that he will let you go.*
> *As I live, sayeth the Lord God, surely with a mighty hand, and with a stretched out arm, and with fury poured out, will I rule over you (Ex. 3:19, 20).*

Wow. Whenever God works by His hand, something spectacular and supernatural happens. Whatever God chooses to do with His hand is beyond what any human could have done.

God Performs By His Spirit

> *And the earth was without form, and void; and darkness was upon the face of the deep. And the Spirit of God moved upon the face of the waters (Gen. 1:2).*
>
> *...When the enemy shall come in like a flood, the Spirit of the LORD shall lift up a standard against him. (Isa.59:19*
>
> *And it shall come to pass in the last days, saith God, I will pour out of **my Spirit** upon all flesh: and your sons and your daughters shall prophesy, and your young men shall see visions, and your old men shall dream dreams: And on **my** servants and on **my** handmaidens I will pour out in those days of **my Spirit**; and they shall prophesy: (Acts 2:17, 18)*

The above passages record how the Spirit moves and causes events to happen. Earlier, in our discussion on God we mentioned the Holy Spirit as the third person in the Trinity.

The name 'Holy Spirit' is noted in the Greek as "pneuna" [Strong's 4151], which translates as "wind, breath, or spirit." (Never should we reduce the Holy Spirit to a force, or 'higher power.')

The work of the Holy Spirit is complex and comprehensive; beginning with His work in creation, to inspiring the writing of the very Word of God. The Holy Spirit works in the universe to create, to convict and intercede; and through human-kind by baptizing, comforting, filling, helping, guiding, empowering, strengthening, and sealing believers until the day of redemption.

Praise God!

Is praise what you do?

I don't know about you, but without the revelation of the Word of God, I would never have known to include the work of the Holy Spirit in my praise. Excluding the Holy Spirit would be an egregious error. Friend, please don't be afraid to call out the names of the Holy Spirit and to speak of His mighty works.

I trust by now you are beginning to see that praise consists of many more dimensions than applauding on demand or a, *thank* you *Jesus, yes Lord.* The goal is to connect you with the Spirit of God, and this is accomplished when you pour praise out of your soul.

God Performs by His Word

No doubt when you hear the phrase "the Word of God" you think of the Word of God in textural form as recorded in the bible or perhaps you think of Jesus, the Living Word. Every time God 'said,' His Word was at work. When God praised Himself, His Word was in operation. When God commands, He is performing by His Word and His Word always yields intended results.

> *And God said let there be light and there was light.*
> *And God said, let the waters under the heaven be gathered together unto one place, and let the dry land appear: and it was so.*
> *And God said, Let the earth bring forth grass, the herb yielding seed, and the fruit tree yielding fruit after his kind, whose seed is in itself, upon the earth: and it was so.*
> *(Gen.1:1.9.11)*

In praising, we do as King David and others did: we speak out loud the great, mighty, and sometimes terrible things that God has done by His hand, His Spirit and by His Word. God has done things that are innumerable and eternal. The greatest of these being God's plan to redeem creation back to Himself.

The Book of Luke records, that Mary the Mother of Jesus honored the works of the Lord's hand. She magnified the Lord and sang at length:

> *And Mary said, My soul doth magnify the Lord,*
> *And my spirit hath rejoiced in God my Saviour.*
> *For he hath regarded the low estate of his handmaiden: for, behold, from henceforth all generations shall call me blessed.*

For he that is mighty hath done to me great things; and holy is his name. And his mercy is on them that fear him from generation to generation
He hath shewed strength with his arm; he hath scattered the proud in the imagination of their hearts
He hath put down the mighty from their seats, and exalted them of low degree.
He hath filled the hungry with good things; and the rich he hath sent empty away.

Mary's praise is an excellent example of how to incorporate the acts of God in our praise. Mary breaks it down and mixes it up; she called Jesus LORD before He was even born. She loved Him as her child, but recognized she was being used by God as a vessel and that He was the Savior of the world.

The Word of God details the acts of a Sovereign God from the beginning of time. Who God is, is demonstrated by His hand, His Spirit, His Word, and by His Will. God acts toward human kind and on behalf of human kind. God is a hands-on God. He is not occupying his throne in eternal rest, as the center of attention for the heavenly hosts, waiting for us to get there. God is involved in everything that moves. Not only that, God is in control, which brings up the subject of the Will of God.

The Will of God

The Will of God is what God wants to be carried out. As this simple definition suggests, God wills action that produces an affect. This affect could be goodness, or righteous judgment when we are disobedient [the law], or vengeance.

God's Will is manifested as perfect or permissive, but no less divine or sovereign.

The subject of the Will of God is sometimes elusive to Christians who are seeking to know their purpose in life. Though hundreds of books have been written to instruct people on the Will and purpose of

God, **God's purpose never exceeds the corners of the written Word**. The subject is well explicated by Dr. R.C. Sproul in his book "*Can I Know God's Will?*" In addition to the perfect and permissive Will, Dr. Sproul expounds the decretive Will of God:

> Theologians describe as the 'decretive will of God' ('boule' in the Greek) that will by which God decrees things to come to pass according to His supreme sovereignty. This is also sometimes called 'God's sovereign efficacious will;' by it, God brings to pass whatsoever He wills. When God sovereignty decrees something in this sense, nothing can prevent it from coming to pass.[54]

God's Will is an attribute which commands and accomplishes intended result. Thus we should marvel at these divine acts in our praise because this characteristics distinguishes the God of our faith from any other; therefore He is worthy of praise. "F*or it is God who works in you to will and to act in order to fulfill His good purpose" (Phil. 2:13, NIV)*.

The acts of God are deliberate, intentional, purposeful, and glorious. He has no problem taking responsibility for what He has done. Oh magnify the Lord with me! Exalt His name(s)! Applaud God! Laud the Lord for the marvelous things He has done by His Hand, His Word, by His Spirit, and by His Will. Right now, appreciate God for shedding His royal garments to be homeless, oppressed, stricken, smitten, afflicted, wounded, despised, rejected, bruised for our gross wickedness and for entrusting His soul into His Father's hands and then vacating the grave. What an awesome God.

Ministry Tip

No matter who you are or what your position, God has done something for you or someone you know. For this next exercise get together with a few friends or family members:

1) Get a large piece of paper.

2) Draw a circle and make pieces of pie.

3) Take turns writing in the pieces what you believe was done that could not have been done without divine intervention. You can also ask everyone to take turns writing the acts on small pieces of paper and place the pieces in a box or hat.

4) Go around a second time and try to match the Acts of God with a person.

5) Mix them up and share them one at a time. You may also do this exercise as a part of a lesson during praise and worship rehearsal or a choir rehearsal. But go ahead and incorporate this information in praise.

Summary

The bible records the many acts of God as He performs them by His Hand, by His Spirit, by His Word, and by His Will. Take a moment and direct your thoughts toward the acts of God. Confess your sins and faults before the LORD God so that He will look upon you. Now, invite the Presence of the Holy Spirit into the space where you are, and the space that is you. Give yourself over to consider the great and marvelous things that God has done on behalf of your life and the lives of those you know. If you can begin to think on His acts your praise will be more relevant.

Has God answered your prayers? Has anyone you know been healed? Are you saved? Did He deliver you? Did you ever need Him to be a present help in the time of trouble? Did you call the name of Jesus at the moment your vehicle was about to slam into an eighteen wheeler or a median? Did a doctor shake his head and say there was nothing else he could do, but somehow you or your loved one lived to tell the story? Wait. Did you tell the story, or did you return to life as usual?

The acts of God are still in operation today and He is worthy of the praise. If you have difficulty recounting the acts of God, take a few moments over the next few days and sky gaze: witness the sun rising or the setting sun. Listen to the chatter of the birds at the crack of dawn or the waves swooshing and slashing. Consider how the tide rises and recedes from one day to the next. How many of these acts - which we take for granted - could mankind perform? There is no Mother Nature or Father Time. All phenomenon and natural occurrences throughout the universe are the results of the acts of God by His Hand, by His Spirit, by His Word, or by His Will.

Part Three

Demystifying Praise

Chapter 9

What Praise is NOT

Prayer
Good and Perfect Gifts
Tongues
A Different Dance
Pantomime
Being Quiet

As Christians, there are many tools that God has given us to enhance our relationship with Him. God wants to be close to His people, and He wants us to communicate with Him. Praise consists of complimentary acts directed vertically toward God, with little to do with the praiser. Saints, be encouraged to continue in prayer and the operation of good and perfect gifts including tongues, but understand that praise is separate from these functions.

Prayer

The Word of God says to "*pray without ceasing*" *(I Thess. 5:17*) and that *men ought always to pray, and not to faint (Luke18:1*) but prayer alone is not praise. Prayer should include praise as Jesus did in teaching the disciples how to pray, when He hallowed – or blessed - the name of the Father, but prayer by itself is petition. When Jesus prayed, He called the name of God as His Father, then reverenced and commended God ("*hollowed be thy name")*. In reading the Word of God, you will see that every time someone prayed, there was acknowledgement of the One to whom they prayed. However, prayer alone does not constitute praise.

Good and Perfect Gifts

> *Every good gift and every perfect gift is from above, and cometh down from the Father of lights, with whom is no variableness, neither shadow of turning.*
> *(James 1:16-18)*

The Greek term for 'gifts' in its use, is distinguished as "domata"[55] (Eph. 4:8). In this sense the gifts are manifested to build up the church. The Apostle Paul addresses the gifts of the Spirit and lists them as Word of Wisdom, Word of knowledge, Word of faith, healing, working of miracles, prophecy, discerning of spirits, divers tongues, interpretation of tongues and teachers (I Cor. 14:12, 13). These gifts are abilities given by the Holy Ghost to edify the church. Holman divides the gifts into four (4) categories: 1) Activities (miracles, healing, faith) 2) Manifestations [revelation, vision, knowledge, wisdom, guidance] 3) inspired utterances [proclamation, prophecy, discerning spirits, teaching, singing, prayers, tongues and interpretation of tongues] and 4) service (giving caring, helping and guiding). Yet these gifts are not to be mistaken as consisting of praise.

Praise must compliment, and or favorably express the aspects of God. Furthermore, our praises are chiefly meant to Glorify God, and secondly, to minister to one another.

Praise is the appropriate atmosphere for the indwelling of the Holy Spirit. The Holy Spirit makes His abode in our praise. This is not to say that there is no connection with the Holy Spirit when the gifts are in operation or in prayer. Acts of praise may work interchangeably with the gifts of the Holy Spirit, who is the giver of these gifts.

Some have said, "well, every perfect gift comes from above."

True.

In fact, the bible reads: "*Every good gift and every perfect gift is from above, and cometh down from the Father of lights, with whom is no variableness, neither shadow of turning" (James 1:17).* The gifts themselves are not praise though they are beneficial to the body of Christ. Other gifts are talents. God has given us song, the ability to sing and play music, dance, and a host of creative expressions. Still, the primary mode of praise is the fruit of our lips.

Tongues

Like many subjects, speaking in tongues is a divisive one in the body of Christ. The expectant aim is to unify the body of Christ in our thinking on this important subject of speaking in tongues, as it relates to praise.

Speaking in tongues may precede praise or follow praise; or else praise may precede speaking in tongues, OR follow speaking in tongues, but speaking in tongues is a spiritual gift relative to the revelation of the mysteries of God.

Prior to the second chapter of Acts, the tongues as such, were not mentioned in the bible. The bible mentions four types of tongues: 1) other tongues 2) divers or diversity of tongues 3) new tongues, and 4) unknown tongues. The Book of Isaiah talks about a *"stammering tongue which could not be understood" (ch. 33:19).* The 'tongues' to which we are referring is known as 'unknown tongues' while the tongue spoken in the upper room on the day of Pentecost (Acts 2:4-16) was called '*other* tongues.'

The tongues spoken in the upper room on the day of Pentecost were recognizable languages that indigenous people from foreign lands recognized as strangely being their own. In Matthew chapter 28, Jesus commanded the disciples to go and "teach all nations" (v.19). He then instructed the disciples to 'tarry' in Jerusalem (Luke 24:*48, 49) until they be endued with power after that the Holy Ghost is come upon them" (Acts 1).* You may remember that prior to what is known as the Day of Pentecost, Jesus had charged His disciples to 'tarry' (or wait) until they be endued (clothed NASB, AMP, NIV) with power, after that the Holy Ghost is come upon you." Let's address the tongues spoken on that Day of Pentecost by considering the sequence of commandments:

1) Wait (for power)
2) Go
3) Teach (nations)
4) Baptize
5) Worship and praise (Luke 24:52)

At no time did Jesus command the disciples to speak in tongues, but as they were in one place on one accord, worshiping and continually praising, the Word of God says they were filled with the Holy Ghost and began to speak in other tongues as the Spirit gave them utterance. This profound phenomenon occurred as a result of their obedience to the commandment of Jesus. The Holy Ghost came as promised, fell upon them, and then gave them the utterance to speak in 'other' tongues that were recognized by those in the assembly who were from other nations.

So in the course of speaking in other tongues – they witnessed the uttermost parts of the world by way of those that heard them. Then Peter stood up and revealed what had just happened as a fulfillment of what was spoken hundreds of years before by the prophet Joel.

Unknown Tongues

Tongues in this case is in reference to a tongue also given by the Holy Spirit which ministers only to God and to the speaker but when spoken in public must be done so by two or three speakers and have an interpreter. This is the *unknown tongue.*

The Apostle Paul clearly presents the guiding principles in I Corinthians 14:7-9, 12, 15-19. At first glance verses 7 and 8 are examples, but Paul continues in v. 15 and 16 distinguishing forms of praise with the voice i.e. singing, blessing the Lord, and giving of thanks. His stated position is that believers seek to edify the church (vv. 12, 17, 19). He declares, "*yet in the church I had rather speak five words with my understanding that by my voice I might teach other also, than ten thousand words in an unknown tongue.*"

> *Therefore, the person who speaks in an [unknown] tongue should pray [for the power] to interpret and explain what he says.*
> *For if I pray in an [unknown] tongue, my spirit [by the Holy Spirit within me] prays, but my mind is unproductive [it bears no fruit and helps nobody].*
> *Then what am I to do? I will pray with my spirit [by the Holy Spirit that is within me], but I will also pray [intelligently] with my mind and understanding; I will sing with my spirit [by the Holy Spirit that is within me], but I will sing [intelligently] with my mind and understanding.*
> *Otherwise, if you bless and render thanks with your spirit [thoroughly aroused by the Holy Spirit], how can anyone in the position of an outsider or he who is not gifted with [interpreting of unknown] tongues, say the Amen to your thanksgiving, since he does not know what you are saying? To be sure, you may give thanks well (nobly) but the bystander is not edified [it does him no good] (vv. 12 – 17, AMP).*

The Spirit of God and the Word of God agree. Apostle Paul's teaching demands decency and order as the guiding rule in how we operate in the house of God. Therefore we seek not to impress in praise but to minister with understanding and to edify the church.

No matter how deep a person is in God, we must exercise control over our spirit, and it is the Spirit of God that gives utterance: "*And the spirits of the prophets are subject to the prophets" (I Cor.14:32).*

There are various schools of thought on the subject of tongues, including what is called '*heavenly language.*' I find no scriptural reference (in any translation) for "Heavenly language" and in fact, I find it a bit confusing. The Apostle Paul is clear in his teaching that prophecy is preferred because prophecy is understood. He asserts that the church is not edified by gifts which are not understood.

Like myself, some of you may have encountered feelings of intimidation or feeling left out of the corporate praise atmosphere because you did not join in with speaking in unknown tongues. I have been to churches where people spoke in tongues, prayed in tongues, praised in tongues, sang in tongues – and it just never stopped. Even a good portion of the sermon was in tongues! I have heard people make out like their prayers were on the fast track to heaven because they did it in tongues; as though God, was not going to honor their prayer unless they said it in tongues. I have heard preachers say, "come on saints, go into your heavenly language" or "pray in the Spirit." I believe any language spoken unto the LORD and as the Spirit gives utterance, is pleasing and in order. This is not a book about prayer nor tongues, rather how to fittingly offer praise and worship to God that He will receive.

One time I accepted an invitation to go on a nearly two-hour trip with someone and the individual spoke in tongues the whole while going and coming back, aside from when the individual ate their burger.

On that nearly two-hour long trip the person picked me up and we proceeded up the highway. Within minutes the individual began speaking in some kind of tongue. Over and over I heard the same syllables and sounds. I thought, *What is this? Is this prayer? Is this praise? Is it prophecy? What's going on?* We never had a conversation the whole way there and back; just the speaking in tongues. I have traveled to a lot of places, but that was one of the longest trips I've ever taken in my life and I couldn't wait to get out of that vehicle. Bottom line is that what took place in the vehicle that day was not edifying. There was nothing understood or revealed. It was not even beneficial as an encounter to strengthen the relationship of two friends. There was no bonding. It profited nothing. Sounding brass and tinkling cymbals. A whole 'lotta noise.'

*****

All spiritual gifts are meant to unite the body of Christ and build our faith. The 'other' tongues' consists of speaking recognizable, indigenous languages. Paul was not asking people to abandon their native language, or to learn another language, but referred to 'unknown tongues,' as a tongue known and or revealed by the Holy Spirit for the purpose of ministering to God and the speaker, in the absence of an interpreter. The bible says there are supposed to be two or three interpreters when the Spirit gives someone utterance. If there is no interpreter, the speaker must be silent. Paul was establishing how people were to conduct themselves when the gifts of the Holy Spirit were in operation for the benefit of understanding and edification.

I can imagine that Apostle Paul was quite annoyed with people who took liberties to disrupt the service by speaking in 'unknown tongues.' The issue of tongues 'schizmatized' the early church the same as it does today.

If we praise, let us praise so that our words are understood as intended. If we sing, let us sing so our songs are understood and beneficial to the congregation. Praise in such a way that others will want to join in, and not depart. If you have use of the gifts of the Spirit, continue in those things in their proper place and according the Word of God. However, please understand that the gifts of the Spirit cannot take the place of praise, nor can praise take the place of the gifts of the Spirit.

A Different Dance

How is the holy dance distinguished as holy? What does it look like? Does your dance look like the foxtrot or jive?

I believe the church is coming into a better understanding on the ministry of praising God in the dance. Praise dancers have become seriously engaged in this expression intended to reverence and glorify God. I hope we will continue to apply right-thinking to the dance ministry. By right-thinking, I mean Spirit-led creativity that inspires and calls attention to the message of Christ rather than to ourselves. We cannot simply transfer venues in emulating the 'electric slide' or 'crumping' or 'the wave' and other dances too suggestive and disgusting to reference.

There is a reason why the bible says bodily exercise profits little. Paul indicated in 1Timothy 4:8 that our commitment to God supersedes physical expression or training. *For physical training [Bodily exercise, KJV] is of some value, but godliness has value for all things, holding promise for both the present life and the life to come" (I Tim. 4:8, NIV).*

Not all movement to a so-called gospel song can be classified as good and right in the house of God. I believe Christians should live their lives in the Lord, full of joy and have a good time because it makes little sense to give up having a blast in the world to come over to the Lord's side and live a bummed out, somber existence. At the same time, the church needn't provide the missing beat for people who used to go to the club!

Back in the day when I was growing up, the conversation of the saints was peppered with the word: 'worldliness.' Everything was *worldly.*

I remember the youth convention for our church organization was held in the city of Akron. One of the activities was a play about going to hell. During one of the scenes the actors (the young people of the church) began bucking and dancing and carrying on – to secular music. Next thing we knew a voice rose up over the music, the adlib of the actors, and the excitement of the audience. It was our local Church Mother. Her objections shut down the play in front of everyone. We still talk about that moment, decades later. That Church Mother wasn't very popular because she stood for holiness without compromise. I will always remember her throughout my life when it came to taking a stand for holiness.

The accepted form of dance in the church during those days, and for a long time, was spontaneous jumping around. It had no particular style or finesse. The people enjoyed the Lord without subscribing to any particular choreography. Personally, I have always loved various genres of dance, i.e. ballet and modern dance. I tried to watch any show that came on T.V. with dancing but never got too far in our house. There was *Soul Train*, and *Love American* Style, *American Band Stand* and all the variety shows that, outside of sneaking to watch it, my parents weren't having that *worldliness* in their house.

I believe we know in our spirits what is acceptable before God. What is acceptable is marked by a difference; a set apartness.

Before launching a dance ministry, the young people need to be taught the ways of God and what is holy unto Him. I believe dance is awesome when it is done unto the Lord. I encourage the people of God to keep the focus of your dance, heavenward, because unfortunately, if a person allows him or herself to set eyes on some of the liturgical dance presentations they could actually be seduced. The dance movements and the attire are seductive because the dancers have not been taught the ways of God. The purposes of the dances of the world are to entice and ignite the sensual; in contrast, the holy dance honors the holiness of God.

Plainly, some of the secular dances are the equivalent of sex with clothes. They are degrading and a disgrace to what is pure and holy. People who know nothing of the holiness of God cannot be expected to behave any differently. Those of us who believe on Christ need to employ 'spiritual common sense.' If it looks like a Janet Jackson, Beyonce or Usher Video, then it is not of God.

On Pantomime (Miming)

A pantomime in Greece was originally a solo dancer who 'imitated all' (panto—all, mimos- mimic) accompanied by song narrative and instrumental music, often played on the flute. The word later came to be applied to the performance itself. The pantomime was an extremely popular form of entertainment in ancient Greece and, later, Rome. Like theatre, it encompassed genres of comedy and tragedy. Supposedly, no ancient pantomime libretto has survived partly because the genre was looked down upon by the literary elite.[56]

One characteristic of the pantomime is the make-up. Most of us are familiar with the street variety artists with the whiteface make-up and quirky movements such as the one where he or she pretends to climb an invisible wall. The blackface or whiteface make-up worn by pantomime artists is a style of theatrical makeup that is credited to have originated in the United States, and was used to take on the appearance of certain archetypes of American racism. This genre exploited and perpetuated stereotypes in a subtle, yet entertaining way. In both the United States and Britain, blackface was most commonly used in the minstrel performance, but it predates that tradition, and has survived long past the heyday of the minstrel show. Minstrel shows are recognized by their very physical comedy component as well as some of the other elements of pantomime. In summary, both blackface and whiteface had racial implications as a means of shrewdly criticizing other races, and contained negative connotations.[57]

Recently, I had the occasion to see pantomime performed at a church service first hand. When I'd heard the announcement that the mimers were coming, I was displeased that the church was letting down its guard and its standard to allow something that was not Word-based in the church. Yet, I wanted to see this for myself. The performers entered to very loud beat-driven music and scary whiteface. The performance animated the lyrics of the song being played and incorporated dance. Watching the performance gave me mixed feelings that weren't exactly connected with the spiritual until at the end when each of the performers shared their testimonies. Surprisingly, not one performer professed salvation. They just stated that they were grateful that pantomime saved them from the streets.

On another occasion, the performance was reverential and moving. The music was God-centered, there was no blackface or whiteface make-up, the clothing was tasteful, and the entire presentation seemed to connect with the congregation. Still, this may be an antiquated view, but I believe we must stay on the path of the Word of God. As my mother always says, "stay in the old path," we must continue to be prayerful and watchful that the Kingdom of God is not misrepresented by perverted messages.

Praise is Not Being Quiet

> *To the end that my glory may sing praise to thee, and not be silent. O LORD my God, I will give thanks unto thee forever. (Psa.30:12)*

Being quiet is not praise. Yes, there is a passage of scripture where God commands the people to be still, but in order for praise to be praise, it must be audible and visible to commend. Hymns like *Blessed Quietness* and, *The Lord is in this Holy Temple* (Let all the Earth Keep Silent before Him) and *Hush, Hush, Somebody's Calling My Name* or, *Be Still My Soul*, are well meaning, but since when is quietness Holy? Make some noise with your praise. Be joyful, and exceedingly glad – and yes, get loud about it!

On Theatre

I am not adverse to all theatre. There are Christian entities that produce great theatre as a means of bringing people to Christ, and strengthening and unifying the body of Christ. I appreciate organizations like the *Sight & Sound* in Branson and Pennsylvania and have seen nearly every production produced there. Each time, the audience erupted into praise as the truths of the stories were unveiled. Attending the plays confers a sense of what heaven will be like. Christ centered productions are an excellent method of furnishing wholesome entertainment for the saints and bringing the events of the Word God to life. Neither Hollywood nor Broadway will ever equal the elaborate productions produced there. I would encourage every Christian to make the time and save the nominal ticket price to witness the extraordinary creativity that God has made available to us.

Ministry Tip:

Remember the 3 B's:
For an excellent guide of what is holy, ask yourself
Is it BECOMING?
Is it BENEFICIAL?
Is it BEFITTING?

Summary

Praise is the physical, audible or visual expression of loving thoughts toward God. God has given us many methods of communicating with Him. We correspond with God through worship, prayer, praise and then we edify the church with the gifts of the Spirit. Though spiritual gifts are crucial for every believer and the church-at-large, the acts do not make up or take the place of praise.

Praise manifests in words of adoration, singing, clapping, a whisper, waving of the banner, making a joyful noise, and dance. Praise consists of all of these acts as done unto the Lord.

Some forms of dance, along with other popularized activities such as pantomime are convenient forms of entertainment with a tradition rooted in xenophobia, which are not suitable offerings to a Holy God.

Additionally, pastors are encouraged to accept the role of Worship Leader in your churches so that an uncompromising standard of set-apartness to God is taught and exemplified. People are uplifted when they see their shepherd participating in praise, singing, and lifting their hands in praise.

Holiness is the standard of godliness and purity for a peculiar people, chosen and adopted by God. God told Israel in Leviticus 20:26, *"And ye shall be holy unto me: for I the LORD am holy, and have severed you from other people, that ye should be mine."* The New Testament follows with, *"for it is written: Be holy, because I am holy" (I Peter 1:16, NIV).*

We must render holy praises unto Holy God in addition to prayer, fasting, and utilizing the spiritual gifts. All of these are amazing separate acts given to us to fortify intimate relationship with an approachable God.

Chapter 10

When to Praise

Early in the A.M.
As we Enter His Gates and into His Courts
In the Wilderness
Continually
Always
Forever

Early in the A.M.

I am not a morning person.

Then again, I am not a night person either.

Perhaps, I am an afternoon person.

Okay, maybe I am a 'no time of the day' person.

Spending time with God in the morning is in keeping with putting God first, which is not to say time may not be spent with God at other times of the day.

Perhaps you do not consider yourself an early riser. Perhaps you would simply prefer not to be bothered in the morning.

For a long time I resisted spending time with God early because the flesh said I am not a morning person, but then I realized, "maybe I'm not a night person either!" God would beckon me out of my sleep, and even now, I awaken early but procrastinate communing with God. God has a way of getting our attention. Remember that He is a jealous God. Sometimes - and without warning - circumstances that may be unpleasant will compel us to seek God early, continually, and always.

> *And Abraham gat up early in the morning to the place where he stood before the LORD:*
> *(Gen. 19:27)*

> *I love them that Love me; and those that seek me early shall find me. (Prov. 8:17)*

> *And very early in the morning the first day of the week, they came unto the sepulchre at the rising of the sun. (Mark 16:2)*

You may ask, *what is the difference when I choose to spend time with God in prayer and praise as long as I do it?* Most Christians were reared in a "Now I lay me down to sleep" micro-prayer culture, recited at bed time.

Presumably, bedtime is the end of the day. You've exhausted every desirable activity, watched every television program and engaged in conversation, had your late night snack and now you turn off the lights and settle in with just enough strength over a full belly to utter, *Thank you Lord for another day.* Ironically, this is all you had time to say in the morning before going about the day's agenda.

God desires His children to desire Him, to pant after Him, and to seek hard after Him early.

Have you ever taken the time to just wonder about God? Have you ever risen as the sun is rising and sought Him earnestly?

Seeking God early meets God's requirement of giving the first fruits of our time; not necessarily requesting, but just to enjoy soaking in His presence. Seeking God is seeking the Presence of the Shekinah Glory in our secret closet. We enter declaring that He is the Living God, that He is Elohim, that He is great, awesome, terrible, majestic, and that He is holy, holy, holy.

The secret closet is a place and time of honesty with God. We immerse ourselves in praise no matter whether we have little or no food, or we're about to be evicted, or our houses foreclosed, or if we have to spend our days begging creditors. Call Him out as Jehovah-jireh and know that He is a present help in the time of trouble; that His name is a Strong Tower and as His righteousness, you have safety. Call out the name Jehovah-nissi with the assurance that He will give you victory and make you more than a conqueror.

If we could only comprehend and make the connection that speaking the attributes of God, the character of God, the names of God and the acts of God are key to seeking the face of God, and ultimately His hand.

Look at the life of Hezekiah, king of Judah in II Kings 18. King Hezekiah began to reign at the early age of twenty-five. The bible states that he did right in the sight of the Lord AND he trusted in the Lord (v.5). Hezekiah took office and began *"removing the high places, and brake the images, and cut down the groves, and brake in pieces the brasen serpent that Moses had made: for unto those days the children of Israel did burn incense to it: and he called it Nehushtan."*

The bible says,

> *For he clave to the LORD, and departed not from following him, but kept his commandments, which the LORD commanded Moses.*
> *And the LORD was with him; and he prospered whithersoever he went forth: and he rebelled against the king of Assyria, and served him not (verses 6-7).*

King Hezekiah proceeded to required sanctification and purification of the house of God. And then,

> *And all the congregation worshiped, and the singers sang, and the trumpeters sounded: and all this continued until the burnt offering was finished.*
>
> *And when they had made an end of offering, the king and all that were present with him bowed themselves, and worshiped.*

Note verse 7 says that Hezekiah prospered whithersoever he went. King Hezekiah reserved asking; instead he focused on meeting

God's criteria of purification, removing the unclean things and then worshiping. In turn, God blessed him and he prospered.

As We Enter His Gates and Into His Courts

I am sorry. I must release this: one thing that really aggravates me is getting up on Sunday morning, get ready, purpose in my spirit to glorify God, only to arrive for service to a sea of chatter.

I get it.

I get that the saints love one another and – glory hallelujah!

David said, *"I will enter His Gates [*doors*] with thanksgiving in my mouth, I will enter His courts with praise."*

There was a reason for entering reverentially. The temple of the Lord is supposed to be a place for God's name to dwell; not a smorgasbord of activities which preclude praise and the flow of the Spirit. Exodus 25 records how God told Moses to have the children of Israel build a sanctuary so that He could dwell there (v.8). God then instructs Moses on the architectural details followed by the promise that He would meet His people there, in the tabernacle (v.22).

Back in the day, the old folks would enter the temple, with bible in hand, bow, and then wait prayerfully for the service to begin. How we enter makes the difference in the atmosphere of corporate worship. May I kindly challenge you to think before you enter the doors of the tabernacle? Will you enter with thanksgiving and praise? Will you learn to wait reverentially in his presence and reserve socializing with the saints until later?

When you enter the temple, is praise what you do?

In The Wilderness

> *For the Lord will comfort Zion; He will comfort all her waste places. And He will make her wilderness like Eden, and her desert like the garden of the Lord.*
>
> *Joy and gladness will be found in her, thanksgiving and the voice of song or instrument of praise (Isa. 51:3).*

The Hebrew term for wilderness is 'midbar' or 'midvar' (ancient)[58] or place without speech... The Greek term is 'eremos' or a desert, a desolate, solitary, barren... land area particularly in the southern part, with little rainfall and few people. The words in the OT come close to the English word for desert or rocky dry, wasteland. Wilderness is associated with times of difficulty such as poverty, illness or relationship.

The worse part about the wilderness is the depletion of strength and the emotional disconnection; the emptiness in your soul becomes tangible in the walls of your belly. You may find yourself grasping to survive each moment.

It may seem as though your wilderness experience will never end, and you cannot see beyond the 'midvar' circumstance to a more optimistic future. You must continue to praise in your wilderness. You may also ask the Holy Spirit to intervene on your behalf. Begin to say, "Groan Holy Spirit, groan." I find that this has helped me when the mirage in my spirit is devoid of praise, and circumstances abound beyond my control. Yes, there were times when I found myself telling God "God I don't have a prayer today. I thank you for this day but I have nothing else to say."

This sounds appalling, but when our humanity is tested on a day to day, minute by minute basis, we may not be able to predetermine how the tests will play out; particularly if the time in the wilderness drags on. Like a mountain climber who sets out on an expedition but first prepares and conditions himself. He researches altitude and terrain, weather conditions, equipment, etc. The climber - armed with information - stands a better chance of accomplishing his goal of reaching the top, but there are no guarantees he will not experience sickness, fatigue, or lethargy. He presses on. He re-energizes, but one thing that is discouraged is stopping. Stopping lessens a climber's chance for survival, especially on the higher altitudes.

An interesting dichotomy draws from the extreme conditions of the wilderness and the altitude of the mountains. Both conditions test the human capacity for endurance, in the absence of the appropriate replenishing of nutrients. Similarly, the wellspring of praise provides spiritual carbs, proteins, electrolytes, and oxygen to increase chances of survival in our relationship with God.

Continually

Just as the Lord instructs us to pray without ceasing and men ought to always pray, His praises should continually be in our mouths. "*I will bless the Lord at all times and His praise shall continually be in my mouth" (Psa.34:1).*

Always

> *Rejoice in the Lord Always and again I say rejoice (Phil. 4:4).*

Forever

> *I will make thy name to be remembered in all generations: therefore shall the people praise thee forever and ever (Psa.45:17).*

Ministry Tip: Please Read

1 O God, thou art my God; early will I seek thee: my soul thirsteth for thee, my flesh longeth for thee in a dry and thirsty land, where no water is;
2 To see thy power and thy glory, so as I have seen thee in the sanctuary.
3 Because thy loving kindness is better than life, my lips shall praise thee.
4 Thus will I bless thee while I live: I will lift up my hands in thy name.
5 My soul shall be satisfied as with marrow and fatness; and my mouth shall praise thee with joyful lips:
6 When I remember thee upon my bed, and meditate on thee in the night watches.
7 Because thou hast been my help, therefore in the shadow of thy wings will I rejoice.
8 My soul followeth hard after thee: thy right hand upholdeth me. (Psa. 63 1-8)

Chapter 11

Why Praise

We Were Created by God
To Make Known His Deeds
Because He is Great
For Strength
God Inhabits the Praises of His People
Renew our Minds
For the Joy of it
For Peace

"But ye are a chosen generation, a royal priesthood, an holy nation, a peculiar people; that ye should shew forth the praises of him who hath called you out of darkness into his marvelous light"(I Pet. 2:8-10).

We Were Created to Praise God

The greatest compliment to an artist is his or her work. The work that an artist creates is completely subject to the will and design of the artist. The beauty is that the resulting sculptor merits the creator, fame. For example when artwork is on display, patrons stroll by and then draw close to see who is the author of the piece. The artwork then becomes a reflection of the creator; an extension of the hands which carefully formed it. Isaiah 43:7 declares, *"Everyone who is called by my name, whom I created for my glory, whom I formed and made...The people whom I formed for myself that they might declare my praise" (Isa. 43:7, 21, ESV).*

As Elohim, God the Creator exercises the sovereign right to designate the purpose of His creation, and He does. We ought to consider it an awesome privilege to have been created by God and that He claims us as His own. We ought to inhale every aspect of the life that He allows us to live to glorify Him. God is so completely unselfish in that He made us in His image (Genesis 1:26 NIV).

And if you have ever been near death, to the point where doctors put a percentage on your life, you will appreciate what it means to walk out of the hospital and not care whether it's raining, snowing, or freezing. Things like chattering teeth or a wet perm - that at one time quickly irked your nerves, becomes inconsequential to feeling grateful to God for whatever conditions He chooses to bring and the gift of experiencing it.

The winter of 2014-2015 solidified a place in the record books as one of the most brutal winters on record, according weather reports. All winter New Englanders complained.

I could not complain. I am so appreciative of the Grace of God that keeps me here to witness the wonder of His artistry and handiwork while people are losing their lives in missing planes, fallen planes, train accidents, helicopters colliding, war, random violence, and disease of pandemic proportion.

Begin to think and meditate on the intricacies of your humanity; how your body works with little contribution from you. Consider the multitude of varying species and never again take for granted the complexities of God, Creator: *"I will praise thee; for I am fearfully and wonderfully made: marvellous are thy works; and that my soul knoweth right well" (Psa.139:14).*

We Are Commanded to Praise God

I can imagine someone reading certain verses of scripture and surmising that we have a choice to praise God. There are verses which say 'let,' as in the famous Psalm 150:

> *Praise ye the LORD. Praise God in his sanctuary: praise him in the firmament of his power. Praise him for his mighty acts: praise him according to his excellent greatness. Praise him with the sound of the trumpet: praise him with the psaltery and harp. Praise him with the timbrel and dance: praise him with stringed instruments and organs. Praise him upon the loud cymbals: praise him upon the high sounding cymbals. Let every thing that hath breath praise the LORD. Praise ye the LORD.*

I love Psalm 150, because it covers a number of approaches to praise. You can express praise with an instrument (zamar), you can dance, and most importantly, if you are breathing you are to praise God for (borrowed) breath. Also there is no condition of choice in the passage. The word 'let' in this passage serves as a command (e.g. Let there be light, etc.) rather than an invitation or option. The usage is put forth with the expectation of obedience. We are expected to praise God for His mighty acts, which are alluded to in the Psalm 150. Remember, the Word says, *that if we will not lay it to heart to glorify His name, God will send a curse (Mal. 2:2)*. If praise is not what you do, then why are you saved? If praise is not what you do, what serves as your witness? If praise is not what you do, how do you gauge your happiness in Him? If praise is not what you do, how do you express your love and appreciation for God; how do you acknowledge God?

To Make Known His Deeds

> *Give thanks unto the LORD, call upon his name, make known his deeds among the people*
> *(II Chron. 16:8).*

When we praise, we call attention to the acts of God. For instance, when I praise God for delivering me from death and for healing me from paralysis, I am calling attention to His capabilities and to His power. I am proclaiming to everyone in attendance – and especially others who may be suffering that,

"The God I serve is a mighty God and He will do the same for you."

I call on you to glorify God for what He has done. Often, individuals ask for prayer, the church prays that God will answer, God answers, and then receives no recognition for the good that He has done for that person. Saints this is not right. We owe it to God to make known His deeds. When God delivers you, tell it. It is the word of our testimony that will lead us into eternity.

To Glory in His Name

> *Glory ye in his holy name:* let *the heart of them rejoice that seek the LORD.*
> *Declare his glory among the heathen; his marvellous works among all nations*
> *(II Chron. 16: 10, 24).*

We make God known to those who hear us when we praise and proclaim the His name and His works.

Because He is Great

> *For great is the LORD, and greatly to be praised: he also is to be [reverently] feared above all so-called gods (II Chron. 16:25* AMP*).*

For Strength

> *Seek the LORD and his strength, seek his face continually (II Chron. 18:11).*

I can attest that I know of no one who has experienced praising God and His presence, only to say, "that was lousy. I feel so horrible." Praising God can make you feel like spiritual King Kong and as though you can handle anything. Praising God strips you of the 'downer' outlook on life and gives you 'I-can-do-all-things-more-than-a-conqueror' attitude.

Because God Inhabits the Praises of His People

When one inhabits, one 'lives within; one dwells.' The term in the Greek is 'oikeo' which is from 'oikos' meaning, to occupy a house [Strong's 3611]. I like that the term suggests the length of time one stays as permanent. As long as we praise, the Spirit of God will descend in the atmosphere of our praise and remain! God's presence isn't just limited to a visitation as we sometimes say, but our praise becomes His dwelling.

The evidence of God's dwelling in our praise is supernatural and real because people are praising God all over the world at different times, in diverse ways, and in many languages and God is there for all of us. That God is there for praisers all over the world, is characteristic of His omnipresence.

To inhabit is to reside; to live within. When we praise, God's Spirit makes our praise His abode. How is this possible? How can God take residence in words of adoration, in the sound of sacred music, in a wave offering? How can He place His essence in a dance, or the lifting of hands? The scripture says, "*But thou art holy, O thou that inhabitest the praises of Israel" (Psa. 22:3).*

The verse in Psalm 22 has been popularized in this manner: 'God inhabits the praises of His people. The New American Standard Bible translates the verse thusly, *Yet You are holy, O You who are enthroned upon the praises of Israel.*

The term 'enthroned' has to do with sitting in, or residing in a place or reigning. When we lift up the name(s) of God we invite His Spirit to abide or live in the atmosphere of our praise. People have described the manifestation of the presence of God as a knowing; others have said they feel a warm and pleasant heat. Still others have witnessed a feeling akin to being detached from their surroundings. When we praise God without respect to ourselves and with abandon, being in His presence manifests itself in varied manners. The manifestation of a believer's praise is connected to the emotions. My experience has been a variety of phenomena that occur outside my control, where joy is the spiritual bonus.

We touch God with words of adoration, love, respect, and words of devotion and adulation. Realistically, we cannot see God. The bible states that no man hath seen God and no man can see God and live (I John 4:12).This is why the scriptures declare that we are saved by grace through faith *and that faith is the substance of things hoped for and the evidence of things not seen (Heb.11:1).* Our faith accepts that He is. The NASB and Amplified bibles translate 'substance' as assurance (confirmation); while the New Living Translation reads 'confidence.' We have assurance that living as the bible says, reconciles us to relationship with Him.

Renewing our Minds

> *I beseech you therefore, brethren, by the mercies of God, that ye present your bodies a living sacrifice, holy, acceptable unto God, which is your reasonable service.*
>
> *And be not conformed to this world: but be ye transformed by the renewing of your mind, that ye may prove what is that good, and acceptable, and perfect, will of God (Rom. 12:1, 2).*

Renewing your mind means assuming responsibility for what enters your mind, the gateway to your spirit. The relevance of renewing the mind should not be taken for granted or underestimated. If the devil can ensnare us in the realm of our thinking, then our actions will follow because we are what we think.

Undertaking responsibility for your mind means guarding it. Turn off the T.V. if there are no offerings conducive to a healthy spirit. Guard what enters the portals of your eye gate, your ear gate, the mouth gate, and captivates your senses. Never underestimate the power of seductive images.

Also, the Word of God prohibits a lot of foolish jesting and joking around. This does not mean you cannot laugh and have a good time, but joking and jesting is like eating a dietary regimen of chips, candy bars, gooey brownies, milkshakes, pies, cake and fries. (I can name all these food items because I love that stuff.) You can't possibly eat that way all the time and keep your blood pressure under control, your weight down, and your blood sugar at a healthy level. Sometimes if I eat junk food for too long, I put myself on a purification course to detoxify my body, and then I feel better.

Renewing your mind is a detoxification process. Detoxification in the natural realm rids us of accumulated toxins that cause natural sickness. Purifying our minds from unclean things rids us of toxins in the spirit. Once you have purified your mind, praise becomes part of a healthy spiritual regimen.

Praise also has a preventative function.

Occupying our time with reading the word of God, prayer and praise can help avert temptation. This is where self control comes into play. You may want to see it, you may want to listen to it, you may in fact want to feel it, taste it, smoke it, or participate in it – why wouldn't you?

Church this is about getting real.

Most of us have been saved from more than just the curse of sin. We enjoyed the activities of sin. What the devil has to offer feels good and don't let anyone tell you anything different. No one is tempted by something that produces misery - at least not initially. The devil has plenty to offer and the bible says he tempted Jesus on a seasonal basis.

Apostle Paul struggled with a particular evil. Evidently it was none of our business what it was, nor is it relevant. Evil is evil. However, the passage reads:

> *We know that the law is spiritual; but I am unspiritual, sold as a slave to sin. I do not understand what I do. For what I want to do I do not do, but what I hate I do. And if I do what I do not want to do, I agree that the law is good. As it is, it is no longer I myself who do it, but it is sin living in me. For I know that good itself does not dwell in me, that is, in my sinful nature. For*

> *I have the desire to do what is good, but I cannot carry it out. For I do not do the good I want to do, but the evil I do not want to do—this I keep on doing. Now if I do what I do not want to do, it is no longer I who do it, but it is sin living in me that does it (Romans 7:14-20, NIV).*

The passage in Romans is a perceptibly scandalous passage. The great tower of the New Testament, Apostle Paul, struggled with sin? Make no mistake about it; it takes every spiritual weapon God has given us to wrestle against spiritual wickedness. The old saints used to say, it takes time to live holy.

You can start developing a passion for praise by implementing the methods discussed so far in this book. I cannot promise that praise will alleviate every spiritual adversity, but you will certainly increase in joy, and in strength for the *joy of the Lord is your strength.*

Obviously, there are multitudes of ways that we can access things we have no business. With every invention we are presented with more options for perversion, and these days nothing is hidden or restrained. There is a smorgasbord of activities in the form of entertainment that we can view, or straight up do on our own.

If you had a choice between rutabagas or turnips and your favorite pie, which would you choose? Would you choose something that you are likely to regurgitate into a napkin or something that is so good you are ecstatic to partake in it? Author Joyce Meyer is famous for her "on purpose thinking" philosophy. I like how she says, "…and I had to be firm in my resolve to think right thoughts so I could get right results. To get your mind renewed, you will have to think right thoughts over and over again."[59]

Praise helps to renew our mind. We renew our minds by steadfastly studying the Word, praying, praising, and worshiping. The Word of God says *"we are tempted when we are drawn away of our own lust, and enticed" (James 1:14).* The last line of this passage lets us know that if we delight in the law of God He will strengthen the inward (where sinful desires and inclinations originate) person. Sometimes you may not feel like doing it, but I encourage you to put aside how you feel in your body and in your emotions. Focus your affections vertically and the Lord will be present in your praise.

Joy

No doubt, you or someone you know has faced a challenge this week. Maybe the phone rang late last night or you received one of those infamous early morning phone calls and now you avoid putting on the ringer because you can't take another minute of bad news. There are times when wickedness is against you like a flood hour by hour. God knows we cannot address every distraction and disruption. We cannot straighten everybody out who does us wrong. We cannot police every situation. But these are the subtle means by which we are weakened in our spirit. Demons attack people through people – and usually people to whom you are close - to pick and poke at your nerves. Just know that you must maintain your joy at all costs because the joy of the Lord is your strength. Joy makes us over comers. If you will passionately integrate praise into your life throughout every day, you will be better equipped to cope when you are tempted and tried.

Praise is priceless.

The prophet Isaiah (61:1-3) refers to joy as oil for mourning and praise as a garment for the spirit of *heaviness*. In those days, it was Jewish custom to wear that self-deprecating sack cloth when a person or group was sorrowful or penitent. The cloth - usually accompanied by ashes – advertised that you were suffering. Isaiah speaks of oil and the garment of praise as materials of comfort in addition to an exchange of beauty in place of ashes. Oil is a commodity, which Isaiah uses to describe the worth of joy produced from praise.

One of many metaphors, "beauty for ashes" refers to something that has been burned beyond its original composition or recognition, and then miraculously returned to its luster and glory. Consequently, there is the sense that the 'after' (beautiful to behold) is better than the 'before' (dull, grotesque). God doesn't just give us a superficial make-over, He makes all things become new.

The Hebrew term for 'joy' is "simchah"(Strong's #8057) meaning, glee, festival, exceeding gladness; mirth, pleasure, rejoice." The Word of God also indicates "oil of joy." Oil or "Shemen" (Heb) is,

- An important element historically and presently in terms of wealth.
- Symbolic of the Holy Spirit;
- Described as precious and holy;
- Typically poured or generously distributed.
- Has use for anointing, cooking/baking, as an offering, as fuel, as a demonstration of love, medicinal purposes, as currency or a commodity and given as a gift to individuals of importance.

Matthew Henry credits Jesus as the speaker in these verses which is confirmed by Jesus himself in Luke 4:17-21. *Jesus says in v.21, "this day is this scripture fulfilled in your ears.* Thus Isaiah 61:3 is a passage of hope that Jesus promises to fulfill. The "Good tidings" in verse 1 give us to know that we can praise God that mourning does not last forever. And when it ends, God gives (distributes) joy abundantly. He pours it out to the overflow, running over. Not only that, we will be outfitted with praise.

Again, mourning, depression and heaviness were indicated by the wearing of sack cloth and placing ashes over the garment. Sack cloth was a rough cloth made of camel's hair, goat's hair, hemp, cotton, or flax. I can imagine that as the self-deprecating sack cloth made contact with the skin, it served as a severe reminder of personal loss or sins. Jesus came and said I am here now; all you have to do is believe in me. Jesus has taken the punishment and the shame; therefore the garments are no longer needed.

Perfect Peace

> *"I will keep him in perfect peace whose mind is stayed on me" (Isa. 26:23).*

How is your peace today? I heard a news anchor testify that in all his time as anchor and reporter, he couldn't recall a time when there was such an influx of tragic news and that there was no room to air it all. Fear manifests itself in many ways: depression, anxiety, anger, hostility, sleeplessness, mood swings, and psychosomatic illnesses, etc. I Praise God that we can find refuge for our souls when we pray and praise because He has given us good things to think about in the Word. Our peace depends on our thinking. We can find this peace in the Word of God. The Word says,

> *Finally Brethren whatsoever things are true, whatsoever things are honest, whatsoever things are just, whatsoever things are pure, whatsoever things are lovely, whatsoever things are of good report; if there be any virtue, and if there be any praise, think on these things (Phil. 4:8).*

Christians need to purposefully direct our thought process, rather than allow random thoughts to monopolize our thinking. Think good thoughts. Occasionally pray the scriptures pertaining to the mind such as:

> *Thou wilt keep him in perfect peace, whose mind is stayed on thee: because he trusteth in thee (Isa. 26:3).*
> *For to be carnally minded is death; but to be spiritually minded is life and peace (Rom. 8:6)*
> *Let this mind be in you, which was also in Christ Jesus (Phil. 2:5).*

Praising God Demonstrates Walking in the Light

> *For ye were sometimes darkness, but now are ye light in the Lord: walk as children of light: (Eph. 5:8).*

> *Blessed is the people that know the joyful sound: they shall walk, O LORD, in the light of thy countenance (Psa. 89:15).*

To walk in the light is to walk on the outskirts of obscurity. People know when you know God. There is an illumination and brightness as though one is in a dark room and someone turns on the light suddenly.

Walking in the light means there is an adjustment, such as when we adjust our eyes as light comes into focus. There is no gray between light and darkness. The difference is distinct. This is how we must be in our walk with God: distinctly different in our appearance and in our sound.

Praising God Shows Kinship

> *But ye are a chosen generation, a royal priesthood, an holy nation, a peculiar people; that ye should shew forth the praises of him who hath called you out of darkness into his marvelous light; (I Pet. 2:9).*

When I think of kinship, I think of a group of individuals who are bound by blood, adoption, DNA, marriage, contract, or emotions. Also, somewhere in the mix, individuals are joined by a sharing of experience and thought. In my family, we are joined by blood, but also by the blood of Jesus. As such, no one has ventured into opposing beliefs.

Along the way, kinfolk tend to do things alike. There is a similarity in the way they laugh, the way cuisine is cooked and passed on to generations, as well as consensus of political views and party affiliation. We have shared pivotal moments in each other's lives.

In the family of God, we are joined by grace, faith, baptism, and devotion. We express our devotion in praise and worship. All of us are called upon to show forth the praises of God and to glorify Him in the beauty of holiness by way of proclamation.

Other Reasons Why We Praise God:

We also praise God because it is good to do so, and because of the works of God:

> *It is a good thing to give thanks unto the LORD, and to sing praises unto thy name, o most high:" (Psa. 92:1).*

For thou, LORD, hast made me glad through thy work: I will triumph in the works of thy hands. O LORD, how great are thy works! and thy thoughts are very deep (Psa. 92:4-5).

Ministry Tip:
Read Isaiah 61 in its entirety

Summary

We praise because we were created to praise, commanded to praise, to make known His deeds, because He resides in our praise, and because praise helps to renew our minds and give us joy.

When we come over to the Lord's side, we are not on our own. I believe we can better appreciate the function of praise when we know God for who He is and our purpose as His creation.

We shouldn't have to look too far for a reason to praise God.

We are heavily indebted to God that He reserved a plan of reconciliation after Adam and Eve messed up in the garden of paradise. At the point where God became nauseated by mankind's sins and wicked imagination, He offered mercy instead of annihilation from the face of the earth. God stayed our execution. I owe God because the devil sacrificed nothing for me or the world. Jesus is the only one who gave His life for my sins. He died and had the miraculous power to live again.

In our culture we esteem people who not only save lives but sacrifice their lives; such as soldiers, firemen/women and police officers. We honor them constantly with medals, parades, special applause, and holidays. How much more honor do we owe God?

We don't have to look far to know why we praise. I could have gone on for hundreds of pages with the previous section alone. Christ died for us. He gave us newness of life so that we would not have to taste death. Therefore we are His creation and His re-creation. God commands praise, expects praise, and deserves praise.

The main reason we praise is because we were created to do so. Praise is God's gift that binds us in close relationship to Him. When we praise, God dwells with us. Praising enables us to experience joy, peace, and hope in the Living God.

Chapter 12

What and Whom We Must Not Praise

Other gods
Nature
Angels
Spiritual Leaders
Mary
Ourselves
Other gods

> *I am the LORD thy God, which have brought thee out of the land of Egypt, out of the house of bondage.*
> *Thou shalt have no other gods before me. Thou shalt not make unto thee any graven image, or any likeness of any thing that is in heaven above, or that is in the earth beneath, or that is in the water under the earth (Ex.20:2–4).*

When God gave Moses the commandments concerning other gods, He wrote in stone so there would be no question for generations to come. Worshiping other gods would not be tolerated, and not only that, nothing was to come before Him, including family, children, jobs, possessions, and time. Nothing and no one is more important or worthy to receive glory above the LORD God.

The Elements of Nature

There is no acceptable condition by which we should praise NATURE or any aspect of nature, or CREATION. Nature has no equivalency to God, nor does it possess a spirit. Human beings, creeping things, life in the air and in the sea, depend on God the Creator for their existence. Unlike the beliefs of naturalists and transcendentalist of the 19th century, we are not one with the universe. The Universe has no intellect from which proceeds a thought process or conscience. The biblical premise rejects the naturalists, transcendentalists, and Darwinists premises. As believers, we worship the Living God who is Creator of all things, and all things used to create other things for the purpose of man.

Angels

Angels are not proper objects of worship. There is a broad line of distinction between Jesus and the angels. For by him were all things created, that are in heaven, and that are in the earth, visible and invisible, all things were created by him, and for him. Angels are ministering spirits sent forth to assist and serve those who will inherit salvation. Angels do a great work but are not to be worshiped or revered above God.

> *Then the angel said to me, 'write this: blessed are those who are invited to the wedding supper of the Lamb!' and he added, 'these are the true words of God.' At this I fell at his feet to worship him. But he said to me, 'don't do that! I am a fellow servant with you and with your brothers and sisters who hold to the testimony of Jesus. Worship God! For it is the Spirit of prophecy who bears testimony to Jesus (Rev. 19:9, 10, NIV).*

In Revelations 19, God sent the angel to give John a glimpse into the heavens. John saw an extraordinary sight of people, and beasts, and elders; he heard their voices blasting, "*Alleluia, salvation and glory, honor and power unto the Lord our God.*" John heard voices like many waters and like thunder saying, "*Alleluia for the Lord God omnipotent reigneth" (v.6).*

*With all t*he amazing sights and sounds that John witnessed, the angel would not allow John to worship him. The angel made it known that he was only a messenger. He was not God.

Spiritual Leaders

The pinnacle of the believer's motivation must be to glorify God in all things. I love my mother and father more than anything on earth, but there is no one I esteem higher than God. I firmly believe nothing ought to take the place of the glory of God. This is not to say we cannot honor those to whom honor is due. God is pleased when we bestow honor, as long His glory is not shared with another. Isaiah 42:8 says *"I am the LORD, that is my name; I will not give my glory to another, nor my praise to graven images" (NASB).*

Typically humility was not one of Peter's strongest traits, however he declined to allow Cornelius to bow down to him. He recognized the limitations of his humanity in this passage: "*And as Peter was coming in, Cornelius met him, and fell down at his feet, and worshiped him. But Peter took him up, saying, Stand up; I myself also am a man" (Acts 10: 24-26).*

Mary, Mother of Jesus

The main theme surrounding Mary, the mother of Jesus is that she was chosen by God for the redemptive purpose of God. The awesome thing about Mary was that she was willing to be used by God for His purpose. She considered herself a servant. Her humility and recognition of who she was in the scheme of things is the pivotal point in Luke 1:38 "*And Mary said, Behold the handmaid of the Lord; be it unto me according to thy word. And the angel departed from her."* Mary went on to say, "*And my spirit hath rejoiced in God my Saviour (v. 47). For he hath regarded the* ***low estate*** *of his handmaiden: for, behold, from henceforth all generations shall call me blessed" (v.48).*

Mary never sought greatness for herself. Rather, she worshiped and praised God. She considered herself a servant, and by *"all nations calling her blessed*" she meant future generations would know she was consecrated for the will of God. She knew she was no better than anyone else and not worthy to be praised but, to give praise.

> *And when they were come into the house, they saw the young child with Mary his mother and fell down, and worshiped him: and when they had opened their treasures they presented unto him gifts; gold, and frankincense and myrrh (Matt. 2:1).*

Notice in Matthew 2:1 that they came into the house where Mary was with the Christ child. The visitors did not fall down and worship Mary; they fell down and worshiped Jesus.

Ourselves

The blueprint of our salvation is self denial. We live not to exalt ourselves in any way, but to exalt Father, Son, and Holy Ghost. We must become minimized so God is maximized. Self-denial is the mark of a true follower of Christ; meaning we seek no glory for ourselves.

> *And when he had called the people unto him with his disciples also, he said unto them, Whosoever will come after me, let him deny himself, and take up his cross, and follow me (Mark 8:34).*

> *For whosoever exalteth himself shall be abased; and he that humbleth himself shall be exalted (Luke 14:11).*

The Dead: The Living God is a God of the Living

One sign of inconceivable evil is the worship of the dead or ancestral worship. The bible vehemently labels ancestral worship as an abomination; the most exceedingly terrible class of sin. The NT says it is appointed to man once to die, after that the judgment. Once someone has died, access to that person and their spirit dies also.

> *Wilt thou shew wonders to the dead? shall the dead arise and praise thee? Selah.*
> *Shall thy loving kindness be declared in the grave? or thy faithfulness in destruction?*
> *shall thy wonders be known in the dark? and thy righteousness in the land of forgetfulness (Psa. 88:10 –12).*

Believers are not to participate in ancestral worship; whether the ancestor is dead or alive.

Ministry Tip:

READ: Deuteronomy 18:9-13
Ask God's forgiveness if you have engaged in this activity, and that His blood covers you.

Chapter 13

The Benefits of Praise

Praise Pleases God
The Glory of God
Unspeakable Joy
Strength
Weapon of Our Warfare
The Presence of God

There are many benefits to praising God – in fact, there are only benefits and no detriments.

It should be comforting to know that there is no risk factor in praising God and no disappointment. Praising God is like eating healthy, exercising, and avoiding any substance or activity that is not good for the body: only good can come of it. Praise promotes spiritual well-being. Praise benefits the praiser by giving us hope: *Why art thou cast down, O my soul? and why art thou disquieted in me? Hope thou in God: for I shall yet praise him for the help of his countenance" (Psa. 42:5,11).*

Praise is Pleasing unto God

There are few people mentioned in the bible with the testimony that they pleased God. Jacob pleased God. Enoch pleased God; Noah found grace in the eyes of God because he walked with God; Job was blameless and upright and therefore he pleased God; The Apostle Paul pleased God. Jesus pleased God "well" (II Pet. 1:17). All of these individuals offered unto God sacrifices and Jesus gave Himself as a sacrifice for the sins of God's creation.

It pleases God when we glorify Him. You may ask, "how is pleasing God a benefit?" How does pleasing anyone other than myself benefit me?" The answer is curses are lifted when we praise God and blessings are released into your life. The bible is replete with examples (e.g. Abraham, Job, David, Solomon) of people who praised God and they were prosperous beyond measure. Praising is pleasing, and pleasing is beneficial. Also, praising God when you don't feel like it or when there seems to be no apparent reason why you should (e.g. you're homeless, hungry, heavily indebted, have a chronic disease or illness from which there is no relief, or people have wounded you, etc.) you are activating faith that says you trust God. You trust God enough to keep on praising and declare the promises of the Word of life over your situations.

The Glory of God

Another benefit of praising God is the Glory of God. We have already discussed how God acts: by his Word, His Hand and by His Spirit. Throughout time God has also revealed Himself by the Presence of His Glory. According to *Thayer's Lexicon* there are 590 occurrences of the term glory in the Word of God; plus just under 100 important sub-topics; including God's eternal glory, the glory of His Holiness, and the glory of His Majesty and power.

The Glory of God in the Greek is, "doxa' which means "renown or fame"; there is "haulinos," and refers to an image or reflection, or the degree of brilliant light, such as the brightness of the Glory of the Lord that was shone on Moses' face which he covered with a veil when he was before the people (Acts 7:2, Heb. 1:3). There was the Glory which had to do with the manifest Presence of God, or the Glory (cloud) that filled the temple and from time to time rendered the priest unable to see (1 kings 8:11) which was so encompassing that sometimes Moses or the priests could not enter the temple (Ex. 40:35); or that appeared before the children of Israel as a devouring fire. Finally, there is "doxazo" glory that pertains to esteem or honor ascribed to Him,[60] for instance:

> *And at once an angel of the Lord smote him and cut him down, because he did not give God the glory (the preeminence and kingly majesty that belong to Him as the supreme Ruler); and he was eaten by worms and died (Acts 12:23, AMP).*

'Doxazo' glory is what we do when praise God for His worthiness, when we extol Him and give Him reverence. The "doxazo" is the glory that He said, "my glory will I not share with another.' This is the "doxazo" glory of which He is worthy.

Why did Moses beg God to show him His glory?

The presence of God had been with the children of Israel throughout their wilderness journey in the forms of a pillar of fire by night and a cloud by day. God told Moses His presence would go with them. Still Moses wanted more. The scenario was like two people who are courting: hours spent on the phone talking and listening to each other breathe. Eventually the phone thing gets old. In order to advance the relationship, the two people become anxious for face to face encounters. The two people must be in each other's company. Moses wanted more than conversations with God and the glory of God covered by a cloud or representations of the glory of God. I believe He pressed for the presence of God, Himself.

To know someone is to know how that person will respond in situations, their family, their vernacular, their voice, their characteristics, and possibly their financial situation and associations. We know the person's habits and the range of emotional displays as well as when to approach and when to leave them alone.

When we know God we know His acts, His characteristics, how He responds as well as His expectations of us. God holds nothing back from those who desire after Him and seek out the knowledge of Him through the scriptures and revelation knowledge of the Holy Spirit. God responds to our seeking with His glory. His glory is the sanctioning of intimacy with Him. His glory is as close as we can get.

Joy Unspeakable

Thirdly, we have joy in praising God. Jonathan Edwards writes,

> Though their outward sufferings were very grievous, yet their inward spiritual joys were greater than their sufferings; and these supported them, and enabled them to suffer with cheerfulness. The nature of this joy; unspeakable, and full of glory. Unspeakable in the kind of it; very different from worldly joys, and carnal delights; of a vastly more pure, sublime, and heavenly nature, being something supernatural, and truly divine, and so ineffably excellent! The sublimity and exquisite sweetness of which, there were no words to set forth. Unspeakable also in degree; it having pleased God to give them this holy joy with a liberal hand, in their state of persecution.[61]

There are two things which the Apostle Peter notes in the text concerning this joy: first, the approach, the way in which Christ, though unseen, is the foundation of it, viz. by faith; which is the evidence of things not seen;

> *That the trial of your faith, being much more precious than of gold that perisheth, though it be tried with fire, might be found unto praise and honour and glory at the appearing of Jesus Christ: Whom having not seen, ye love; in whom, though now ye see him not, yet believing, ye rejoice with* ***joy unspeakable*** *and full of glory (I Peter 7-9).*

Secondly, that the Kingdom of God is joy:

> *For the kingdom of God is not meat and drink; but righteousness, and peace, and joy in the Holy Ghost. (Rom. 14:17)*

The Book of Luke pronounces that "*in His presence there is fullness of joy*" *(Luke 15:10)*. After speaking on who He is to the disciples, Jesus explains why He is telling them who He is - that their joy might be full (John 15:11). In Luke 6:23 believers are encouraged to 'leap' for joy. To leap for joy in the Hebrew is 'skirtao' or to skip, jump as in the quickening of a fetus. Leaping for joy is deliberate, intentional and conveys passion. In other words, you want it bad! You are excited for the presence of God. Psalm 16:11 says "in *His presence there is fullness of joy...*" Fullness connotes capacity reached.

These descriptions suggest the joy one experiences in knowing God and praising Him. This joy is something which cannot be emulated by hedonistic pursuit – which Edwards characterizes as prideful, idolatrous, and synthesized by entertainment and popular culture, or gratified by secular humanism (i.e. belief in Universal morality without attribution to anything supernatural, theistic or deistic). The joy in knowing God is soulish, not superficial.

The Joy of the Lord Is Our Strength

Praising God sets in motion His strength when we are weak: *"And he said unto me, My grace is sufficient for thee: for my strength is made perfect in weakness. Most gladly therefore will I rather glory in my infirmities, that the power of Christ may rest upon me"(II Cor. 12:9).*

The text gives us to know that we can maintain a disposition of praise with victorious results. In so doing, we wait on the Lord and He renews our strength. If you are weak, admit your weakness. Honesty effects praise; for example, if you are too weak or going through more than you feel you can handle, confess out loud, "God I am weak. I can't take it anymore," or "I don't know how much more I can take. Please show yourself strong on my behalf." The Prophet Isaiah writes:

> *To grant [consolation and joy] to those who mourn in Zion – to give them an ornament... of beauty instead of ashes, the oil of joy instead of mourning, the garment [expressive] of praise instead of a heavy, burdened, and failing spirit--that they may be called oaks of righteousness [lofty, strong, and magnificent, distinguished for uprightness, justice, and right standing with God], the planting of the Lord, that He may be glorified (Isa. 61:3, AMP).*

We are living in perilous times. Everyday something happens to disrupt our peace and to distract us from being godly and God-minded. We awaken to a beautiful day: sun shining, deep blue skies, birds singing, butterflies skipping about when - crash! Warfare crashes down. In the midst of the struggle we can't seem to remember a prayer, a scripture or praise. Our response is within the means of the flesh: anger, bitterness, strife, or defensiveness. We want desperately to enjoy the Christian life and to simply feel good - but the devil, working through people and circumstances won't let it happen. Negativity permeates our conscience, as well as our spirit.

The impenetrable truth is that the devil does not want us to Praise God. He does not want us to open our mouths and glorify God in the Temple, the public square, or even in private. Satan does not want us to lift our hands or lift our eyes, because if we praise God we will know God more intimately. He knows that if we praise God we will have joy; if we have joy then we will have strength; if we have strength then we are empowered to be living testimonies, and if we have in our mouths a testimony, then the Word says in Revelations, we are overcomers.

> *And I heard a loud voice in heaven, saying, "Now the salvation and the power and the kingdom of our God and the authority of his Christ have come, for the accuser of our brothers has been thrown down, who accuses them day and night before our God. And they have conquered him by the blood of the Lamb and by the word of their testimony, for they loved not their lives even unto death. Therefore, rejoice, O heavens and you who dwell in them! But woe to you, O earth and sea, for the devil has come down to you in great wrath, because he knows that his time is short! (Rev. 12:10-12, ESV).*

From the time of his existence in heaven, the devil wanted the glory that belonged to God and now he is manipulating and recruiting as many people as he can to keep him company in the bottomless pit for eternity. He is the accuser of the brethren whom the Word of God says we will overcome. The prophet Isaiah speaks about satan's pride when he was Lucifer:

> *How art thou fallen from heaven, O Lucifer, son of the morning! How art thou cut down to the ground, which didst weaken the nations! For thou hast said in thine heart, I will ascend into heaven, I will exalt my throne above the stars of God: I will sit also upon the mount of the congregation, in the sides of the north: I will ascend above the heights of the clouds; I will be like the most High. Yet thou shalt be brought down to hell, to the sides of the pit.* (Isa. 14:12,13)

Genesis 3, satan tempts Eve by saying that she shall not surely die (Gen. 3:4). The significance of this is that satan's sole purpose is to tempt people into disobedience. The job of satan comes in the form of the 5 D's:

Distract ⇨ Discouragement ⇨ Disbelief ⇨ Disobey ⇨ Destroy

When we keep the name of Jesus in our mouths and in our thoughts, demons will have to flee because a heart of praise activates resistance to distraction and discouragement. When there is a protective wall of praise in your mouth satan's offensive diminishes. Praising God invites the presence of the Spirit of God; thus the Holy Spirit will lift up a standard against the attack of satan - the enemy - as he tries to operate. Praise is part of our arsenal of spiritual weaponry against all that the devil brings against us.

When we don't praise God, we become easily distracted. When we are distracted then we open ourselves up to discouragement. Discouragement brings disbelief. When we do not believe, we disobey. We actually give obeisance to that which we believe. The ultimate job of satan is to destroy not just our bodies, but our souls so that we will spend eternity in the same miserable existence as him.

The Presence of God

The Ultimate aspiration of every Christian should be to know God and to be in His presence. In praising God, we seek nothing for ourselves except the satisfaction of being in the presence of God.

The relationship between God and man is defined in Genesis 3. Until this time, Eve had only been identified as the woman. At the moment of separation from the garden, the woman became 'Eve' just before she and Adam were booted out of paradise where they had been in the presence of God. By seeking the presence of God we seek restoration of the relationship human kind was created to have with God before sin separated us.

'Presence' means the state of visible, spiritual, or psychological existence. Sometimes the 'presence' of God and the 'Glory' of God are used interchangeably. The presence of God in Hebrews refers to the 'interior' or 'within' [Strong's, 6440]. Luke 1:19 suggests 'in front of; alongside; in the face of;' while 'Glory' is the brilliance or brightness; a distinguished quality or asset; something marked by beauty or resplendence or perfection; to express delight [as in glory in]. Glory describes appearance while presence is the state of being. Greek terms for 'Presence' of God are eno-pe-on [Strong's, 1799] or "in the face of [6440]."

In the Word of God, the presence of God was manifested in the burning bush (Ex. 3:2) a cloud (Ex. 13:21, I King. 4:11) in the fire (Gen. 15:17, 18) and in the smoke Ex. 13:2) a rainbow (Ez. 1:28, Rev. 14:3) thunder (Ex.19:16) and a whirlwind (Job 38:1). In the presence is being in the company of, or simply being there.

Again, obedience plays a major role in seeking the Glory of God. "The manifestation of Love for God is keeping His commandments."[62] We must humble ourselves to the obedience of God if we want to be in the sight of God and experience His glory.

The servant Moses said, "I beseech thee, shew me thy Glory" (Ex. 33:18). Moses had an awesome relationship with God that I believe entailed a dialogue which was audible. In chapter 33, v. 12, God extends an invitation to Moses to come up to the Mount (Sinai). He and Aaron and his sons and seventy elders of the congregation went to the mountain top where the Glory of the Lord covered the mount in the form of a vast cloud. The cloud appeared as a devouring (consuming) fire (Exodus 33:7-23). Moses was allowed to be in the company God but only to view Him from the back side.

Seek to glorify God in praising Him. Do not seek blessings and material things in praising God. Do it because His glory is your reward. Seek to have intimacy with God and to be in His presence. There is nothing more pleasing to God and no greater benefit us.

Summary

Everything That Has Breath

This book was inspired in part by the final verse in Psalm 150 that reads, "*Let everything that hath breath praise the Lord, Praise ye the Lord (v. 6).*"

Have you ever just paused to listen to the sounds of other life forms; including the sounds of the vegetation as the wind caresses the leaves? If you listen intently, even a gnat produces sounds; species of birds have individual and unique sounds to communicate with one another. I believe in their own way these creatures honor their creator, God, Elohim. I believe when fowl assemble in formation and soar south, through the heavens, they are extolling God. When robins sing in the Spring, they are praising. Will you allow a gnat or a scorpion to praise God more than you?

Humans customarily talk about the weather, usually as an opener for small talk or to establish a level of comfort in an effort to be cordial. Most likely, you have given little if any, thought to the notion of inanimate things such as astronomical elements, praising God. Instead, we use those exchanges to complain. But the good news is that all the heavenly elements belong to God and exists to glorify Him.

I know few people who have an appreciation for a thunder storm, or a blizzard, or floods that threaten life. A nonscientific-minded person, may not be able to explain the phenomenon of inanimate things, but there is no reason to fear. The earth, the seas, the floods, the heavens, and the fields all have a place in glorifying God. The plan of God incorporates the weather and all things in nature to accomplish His will, for our good.

> *The earth is the Lord's, and the fullness there of, the world, and they that dwell therein,*
> *For he hath founded it upon the seas and established it upon the floods.*
> *Who shall ascend into the hill of the Lord? Or who shall stand in his holy place?*
> *(Psa. 24:1-3)*

And,

> *Let the heavens rejoice, and let the earth be glad; let the sea roar, and the fullness thereof.*
> *Let the field be joyful, and all that is there: then shall all the trees of the wood rejoice*
> *(Psa. 96:11, 12).*

Finally, seek to praise God because of the many benefits. The benefits of praising include pleasing God, the Glory of God, joy unspeakable, strength, and because praise acts as a weapon against spiritual warfare. The best benefit is that praise invites the Presence of God.

Part Four

The Music of the Church

Chapter 14

Music of the Church

Biblical Origin
Goal of the Church Musician
Gospel Music

Origin

Music is and always will be a vital part of praise and worship in the lives of most Christians and in churches. Biblically, music involved multiple purposes: to accompany sacrificial offerings, as a part of the Levitical Feasts (i.e. of unleavened bread, and the Passover); and as a backdrop for the work on the House of the Lord under Josiah (II Chron. 34:8-12).

Miriam sang and the women sang songs celebrating David's victories at war; Moses sang a song about God bringing the Israelites out of Egypt, while the boy David was called on repeatedly to play on the harp for King Saul to ease his troubled mind.

Access to musicians during that period was a sign of prosperity in the instance of Solomon (Eccl. 2:1-8). In those days, the only access to music was live performance; unlike today where people can acquire music through multiple digital outlets such as YouTube, iPods, iPads, Mp3 players and for a little while long, CD's.

Genesis 4:2 credits the organist Jubal as the inventor of music in Genesis 4:2: *And his brother's name was Jubal: he was the father of all such as handle the harp and organ.*

Jubal was mentioned as a descendent of Cain, son of Adam. Nothing else is spoken about him, however, by this verse we know that music was expressed near the beginning of time on earth. Right away mankind discovered the need to express himself musically. Also, music was used exclusively for God during this time.

We know that before God created the earth there was Heaven, the place of His dwelling and the heavenly hosts, including the angel Lucifer. Lucifer would later be demoted to the devil because he became prideful and wanted to be like the Most High God. God created Lucifer - as he was originally known - with musical instruments and exquisite jewels in his body. For that reason, we should know that music is a medium by which the prince of the power of the air – the devil works to deceive. Early on he perverted something beautiful, made by God.

> "I*t came even to pass, as the trumpeters and singers were as one, to make one sound to be heard in praising and thanking the LORD; and when they lifted up their voice with the trumpets and cymbals and instruments of* ***musick****, and praised the LORD, saying, For he is good; for his mercy endureth for ever: that then the house was filled with a cloud, even the house of the LORD."*
>
> *II Chron. 5:13*

Jubal was a musician (organist) who used music to praise God. Before he became king, David was a virtuoso musician, who ministered to the needs of the trouble-hearted and unto God. (We need Spirit-filled musicians to serve exclusively in the body of Christ who minister the music under the power and anointing, of the Holy Ghost to destroy yolks.)

Goal of the Church Musician

As musicians, the primary goal should be to offer ourselves as living sacrifices of praise, holy and acceptable - and then offer our praise as an extension of a living epistle.

Next, God is glorified when the church is edified so we must keep the people in mind when it comes to supplying the music. It should be easy to distinguish the sacred and holy from the expressions of the world with respect to music. Praise is the favorable view of; to acclaim; to venerate by admiration of affections. Additionally, "praise being derived from the Latin 'value' or 'price' is to give praise to God and to proclaim His value or merit."[63] Music that is of God is about God, unto God. God is the supreme praiser. He praised Himself and knows how He wants to be praised.

No flesh should be glorified in music offered unto to God. God created mankind with the need to express ourselves musically, and He placed within us the desire and ability. I like the view of Martin Luther, who said,

> "...I truly desire that all Christians would love and regard as worthy the lovely gift of music, which is a precious, worthy, and costly treasure given to mankind by God. The riches of music are so excellent and so precious that words fail me whenever I attempt to discuss and describe them. In summa, next to the Word of God, the noble art of music is the greatest treasure in the world. It controls our thoughts, minds, hearts, and spirits. Our dear fathers and prophets did not desire without reason that music be always used in the churches. Hence, we have so many songs and Psalm. This precious gift has been given to man alone that he might thereby remind himself that God has created man for the express purpose of praising and extolling God."[64]

Martin Luther was saying that we were made for music and music was made for us. Music was meant to be for the purpose of praising God. We do this individually and as a part of the collect.

> Within the context of the historical liturgy, music functions not as an ornament or entertainment, but rather as an integral part of the liturgy, carrying prayer and praise and illuminating the proclamation of the Word. The music of the liturgy invites all — congregation, choir, instrumentalists and pastors — to participate. Because each group is a part of the whole, each has its own role as it takes a turn leading prayer and praise with the entire assembly. Music's most important function is to illuminate the text that allows us to see Christ and the action of God in our lives. Music that overshadows the text and draws attention to itself violates its purpose...[65]

We should be pleased to live during a time of great anointed music that glorifies God, irrespective of styles. I tell you, I can hardly keep up with recorded music. I want to commend recording artists like Chris Tomlin, Israel Houghton, Michael W. Smith, the Crabb Family, Dietrick Haddon, William Murphy III, Lincoln Brewster, Tasha Cobbs, William McDowell, the Brooklyn Tabernacle Choir, and so many others that have kept God at the center of their music. In spite of disparagement in some fundamental circles – these people have blessed the body of Christ with music that ministers to the spirit.

As Christians, we need to be aware that influences pervade the church; including popular culture and lifestyles. One day, take the time to listen to the offerings on various Christian channels. Perhaps you already listen to Christian music programming. How many times have you said to yourself out loud, "What in the world are they singing about?" or maybe you have found yourself driving along, you select a radio station and settle in, when you have to look at your radio to double check whether it's a gospel station.

God is moving all over the world, in the medium created by Him for His glory. Music is something that should be enjoyed to lift our spirits irrespective of style preferences. There are as many dimensions among believers as there are anywhere else. The good thing is that the same God who confounded language receives all praise in song which is done unto to Him. Praise the Lamb of God!

Again, God created Lucifer with instruments contained in his body. (This could be the basis for the cliché, 'when the devil gets busy he always starts with the choir or the music department because he was a choir director in heaven.') With an angelic, one-of-a-kind outfit of what would have been called, 'bling-bling.' The devil committed the sin of pride, or conceit in heaven, and then waged a coup d'état against Almighty God. His defeat terminated his position as worship leader, and determined his future in torment.

Gospel Music

Thomas A. Dorsey is credited with creating gospel music by marrying "the Blues with sacred text in 1932."[66] The music was described as 'Good news' music for its messages of hope, coupled with upbeat syncopations and walking bass lines. Prior to that time there were sacred hymns, and spirituals. Gospel music was introduced as foot stomping music to lift the spirit and cause one to clap glad hands. This was particularly common in the black church where people didn't mind getting rowdy. This music was a coping mechanism for life's insurmountable suffering, poverty, and oppression. As time progressed Gospel music became more of an umbrella for a variety of musical influences used in the church, including gospel jazz and Contemporary Christian Music (CCM) R& B gospel, southern gospel and Hip-Hop which was distinguished as sacred only by the lyrics.

Music Uses in the bible:

- Celebration
  "And David and all the House of Israel played before the Lord on all manner of instruments made of fir wood even on harps, and on psalteries and on timbrels, and on cornets, and on cymbals"
- Drive Evil spirits away
- A weapon against spiritual warfare
- Make announcement or call attention to
- Accompany worship
- Praise

Popularity of musical styles come and go. Songwriters and musicians are always looking for ways to innovate and break the monotony that sometimes plagues their playing. The different flavors of music are dictated by geography, culture, availability, and personal taste. More importantly, worship music is supposed to commend and celebrate the true and living God. I used to hear my mentor and brother-in-law say, "That music has no Jesus in it" or "it's too hollery" or "it's not singable; It's too dissonant" in reference to the fact that a lot of gospel music seemed to be in a minor key. At the time I thought he was being overly critical, but actually he discerned that the music didn't honor God nor edify the soul. Lyrically, the music lent itself to persistent metaphors lamenting about problems and the human condition (songs like *Jordan River, I'm Goin Home on the Mornin' Train*, and *Evenin' Train*).

Christian music, gospel music, and hymns should first reflect God; secondly, songs should direct people to know God; and finally the songs should compliment God in terms of who He is, His attributes, and his acts. And in all that we do in praise and worship there should be an effort to draw nearer to Him that your joy be fulfilled. These principles are applicable to leisurely listening as well. The music of the believer should be about God.

I encourage you to put forth the effort to acquire Christian music and learn the hymns and worship songs. If you really have a heart for God, why fill your spirit with music containing lyrics with sex-talk, shallow romance, violence and references that profane God's name and denigrate sectors of society? How can my mind be pure if it is filled with filth all week, day in and day out?

I hearken to you as a reader, and hopefully as a believer, to guard your mind, your eyes and your spirit as well as your senses. When you are driving through the city, and you roll up next to someone with hip-hop rattling their windows; feel free to crank up your best 'Jesus saves' CD or 'Nothing but the Blood of Jesus' recording, or 'There is Power in the Blood.' Filter out music that is unbefitting.

I know how it is to have difficulty in the area of filtering out music. It's still a natural response for my neck to start moving to anything musical. There was a time in my life that I chose music in ignorance of demonic influences, until the Lord opened my eyes in dramatic fashion.

Though I played the organ nearly every time the church doors opened, at home I listened to Jazz fusion and rock'n roll – the harder and the faster the riffs, the better. I sought out jazz with the excuse that I was trying to improve my playing because gospel music was predictable and repetitious, I had said.

My pursuit led me to a second job as security at a new amphitheater in the city where I worked. I got this job so I could see acts for free. I was in awe of the stage, the equipment – especially the stacks of speakers. I got a kick out of counting the speakers and the number of sound boards the bands used as well as the lighting or the lack there of. I saw chart toppers past and present; and the different festivals and 'paloozas.' Keep in mind there was non-stop alcohol and marijuana that I know the police could smell a mile away but did nothing about it.

One night a hard rock band called *Nine-Inch Nails* and David Bowie were scheduled to perform. As usual, I arrived early to watch the set up and sound check, before assuming my assigned post. That night I practically begged my boss to assign me near the stage and the mosh pit. Nine-inch Nails was up first. Their music was deafening, crazy, and brash. The lights consisted of white strobe lights against the blackness. I peered into the mayhem and spotty darkness; mesmerized at the sight of a young man appearing to have fangs, banging his head on the massive columns of the place. I had become so taken by the sight of the kid, that I was not paying attention when two men grabbed me and swept me into the thick of the head-banging crowd.

As I was being carried, I felt another hand pulling me in the opposite direction. That person turned out to be a uniformed police officer.

I asked him, "how did you know I was in trouble?"

He stated, "I was put here to watch you. I've been watching you all night."

I thanked him, and left that night before the concert was over, shaken.

Before leaving, I turned in the direction of the officer and he was nowhere to be found.

I returned another day only to submit my resignation. My boss, a very kind and mild-mannered gentleman looked at me from his desk as I entered and said,

"What took you so long? I knew there was something about you. You don't belong in a place like this."

He added, "You know that night after you left, a girl jumped off the stage into the mosh pit. She tried to ride the 'wave' but people parted and she fell and broke her neck."

The experience convicted me and I remembered the passage, "*come out from among them and be ye separated, saith the Lord and touch not the unclean thing; and I will receive you*" (II Cor. 6:17).

I have never sought fame to the degree of those recording artists, but secretly I wanted the fortune. I was confident that I had something to say as an aspiring songwriter, but I was not going about it God's way. The bible says that gifts come without repentance. And what the world has to offer can intoxicate a carnal-minded believer. I thought I loved God but I was not demonstrating love by set-apartness. My relationship with God was intellectual; it consisted only of knowledge.

The time has come to remove the gray from our lives as musicians.

The truth of God must stand alone.

Musicians have been given a charge to keep and a God to glorify. My dad used to say, "If it's not beneficial, becoming, or befitting, then you shouldn't do it." God knows we all come from different cultural and ethnic backgrounds that factor into what style of music to which we are inclined. The issue is not about style as much as it is about how praise functions in the believer's way of life and the requirements that a Holy God remains the focus of our song. If we are to be like Christ, all that He did was to glorify the Father. We must do the same.

If you are a Christian musician, there should be no question in anyone's mind whom you represent. The best way to avoid other people judging you is for you to judge yourself. Is it becoming, befitting or beneficial?

Is Praise what you do?

Instruments (Zamar)

The scriptures state that we must praise God on the stringed instruments, the organs, on the cymbals, etc. Therefore, our means of musical expression is with few limitations. Some churches are graced with orchestras, while others praise to music provided by a band with a banging rhythm section; others include digital instruments like synthesizers, work stations, and assorted modules, drums, or tracks. There is no error in any method that is done unto the glory of God and to the edifying of the saints.

Songs of the Church

From my observation of liturgy, customs vary depending on specific traditions, demographics, denomination, or personal taste and culture. I can visit ten different churches and hear ten different styles of sacred music, or visit ten churches in the same community and hear the same vibe. The flavor never diminishes the Savior! From a Capella and basic piano accompaniment, to full orchestral arrangements of hymns and cantatas to digi-sound CCM, I have always believed in the musical paradigm that expresses a body of believer's faith and devotion and sets the tone for the Holy Spirit to work in preparation for the seed of the Word of God.

I considered three polls which indicate that people primarily choose a church based on overall Pastor/preaching.[67] The poll asks three questions such as, the top 13 reasons that un-churched people choose a church; the top nine reasons that church-attendees choose a church; and the top six things that keep them there. Overwhelmingly, many responders answered, "Music/worship services." [Note; total number of people polled was not given and the percentages are on a question by question basis vs. 100%] Author and Pastor Rick Warren concluded, "Few people choose a church on the basis of the denominational label. They choose the church that best ministers to their needs."[68] In one-on-one discussions, people always cite the music and activities like dance more than the preaching. They will go on to list any number of events at the service and not even remember the text or subject of the sermon.

The Songs of the church should be by characterized by,

- The Psalm
- Teaching the Word of the Lord in song

- From a heart of grace
- Spiritual, melodious, rhythmic

Consider the verses below,

> *Speaking to yourselves in Psalm and hymns and spiritual songs, singing and making melody in your heart to the Lord (Ephes. 5:19). Let the word of Christ dwell in you richly in all wisdom; teaching and admonishing one another in Psalm and hymns and spiritual songs, sing with grace in your hearts to the Lord (Col. 3:16).*

Around the early 20th century there was a shift in Christian music and the songs began to emulate secular music. Every generation creates new ways of expressing their particular experience., however, the songs in the above verses were not songs disguised as gospel with 'thugged-out' artists talking about sneakers, rims, grips, guns, bling-bling, cars, radios, and stereos. The lyrics referenced in the above passages were of the Word of God, which transcends trends or what classifies as hip at any given time. Jesus' name was in the songs, not buried beneath the rat-ta-tat-tat-ta-tat chatter, samples, beats, riffs, and bass lines. The songs in the above passages were spiritual and they were unto the Lord. The songs of the bible were more like Revelations 5:9: "*And they sung a new song, saying, Thou art worthy to take the book, and to open the seals thereof: for thou wast slain, and hast redeemed us to God by the blood out of every kindred, and tongue, and people, and nation.*"

Or Revelations 19:6,

> *And I heard as it were the voice of a great multitude, and as the voice of many waters, and as the voice of mighty thundering, saying Alleluia: for the Lord God omnipotent reigneth.*

Or Revelations 4:8,

> *And the four beasts had each of them six wings about him; and they were full of eyes within: and they rest not day and night, saying holy, holy, holy, Lord God Almighty, which was and is, and is to come.*

Uses of Songs

Drive Evil spirits away

The songs of the bible were lyrical but did not necessarily recognize the organization and structure of contemporary songs as we know them today. For example, the arrangement may not have been A-A-B-A-C-D or verse, verse, second verse, chorus, verse, bridge, vamp. Songs of the bible – whether lyrical or instrumental - were effective to drive away evil spirits. King Saul called on a young David to play before him when the spirit of madness came upon him (I Sam. 16:14).

Celebration

Songs of the bible were used for celebration. For instance, there is the familiar story of David rejoicing as the Ark of the Covenant was returned to the camp or the celebration of the temple. There is the Song of Moses in Exodus 15, which may not contain the rhyme and repetition to which our ears are accustomed, but it honored God and recognized His acts, as did the song that Mary, the mother of Jesus sang in the Luke 1:46.

Weapon of Warfare and Victory

I am a witness that singing, and praise in general, are spiritual weapons. For the bible says in Ephesians 6:12, *"we wrestle not against flesh and blood but against principalities, against powers, against the darkness of this word, spiritual wickedness in high places."* Also, *"For the weapons of our warfare are not carnal, but mighty through God to the pulling down of strong holds" (II Cor.* 10: 4).

Songs of the bible

Miriam's song
Deborah, Judges 5
Zachariah, Luke 1:68
Of Angels Luke 2:13
O *the Redeemer, revelations 5:9*
Revelations 19
Glory Isaiah 60: 1- 9
Mary Luke 1:46

Joshua used big music to bring down the wall at Jericho (Joshua 6: 1-20). Another time the enemies were put to flight when the people sang, shouted and made a joyful noise (see section on Shout). The people shouted in unison at the time they were instructed, which was so powerful the wall of Jericho fell down flat. Lisa Bevere of Messenger International said,

> I want to talk to you about what you carry, because if there is a war then that means you better have a weapon… My bible describes the Word of God as a sword of the Spirit. As we speak the Word of God [and] as we sing the Word of God… we send something into motion… as we begin to lift up songs, things begin to shift in the heavenlies. Things begin to open up that were closed. As we worship the enemy scatters; impregnating you with praise gives birth to worship.[69]

When we praise in song, we have an anchor in the Word of God. So whether you feel you are good singers or not, sing. Sing until you have the assurance of the power of God. Sing with abandon even if you are off-key. Sing as though you have a hope even though things seem hopeless.

When you sing in faith you are effectively speaking things that be not as though they were. You can begin to sing *"I Love You Lord"* or any song. You can make up your own lyrics and your own melody. You needn't worry or be concerned about whether what comes out of your mouth makes sense to others.

Additionally, there are a variety of avenues to obtain Christian music. You can listen to music on XM and Sirius radio, digital television (Dish Network, Direct TV, Comcast) or radio, or radio stations on the web, CD's, MP3 players, iPods, or live. Find a medium to get the music of gladness and good news music down in your spirit on a daily basis. This will help you to overcome some of life's challenges. Listening to artists that sing the Word of God helps reinforce that Word in your spirit.

Ministry Tip:

Try this:
Select your favorite passage in Psalm or another verse.
You don't have to be a prolific songwriter
with knowledge Composition or theory.
Begin to hum the words of the text.

Music Ministry – A Practical Guide

As a child I had the privilege of growing up and watching musicians of the church and how they conducted themselves. I am especially glad for that time because it taught me issues like protocol, musicianship, choral performance, and repertoire. Most of those musicians were professionals in the field(s) of music education as opposed to career church musicians. They had families to support, so they did not depend on the church as a 'gig' but their position was a manner of contributing to the church out of a love for music.

The application of what I observed would begin as soon as our family arrived at home. As my mother made fried chicken, baked macaroni and cheese, corn bread, greens and pineapple upside-down cake, and while the rest of the family went about their Sunday afternoon or weekday activities, I would go to my favorite walk-in closet and set up shoeboxes in drum kit formation. I used those old metal ice trays for cymbals and the sticks from the dry cleaner's hangers for sticks. I used go back and forth from air piano to broomstick microphone; air guitar then back to shoe box drums. Eventually, my dad bought me a white baby grand Baldwin® piano; but for some reason I steered clear, in favor of air piano. My favorite play activity was emulating the church musicians.

I remained faithful in my desire to make music for God - and by the laying on of hands - came to fulfill prophesy spoken over my life to become my father's organist and later, Minister of Music.

I thank God for the people God placed in my path who exemplified proper conduct in the house of God. Hence, the necessity to forward a code of practice to present-day musicians as the Apostle Paul wrote to Timothy,

> *These things write I unto thee, hoping to come unto thee shortly: But if I tarry long, that thou mayest know how thou oughtest to behave thyself in the house of God, which is the church of the living God, the pillar and ground of the truth*
> *(I Tim. 3:14, 15).*

The above scripture was spoken within the context of setting in order the qualifications for the offices of the church (i.e. Bishop, Deacons). The ministry of music is more than proficiency of skill or the complexity of your improvisation. This guide draws from nearly 30 years of experience (mistakes included) as a church musician, band leader, and singer. This guide is intended to equip music ministry people with fundamental 'hands-off' skills, or protocol.

The attitude of church musicians has shifted to the extent that rather than hold down a secular job, musicians look to work full time for the church. There is nothing wrong with a life's work serving in ministry. But remember attitude is reflected in every aspect, including from when we show up, to our attire, to how we interact with each other as well as Pastors. We must do our best by God, by the pastor, and by the church.

I contend that the music ministry is an integral part of a church's success. Therefore, below I offer some suggestions to encourage music ministry people who want to please God and help build your church.

Musician's Guide

1) Accept and know Jesus as your personal Lord and Savior, if you have not already done so.
2) Walk worthy of your calling,

   I therefore, the prisoner of the Lord, beseech you that ye walk worthy of the vocation wherewith ye are called,
   With all lowliness and meekness, with longsuffering, forbearing one another in love;
   Endeavouring to keep the unity of the Spirit in the bond of peace (Eph. 4:1-3).

3) Be willing to obey those that have rule over you in the church and save yourself a lot of heartache.
4) Be willing to esteem others higher than yourself. Remember the most important instrument is the voice. You are there to accompany, not to be featured.

5) Before you play, pray.

Pray,

- Your sins be forgiven
- That your flesh be crucified and God be Glorified
- That He will make you a living sacrifice of praise, holy and acceptable
- For the anointing of the Holy Ghost; that yolks will be destroyed
- For the people to whom you are ministering, that they will be changed.

6) Be on time for service. This means, get to the church at least 45 minutes before the scheduled start time of the service. This will give you time to pray, set up your equipment, and troubleshoot in the event something's not quite right. It is simply not right for drummers and keyboard players to arrive while the service is in progress and begin setting up cymbals and tuning toms; or for an organist to start blasting the other musicians and singers in the middle of a hymn. If you didn't get there on time, at least wait until the song is over to begin playing! Being on time includes all sound and technical support personnel.
7) TURN THE VOLUME DOWN!!!! Please, please, please, please, please stop playing so loud. If you can't hear the voices YOU'RE PLAYING TOO LOUD! Sometimes the people trying to sing look like the equivalent of a ventriloquist act. We see only their mouths moving, and veins popping out of their necks from the strain, but no sound. You are there to accompany and when voices are present, the voice is the most important instrument. If you can't hear the singers, you are playing too loud. Humble yourself and bring the volume down.
8) Assist in the flow of the service and in keeping the singers/congregation on track with the songs by playing the melody on top rather a lot of complicated chord progressions. Play the song. If you want to jam out and demonstrate to everybody that

you've got skills, kindly find a garage or stage somewhere and knock yourself out, but the service is not the time.

9) For God's sake, practice alone and then rehearse with the other musicians. If you don't have time to practice, you shouldn't have time to play. This includes the Directors and Minister of Music.
10) Learn to read music so you can play hymns properly as well as the top 40 contemporary and traditional releases.

    A popular strategy among many musicians is to learn one song from the top-40 gospel or Christian charts a week so they are prepared in the event they are called. Also, if you are struggling with chords, there are excellent on-line resources such as Earnest and Roline's ministry (www.earnestandroline.com); Gospel Skillz (gospelskillz.com); Musician's Friend; Learn Gospel Music (www.learngospelmusic.com), Gospel Keyboard (www.gospelkeyboard.com), pianoclubhouse.com; and hearandplay.com. For a nominal fee you can watch the tutorials and play along. Also, some of these may be found on YouTube in part. There is an extensive list if you search "gospel chords" you will find many tutorials – a portion or all of which is free. [Not recommended if you are not a musician. Many times in contemporary gospel the playing chords are not the same chord patterns for the vocals.]

11) Pu-lease don't be one of those annoying musicians who is so grand that you keep strolling in and out of the service to raid the church fridge for breakfast and snacks, or to check your cell phone messages. Remember, everybody can be replaced - by God. No one is so important that he or she is exempt from remaining in the sanctuary to listen to the Word of God. Too many musicians habitually excuse themselves when the Word comes forth, and then miraculously reappear when it's time to play again. Musicians need the Bread of Life as well as everyone else.
12) This shouldn't need to be said, but PUT AWAY THE BLACKBERRY/i phone/video game/tablet!

13) Do have fresh breath. Mints, not gum.
14) Smell good, look good, and sound good.

As a final point, unless your church is casual, lose the basketball shirts, dark glasses, and/or sneakers. Everywhere you go, there is a dress code. Every work situation requires specific attire and we comply, but when it comes to God we present to Him our 'just got-out-of bed-and-I don't-care-just-as-I-am' clothes. *Are you kidding*? God is about the best. He is about things being overlaid with gold, and the best wood, exquisite jewels, things being clean and pure. God is a particular God and we can honor Him with our best. Dressing with Him in mind does not mean to go out and spend money you don't have or stress about what you are expected to have if you don't have the means. But I find that people always use the 'don't have' excuse when it comes to God's house, but when they were out clubbing, they went all out to make sure they sported the latest and the greatest available, to suit their agenda.

The musicians in the bible were essential to the worship, to celebration, and war. The musicians/singers were the Levites of the priestly order. These men were not just anybody; music was their office. They were consecrated for praise, and the Lord God was their inheritance.

"But unto the tribe of Levi Moses gave not any inheritance: the LORD God of Israel was their inheritance, as he said unto them" (Josh 13:33).

The Levites' post was at the door of the temple or at the gate. First, they were to offer sacrifice for their sins and purify themselves, then begin playing the instruments that were made and dedicated by David the King (II Chron. 5:1). These instruments were kept as a part of the treasure in the house of God. My guess is that these instruments were meticulously maintained for the purpose of praise because Solomon used the instruments of his father's reign and they were passed on to Ezra and Nehemiah's generation.

I cannot tell you how many churches I've played, and my fingers were black from the crud on the keys. One church, there was a half inch of dust beneath spider webs. I've seen beautiful Hammond organs used as a shelf to park everybody's stuff - including lattes', cappuccinos, and breakfast croissants, in part because not everybody that plays the organ knows what they are doing, and some just want to play and they don't care.

Thus:

- Before you begin playing the Hammond, take your left street shoe off for better foot mobility and to prevent gouging the wood of the base pedals.
- Sparingly switch the fast-slow function of the Leslie. At least let the rotors complete the cycle before switching. I've watched organists working that switch like they were changing gears in a vehicle or racking it back and forth like a video game joy stick.
- Turn the Leslie tremolo off or on slow when not in use for long periods unless you or your church want to fork out $3 - $4,200.00 to get another one.
- Respect the space, the instruments, and the opportunity. Maintain your instrument including dusting as needed.
- Apply what my mother used to refer to as 'stopping sense.' It is not always your time. Unless the minister or speaker requests that you play while they are talking or preaching, do not play. Remember the Word of God is still powerful and effective without accompaniment. Musicians in the black church and charismatic churches, in particular, have fostered the tradition of 'tuning up' or revving up the preacher and the congregation into this call-and-response frenzy where the preacher ad-libs an exhortation in rhythmic fashion and the organist follows with preacher chords and the drummer/other musicians hit each time. Just remember that not all churches or preachers adopt the same style of preaching so be prepared to adapt and go with their special flow.
- Don't force your style preference on the congregation. I've had occasion to play with guys and didn't know what they were playing. I don't hate on them for having skills, but the service is not the time to show off. Again, please play the song.
- Don't complain, volunteer, or give unsolicited advice. Stay in your lane and focus on doing your assignment well. You may

not win a popularity contest, but let your performance, your word, and your life be your witnesses.

- To keep down confusion, avoid duplicating the same sound. If one organ is playing, the other should rest. If one acoustic piano sound is playing, then another one is not needed. If a bass player is playing, the organist shouldn't be creating his/her own bass lines. The sound becomes muddy and downright nasty on the bottom.
- Generally, the organist is the lead instrument. The organ or keyboard accompanies the vocals, the drums accompany the organ/keyboard and the bass plays with the drummer. That means everyone else in the band should take their cue from John or Jane Q-organist. You may get a consensus of who everyone will look to for the cues but a cue person needs to be established if there is an ensemble.
- Eye contact is essential. Try not to hibernate in your own musical world, doing your own thing. And do not ignore the director.
- Be sure to allow the Holy Spirit to lead when it comes to exhortation or you'll just annoy and provoke a rebellious spirit in people. As musicians and praise leaders, we cannot make people participate. Sometimes it's best to just sing or play because we cannot change people's hearts.
- If you have a dispute with another musician, settle it the bible way, according to Jesus in Matthew (Matt.5:22-26). Please read.
- As it relates to disagreements among musicians (trust me, people have egos) There is no excuse for getting caught up in the flesh and getting loud and having confrontations in the public space of the sanctuary. This is not the Spirit of God, but rather an evil spirit that needs to come under the blood of Jesus.
- Prayerfully, you are a musician that is sold out to Christ, which is your main motivation for doing what you do. I served at one church for more than 25 years before I was ever paid a dime. And then I received $100.00/month. This included all services and rehearsals. I have remained at a church even when checks bounced or showed up on pay day only to be told, we can't pay

you. I have had more than one occasion to play for a full week of revival followed by a week of conference, only to receive less than $24.00 plus some loose change. (Okay, I'm not going to lie. At that point I lost it!) Shamefully, these circumstances come with being a musician in the secular world as well as the church.

I don't know why churches are resistant to paying musicians in ministry, and make it difficult for musicians to discuss discrepancies. As musicians, you have to remain prayerful because criticism and getting 'stiffed' is truly an occupational hazard, but also serve as an alert for imperceptible, underlying issues. I want to encourage you to continue being faithful in service, in humility, and in prayers. Humble yourself before Almighty God and the church. Try not to murmur and complain, especially to other musicians or people in the congregation. Do all you can to have a healthy working relationship with the Pastor – and if this is a challenge, God will handle that matter exclusively. But if they do you wrong by not keeping their word, forgive them and pray for them.

- ABOVE ALL SERVE. I have been called by our Presiding Elder to go to churches and told, Sister LL. "go and serve." There is a biblical basis for this instruction. Jesus sent His disciples and told them to go without purse, script, or shoes. However, later He tells them to take a purse, a script, and shoes; and if you don't have one (a sword) to sell a garment and buy one (Like 22:34-36). At the first command, the disciples were with Jesus, who was about to become the sacrificial Lamb of God and die a criminal's death. By the time of the amended instruction Jesus was saying, you're going to need to be equipped for the task and the journey.

o P.S. Please do not rob God. Tithe your salary as a musician, to the church that sowed into you. Brothers and sisters – this is right. This act of obedience is your first form of worship. If you do not tithe, you will never experience the fullness of what God has for you or what He can work through you. Your pocket will be as a bag with holes (Haggai 1:6). Perhaps this is why so many musicians suffer and is among a number of reason musicians don't receive respect.

I respectfully submit that if musicians and Ministers of Music will be proactive in their assignments, there will be stability concerning musicians and an atmosphere created for the presence of God and the Spirit of God to work His work.

Again, the Levites were of the priestly order and were the musicians and singers. The Bible states the Levites were more upright in heart to sanctify themselves than the priests. Hezekiah the King required them to consecrate themselves unto the Lord. This means they didn't come staggering in red-eyed from the night before to play on the instruments ordained by God with liquor and cigarettes on their breaths. The Levites weren't just utilitarian, they loved God with all their hearts and were dedicated. The Levites didn't create a scene and threaten the high priest when the pay was short; nor was their service put out to the highest bidder. This is the example by which we can pattern our conduct with a heart to give God the highest reverence. A-men.

Sound Reinforcement Personnel Guide

Thanks to all the people who operate sound equipment. Sound operators can either help or hinder the service. Therefore, I find it crucial that we include some tips to steer this task in the right direction, in the event it is needed.

1) Accept and know Jesus as your personal Lord and Savior.
2) Please do all you can to know the equipment.
3) If you do not know what the knobs, buttons, and faders are for, DO NOT TOUCH THE SOUND BOARD until you do!

   Feedback and screeching and squealing microphones throughout the service when people are singing and or preaching serves only as a distraction and will not save a soul.

   As a tip, many music stores gladly offer free tutorials or workshops to familiarize you with today's equipment. As it relates to the particular parameters of your edifice, you should take the initiative to investigate and don't be afraid to experiment OUTSIDE of service time. But please learn your craft so you can get it right for ministry sake.

4) If God didn't call you to be the sound engineer, kindly take your seat in the pews.
5) Take a class and always read up on new developments in sound reinforcement equipment.
6) Know the equipment, building specs, and factors that may alter or affect the sound.
7) Less is more. This means you shouldn't need to be micro adjusting throughout the service. Do feel free to be stingy with the effects.
8) The aim of sound reinforcement is just that – reinforce! The church is not a recording studio. Sound effects are not needed

and if so, at a minimum. You want to augment the natural tone and timbre of the voice. People should sound like themselves.

9) Attend all rehearsals.
10) Arrive well in advance of the service to test the equipment. Know the proper way to test the equipment. (Don't pound the microphones; speak into them).
11) Be a part of the opening prayer for the music ministry and remain alert and watchful throughout the service until the benediction.

Guide for Praise and Worship Leaders

We have addressed musicians in the church relative to conduct. Also important are the Praise and Worship Leaders as they are called. By this term I am referring to the people who actually lead the people into praise and song, etc. Please keep in mind that the purpose of Praise Leaders is to lead the people into halal, shabach, barach praise unto the Lord. Therefore, following are suggestions which I hope you will find helpful in your ministry:

Do,

1) Arrive on time – meaning in advance of the service to get yourself together and be in prayer with the other musicians and singers. There's a cliché (I don't know where or by whom it originated) "If you are on time, you are late."
2) Pray. Before you sing or play a note, consult Almighty God and humbly solicit the help of the Holy Spirit. Please remember that what you are about to do is profoundly spiritual. You are about to engage in spiritual warfare. In your prayer,

o Pull down strong holds.
o Call out hindering spirits and distracting spirits. Order those spirits of distraction, discouragement, disruptiveness, and rebellious unreceptive spirits (witchcraft) out; pray for the hardened heart, the heavy hearted, the broken and unsaved.
o Pray that the blood of Jesus will cover you and that the anointing of the Holy Ghost fall upon you. You will want to strive for excellence in praise.

3) In the event of a lot of activity, stop – according to the leading of the Holy Ghost – because it will become too much of a struggle and a pull when you're trying to glorify God and edify the church amid confusion.

4) Once the prayer has been said, be ready to begin with a song that invites the Presence of the Holy Ghost.
5) Refrain from chatting before the service. It will be difficult for people to take you seriously when they've witnessed you conversing, finishing your cappuccino and muffin, and chewing gum in the sanctuary.
6) Wear appropriate attire which covers your body parts. It is unacceptable to draw attention to yourself with revealing clothing or form-fitting clothing. Neither God nor the congregation needs to be privy to what's beneath your clothes, including you tattoos and piercings (and the occasional thong). Attire is another subject that will make folks fight and storm out of the church if you're not careful, but it must be addressed.

   I have no personal preference for pants v. dresses or skirts for sisters. I think traditionally we spend far too much time stressing standards that God Himself did not set. The Word of God says we are to dress modestly as becomes of saints.

> *I will therefore that men pray every where, lifting up holy hands, without wrath and doubting. In like manner also, that women adorn themselves in modest apparel, with shamefacedness and sobriety; not with broided hair, or gold, or pearls, or costly array;*
>
> *But (which becometh women professing godliness) with good works (I Tim.2:7-9).*

The operative word in the scripture is <u>modestly.</u> We shouldn't need someone to preach a sermon about twenty earrings in our ears, breast tats, back tats, low ride pants to accommodate rear-end tats, shorts, and street lumpish outfits. Saints this is serious and directly connected to the 'set apartness' referenced throughout this book. If we love God we will honor and reverence him with attire that represents him; not drawing attention to ourselves. If you haven't gotten a tattoo, do read what the Word of God has to say:

> *Ye shall not round the corners of your heads,[Mohawk?] neither shalt thou mar the corners of thy beard.*
>
> *Ye shall not make any cuttings in your flesh for the dead,* ***nor print any marks upon you: I am the LORD.*** *(Lev. 19:27-29)*
>
> *From henceforth let no man trouble me: for I bear in my body the marks of the Lord Jesus. (Gal. 6:17)*

7) Remember to be separated unto God. We are His righteousness.
8) Remember to be holy as He is Holy.
9) Come prepared with a list of songs to perform - preferably from the pool of songs you rehearsed.
10) Come with a ready repertoire for all aspects of the service that prepare the heart for the seed of the Living God, which is the Word of God, the Bread of Life.
11) Unless the Holy Spirit moves on you to do otherwise, minister what you rehearse because no one can follow you if you go off course, and it will be a mess that will not save one soul. This is why it is important to rehearse your Holy Ghost inspired list of songs. To achieve a flow in the service, please avoid intervals of silence in between songs while the congregation waits. The organist keyboard player may want to plat appropriate interludes.
12) Focus your repertoire on songs that are uplifting and center on the goodness of God. Try at least to have the chorus/vamp be something people can join in to sing (but remember, do not coerce participation). Don't be afraid to incorporate the old hymns of the church. KNOW YOUR AUDIENCE. It makes no sense to sing all contemporary stuff and no one in the congregation is getting with you because that's not the music of their generation. Conversely, if everyone is under thirty it makes no sense to sing Chancellor material (i.e. arias and spirituals, canons. Trust me, I learned this the hard way – there

will be a revolt, and you will be fortunate if there's anyone left that's willing to sing at all).

13) Show, don't tell. If YOU lift up Jesus, and YOU begin to laud God and call out His names, speak of His attributes and His mighty acts others will follow. Open up YOUR mouth and allow the Holy Spirit to do His work to move upon the people. This is entering into His presence. [Also see the next section on Praise phrases]
14) Smile and enjoy complimenting the Lord.
15) Know when to quit. A good praise leader maintains eye contact with the pastor or person presiding over the service, rather than dragging it out because you feel like it. I realize that many times praise and worship teams are subjected to extending the service because the clergy is late or hanging out in the office. Try not to get flustered, and make the best of it. Remain focused and keep a meek spirit so the Holy Spirit will continue to move in their absence. Remember, people are watching you.
16) Remember gentleness characterizes the Holy Spirit. The Word of God says,

> *Put on therefore, as the elect of God, holy and beloved, bowels of mercies, kindness, humbleness of mind, meekness, longsuffering;(Col. 3:12).*

And,

> *The LORD hath appeared of old unto me, saying, Yea, I have loved thee with an everlasting love: therefore with loving kindness have I drawn thee (Jer. 31:3).*

Do not,

1) Join the choir or the Praise and Worship Team if you cannot sing. If you are an exhorter, there is another time and place for that, but this is typically the time for corporate praise; the objective being to lift up the name of Jesus in song, edify the saints, and set the atmosphere for the soul-saving Word of God.

2) Bully people into praise.
3) Fuss at the people.
4) Criticize the people.
5) Ridicule the people for not responding.
6) Get angry and begin singling people out who do respond as a strategy to get others to partake.
7) Get caught up in showing off your vocal ability with the equivalent of vocal back-flips and vocal calisthenics.
8) Keep begging and twisting people's arms like a drill sergeant, barking instructions to "stand-sit-stand-sit; hunch-your-neighbor-punch-your-neighbor-slap-your-neighbor-tap-your-neighbor, etc." So many times I see praise leaders get frustrated, and actions become less worshipful. Understandably, one of the most discouraging things for a musician or singer is when people don't respond to what you are doing; but we have to remember that we are not performers, and the congregation didn't pay a ticket price to get in. Moreover, we don't know what people are going through. Often people do their best to press their way, so just execute the task. I always say you cannot control your audience.

Finally, begin by inviting the Presence of the Holy Spirit so He will manifest Himself. To God be the glory.

Most praise and worship folks know the serious nature of the task at hand; that the ministry of praise is not a performance. Our main objectives are two-fold: to set the atmosphere for worship, and to prepare hearts for the seed of the Word of God. When we carry out those objectives we are ministering to the saints and to unconfessed sinners because the Word will accomplish what it was sent out to accomplish.

The Holy Spirit moves in an atmosphere of liberty, rather than one of coercion. *2* Corinthians 3:17 says, *"Now the Lord is the Spirit, and where the Spirit of the Lord is, there is liberty" (NASB).* The Amplified says,

> *Now the Lord is the Spirit, and where the Spirit of the Lord is, there is liberty [*emancipation from bondage, freedom*].*

The Message expounds further by stating,

> And when God is personally present, a living Spirit, that old, constricting legislation is recognized as obsolete. We're free of it! All of us! Nothing between us and God, our faces shining with the brightness of his face. And so we are transfigured much like the Messiah, our lives gradually becoming brighter and more beautiful as God enters our lives and we become like him.

Begin to set yourself apart during the week leading up to the day and time you are to minister. Be that Levite in your lifestyle and your routine by habitually praying, fasting, devouring the Bread of Life, and spending time in the Presence of God. Doing this individually and as a team will make all the difference because you won't have time for foolishness before ministering. If you follow these suggestions, I promise God will move in a marvelous way as He uses you to bless God and bless the people.

Summary

Music is the science or act of ordering sounds in succession, in combination, and temporal relation to produce a composition. Music is also described as the creation of favorable rhythmic and tonal sounds. We found that the bible credits Jubal as being the father of Music. Also, music of the bible consisted of Psalm and Hymns. The most important features of music of praise must be,

- Unto the Lord
- Spiritual
- Have grace and gladness in the heart.

In addition, music ministry folks should purify themselves for the purpose of walking worthy of the vocation. We should present ourselves as living sacrifices, Holy and acceptable.

This section offered a practical guide for musicians, singers and technical support people so we can serve in a manner pleasing unto God and which edifies the church. God accepts music such as the orchestral renderings of the Crystal Cathedral and the Brooklyn Tabernacle Choir; the contemporary praise songs of Hillsong, Michael W. Smith, and Jars of Clay; Southern Gospel of the Gaithers; worship music of Chris Tomlin, or Don Moen; the Urban sounds of 21:03 or Fred Hammond, or the eclectic music of Tye Tribbett; as well as traditional gospel of Mississippi Mass Choir. The fundamental element and defining denominator is that the music must be about God and must be unto the Lord.

Serving as a church musician or praise leader should be an enjoyable experience but make no mistake, working for the sake of Christ comes with difficulties. Many of us have chosen the church over the club; righteousness over recognition, and sacrifice over selfish desires. Most of us will not achieve fame. Trust me, I know. Aside from that, you just want to get paid for doing what you love so you can climb out of survival mode and not have to compromise the quality of your craft by working several unrewarding jobs.

On too many occasions I have suffered the most devastating hurt while serving as a musician, but I am determined to finish my course.

If you are experiencing challenges, do not give up. Please continue in the Lord and I promise He will never leave you or forsake you. More importantly, this is God's promise.

For most of my 30+ years as a church musician and Minister of music I was not paid a dime. It took nearly 24 years to finally get paid $100 a month. People I knew in the music community laughed and made jokes about how those one hundred dollars broke down, hourly. But I continued to serve until I became like one of the light fixtures. A relic. Utilitarian. Someone else – not someone better – came along and I felt myself fighting to stay. I actually tried to physically remove that individual from the organ who refused to get up. I knew then it was time to go. I had to repent and move on to serve again and endure the not-so-subtle hints that I was not good enough and that they needed someone from a "Kirk Franklin generation, not C.L. Franklin." (A pastor actually used this metaphor of Aretha's famous preacher father to insinuate that it was time for replacement.)

I continued to serve.

Though disappointed and deeply wounded by pastors who hadn't a clue about keeping their word or telling the truth, I served, until the point I vowed never to step foot in a church again. I was hurt over and over by pastors and the church more than people in the world. I no longer believed. But then that same Elder called me and said,

"Serve."

I was obedient and went to serve. Not only did I serve, I trusted God that He would use me and provide.

My unsolicited advice is, serve. Serve God, serve the church, and serve the sinner. Don't be concerned about how much.

Serve.

Also, we must forgive. We must forgive so we will be forgiven and to stave off bitterness. When the church secretary hands you a check and later the teller announces, *I'm sorry no funds are available. You need to call the issuer,*

Serve.

Ministry tip:
Be appointed, be pure, prepared, be professional.

Phrases and Words of Praise

- Praise Yaweh
- Acknowledge
- Adore
- Appreciate
- Awesome
- Bless
- Extol
- Glorify
- Holy, Holy, Holy are you Lord, God Almighty
- Honor
- Thank you
- King of Kings
- Lord of Lords
- Love
- Mighty
- Majesty
- Thank you
- Thank you for your grace and mercy
- Thank you for the work of your Mighty hand
- Thank you for your ear
- Thank you for your eyes
- Thank you for mouth, Lord and all that you have spoken that is life
- Thank You Lord for being a Strong Tower
- Thank you that you have given us the inheritance of the Power of the Holy Ghost
- You are worthy to receive glory and honor
- You are my Deliver and my Banner Jehovah-nissi
- You are the everlasting, immutable God
- You are Jehovah-rapha
- You are my Peace, Jehovah-shalom
- You are my Provider, Jehovah-jireh
- You are my Strength (El) and Redeemer

Praise Phrases

- You are I AM that I AM
- You are the Way
- You are the Living Bread
- You are the Living Water
- You are Light and in You is no Darkness
- You are the Alpha and Omega
- Holy, Holy, Holy Lord God Almighty, which was and is, and is to come (Revelations 4: 8).
- Worthy is the Lamb that was slain to receive power and riches and honour, and glory and blessing (Revelations 5:12)
- Thou are worthy, O Lord to receive glory and hour and power: for thou hast created all things for thy pleasure they are and were created (Revelations 4:11).
- Honor

  (Respect, Tribute)
- Awesome

  (Splendid, Grand, Amazing)
- Mighty

  (Potent, Impressive, Powerful)
- Majesty

  Magnificence, nobility, aristocracy, dignity
- Hallelujah or Alleluia

  An exhortation in the Hebrew meaning: let the people praise Him; praise Jehovah.
- You are the Faithful Witness
- You (Jesus) are the Over comer. You overcame persecution, tribulation, homelessness, abandonment, humiliation, degradation, death and Hell.
- Thou art worthy to receive glory and honor and power, for thou hast created all things…
- The Lion of the Tribe of Judah
- Worthy is the Lamb that was slain to receive power, and riches and wisdom and strength and honor and glory and blessing.

- Blessing and honor and glory, and power be unto Him that sitteth upon the throne and unto the Lamb forever and ever.

Praise, Revisited

Now that you know praise is to compliment; to speak approvingly of someone's attributes, appearance, or a positive deed; and now that we know we were created to praise God and Him alone, and who we are not to praise, it is time to incorporate the principles into a life of praise.

Praising God means practicing compliments, contemplation, and consideration of the attributes of God and His wonderful acts.

Praise is uncomplicated.

Praise is synonymous with commend, congratulate, pay tribute to, applaud, approve, speak well of.

If we can think of nothing else for which to thank God, we can thank Him for His grace. A wonderful song entitled, "*If Not for Your Grace*" by worship leader Israel Houghton suggests that grace leads us to the place of worship. In the song he asks "Where would I be if not for your grace?" He answers: "Grace restores, redeems and releases one to worship; grace repairs, and releases miracles."[70]

There is so much for which we can compliment God. We are not limited to saying 'thank you Jesus' and "yes Lord' or 'hallelujah.' When we praise we make mention of His goodness. We go on to speak to God at length about what he means to us. For example:

"God I love you. I love you for your wondrous work; for sending your Son Jesus to be the propitiation for my sins. Thank you for staying my execution."

"God, you are my provider, you are my healer,. Thank you for sending a comforter, that Angels protect me and are here on earth working on my behalf."

Praise is something that increases the more we purposefully put it into practice.

The best example of how to praise God comes from an audacious God, Himself. Below are two examples, the first is a response from God to Job; the second is God praising Himself before Moses:

> *Who is this that darkens counsel by words without knowledge?*
> *Gird up now your loins like a man, and I will demand of you, and you declare to Me.*
> *Where were you when I laid the foundation of the earth? Declare to Me, if you have and know understanding.*
> *Who determined the measures of the earth, if you know? Or who stretched the measuring line upon it?*
> *Upon what were the foundations of it fastened, or who laid its cornerstone,*
> *When the morning stars sang together and all the sons of God shouted for joy?*
> *Or who shut up the sea with doors when it broke forth and issued out of the womb?--*
> *When I made the clouds the garment of it, and thick darkness a swaddling band for it,*
> *And marked for it My appointed boundary and set bars and doors*
> *And said, Thus far shall you come and no farther; and here shall your proud waves be stayed?*
> *Have you commanded the morning since your days began and caused the dawn to know its place,*
> *So that [light] may get hold of the corners of the earth and shake the wickedness [of night] out of it?*
> *It is changed like clay into which a seal is pressed; and things stand out like a many-colored garment.*
> *From the wicked their light is withheld, and their uplifted arm is broken.*
> *Have you explored the springs of the sea? Or have you walked in the recesses of the deep?*
> *Have the gates of death been revealed to you? Or have you seen the doors of deep darkness?*
> *Have you comprehended the breadth of the earth? Tell Me, if you know it all.*

> *Where is the way where light dwells? And as for darkness, where is its abode,*
> *That you may conduct it to its home, and may know the paths to its house?*
> *(Job 38, AMP)*

And,

> *Then the LORD came down in a cloud and stood there with him; and he called out his own name, Yahweh.*
> *The LORD passed in front of Moses, calling out, Yahweh! The LORD!*
> *The God of compassion and mercy!*
> *I am slow to anger*
> *and filled with unfailing love and faithfulness.*
> *I lavish unfailing love to a thousand generations.*
> *I forgive iniquity, rebellion, and sin.*
> *But I do not excuse the guilty.*
> *I lay the sins of the parents upon their children and grandchildren;*
> *the entire family is affected—*
> *even children in the third and fourth generations.*
> *Moses immediately threw himself to the ground and worshiped.*
> *(Exodus 34, NLT)*

I encourage you to study the passages where God praises Himself, including the ones mentioned above. He praises Himself in the book of Genesis, for each time He created something He said, "*it is good.*"

For your information, the *'goodness'* of God is the same as His 'Glory' as evidenced by His response to Moses' request: "*I beseech thee, show me your glory.*" God's response was "*I will make all my goodness pass before thee.*"

In your study, begin to write down key passages or to look at the phrases during your time of praise. Be sure to include complimentary words about His goodness and His essence.

As believers we should make a habit of meditating on all that there is about the Lord God. We think lovely thoughts about him on purpose.

With so much negativity in every facet of life, God yet promises to keep us in perfect peace whose mind is stayed on Him. This is the benefit of purposeful praise.

Quietly utter compliments to God, to His Son Jesus, and to the Holy Spirit throughout the day. Laud Him. Extol Him. For every complaint, replace them with praise. Don't wait until you are in trouble and need a lawyer or a doctor. Do not wait until your financial situation is too bleak to think about God. Don't just thank God for material things. Don't just thank Him at income tax time or when you receive a settlement (but forget Him when it's time to bring in the tithe, which belong to Him).

Heretofore, purpose in your heart to love God enough that He is present in your mind at all times. This means you are never separated from Him, but separated unto him. You are speaking praise phrases over yourself and into your situations. A 'situation' or an issue needn't present itself for you to begin praising. Praise Him because He is worthy. Praise God for His everlasting mercy and His kindness toward us and that He is righteous judge, yet slow to anger.

You needn't concern yourself with being repetitious or not getting it right. Say them out loud as many times as you need to. Remember, there is still an attitude with which you apply these exercises of reverence and worship. Be contrite and broken before the Lord as you say these phrases. If you desire to combine singing, dancing, or playing an instrument, seek God for it and ask for the help of the Holy Spirit. For the Word says to covet earnestly the good gifts. Ask your Spirit-filled Pastor to anoint you with precious oil and speak over your life.

I trust this section has been particularly helpful to you and I hope you will go before the throne and before mankind, passionate in your proclamation. The bible is packed with phrases to offer unto God; such as the books of Psalm, Isaiah, and Revelations. I encourage readers to put these phrases into practice and commit them to memory. You may have to read them several times, or open your eyes during your time of prayer and praise to read them. The objective is to enhance your connection to God. Take special care with how God praised Himself.

God is God. He is supreme at everything, including praise.

Press in praise. Begin to love doing it [will to do it] and make it your passion. The more often you praise, and the more you add words and phrases to your praise, the closer you will be to the Living God. I encourage you to search the Word of God. As you read, you will find words of praise that you can enhance you praise life.

Ministry Tip

Read
Job 38
Isaiah 60:1 – 9
Isaiah 54:10
Isaiah 35 1-10
Luke 1:39 - 79
And the Book of Psalm is filled with words of praise. Add one to your praise everyday.

Part Five

Will to Worship

Introduction

In parts one through five, we discussed 'praise 'as it leads to intimate relationship with the Almighty Living God. This section will endeavor to differentiate worship as a separate activity from praise. Praise may lead to worship or worship may lead to praise, but our discussion will revealed that praise is activity and worship involves that place of being still and surrendering to the Most High God as Lord.

- Praise is visual, audible, physical movement. Worship is primarily the internal, coupled with the lowly posture of bowing the knees, the head, or the face, or laying prostrate, in humble adoration or awe of God.

In his book *Exploring Worship* Bob Sorge claims that "worship must be taught or that to attain it we must seek God, or that we can come to a place of worship by speaking in tongues."[71] Sorge goes on to say, "Learning the fullness of worship is a lengthy process and does not come easily."

Truth 1: Worship is easy.

I contend that worship is so much easier than that. If you are discouraged with your worship because people keep imposing parameters on you that are based on a rationale absent in scripture, don't be disheartened. God has made His way and His expectations plain and easy. He is seeking those who are willing to recognize Him as God and surrender to Him every aspect of our being, and in turn, He will respond with His presence.

Truth 2: We must humble ourselves in adoring contemplation or in awe of the magnitude of who He is.

Demonstrate a willingness to reverence Him by bowing down. The wise men who went in search of a child – who was not yet old enough to walk - but they saw Him, knew who He was and fell down to worship Him. The wise men then 'praised' him by giving gifts (Matt. 2:11). So we must humble ourselves in recognition of His Lordship and God-ship. To worship we must bow down in submission and adoring contemplation of who he is.

Do you want to know the truth? Worship is not complicated.

Worship is simply our souls surrendering to the majesty of God – the royalty – the presence and glory of God. Worship is bowing in humble submission and recognition of magnitude of who He is.

You may not be physically able to bow your knees, but you can express an attitude of gratitude, and a heart for worship by bowing your head and lifting your hands. You can tremble before Almighty God. You do not have to study or have a degree. You don't have to spend money and time on seminars, conferences and workshops – or even books to know about worship. Worship is the spirit of the person surrendering; worship is the creature becoming nothing in the presence and brightness of the Creator.

Truth 3: worship is not intellectual. Worship IS spiritual.

Truth 4: worship is not a skill. Worship IS an immediate response of the convicted soul, to the Lordship and majesty of God in His splendor.

The bible records that every instance of worship was preceded only by recognition that He is God. Worship was virtually instantaneous. There were those who followed Jesus - at times by the thousands - to hear His profound teaching, but there were no seminars or conferences or how-to books on worship. It was simply a man or a woman or a people immediately in awe of a majestic God.

At the outset, people saw Jesus as a man or they weren't certain who He was (perhaps a prophet) but when He healed them and revealed Himself as Lord, they bowed and worshiped. The similarity between praise and worship is that both are vertical or directed upward, with God as the focus of our rendering. The posture of worship is horizontal but the reverence is directed upward. The difference is that praise is audible or involves motion that compliments or commends; whereas worship involves less emphasis on action and more on humble submission in the form of bowing the head, bowing the knees, and raising of hands to worship and adore Him.

Truth 5: Humankind did not define worship; God did.

Overall, the main criteria are Spirit and truth. Awe and reverence are manifestations of worshiping the matchless magnitude and majesty of the Almighty God. Our worship journey begins with believing in the truth. We have to know like the blind man who Jesus healed, that Jesus is the Son of the Living God, sent to glorify God. We have to believe that Jesus is the promised One. We no longer have to wait for a revelation or sign; God has been fully revealed in the Father, Son, and Holy Ghost. Only when we believe can we assume the posture of worshiping in Spirit and truth.

Often, I have heard the biblical story recounted in sermons, about how the disciple Thomas did not believe Jesus had risen from the dead; in fact, Thomas is persistently dubbed as "Doubting Thomas." Thomas only called Jesus Lord after he saw proof in the nail-pierced hands. The level our faith and how that faith is translated in worship is determined by our belief.

Martha, the sister of Lazarus and Mary, had the same problem as did Thomas: she did not believe. Martha was Jesus' friend, and she did not respect him as Lord. In John, chapter 11 Mary and Martha summoned Jesus to heal Lazarus. In the minds of Mary and Martha, the situation was a 911 moment. Jesus knew Lazarus was not sick unto death, but rather unto the glory of God, the Father. Martha met Jesus en route and complained that her brother was already dead. She returned with an attitude to their house to tell Mary *"The Teacher has come and is calling for you"* [v.28]. Martha's sarcasm exposed her unbelief. To the contrary, Mary went out to meet Jesus, and guess what she did? Mary fell at Jesus' feet, wept and called Him Lord! Jesus arrived at the tomb where Lazarus lay and Martha was there like a big black cloud. Again, Martha's unbelief was revealed when she scolded Jesus. Jesus *replied, "Did I say to you that if you would believe you would see the glory of God?"*

Saints of God, when we believe, we will worship. When we believe we will reverence, and we will bow. I pray as you read this next section on Worship, that your faith will be reinforced, and you will reach new depths in your time with God. You can begin right now by proclaiming, "Lord I believe."

Chapter 15

Worship

The Nature of Worship
Attitude of Worship
The Posture of Worship

To 'worship' is to show reverent love and devotion to something or someone by bowing down; worship is to esteem, extol, exalt one higher than one's self to the extent there is no one higher. Worship in the "Greek is 'λατρεύω' or 'latrevo.' However, originally, the meaning of the English word 'worship' was different from today's usage. In Old English, the noun 'wurðscip' (Anglian) or 'weorðscipe' (West Saxon) referred to 'the condition of being worthy,' 'honour,' 'renown,' to 'esteem,' 'regard' and 'respect,' in general. The English word humble means 'close to the ground.' It comes via Old French 'umble' from Latin 'humilis,' 'low, lowly.' The word derives from Latin humus, "earth," and is related to the English word human and in its original sense, being human meant being an "earthly being…."[72]

Once more, the act of worship in the bible always involved bowing one's knees, or bowing one's face or head. Worship is that state of '*yieldedness'* – not just physically but in essence. By essence, I mean the spirit. To put it in other terms, we acknowledge our weightlessness or our smallness, to His largeness or vastness.

Worship is akin to hiding ourselves - our humanity – the measure of who we are in honor of the magnitude of who He is. Worship is shrinking, becoming smaller. In theory, and as it correlates to "close to the ground," worship returns us to humble beginnings as dust in God's hands.

Some people refer to 'going to church' as worship. Or perhaps the paper program that one receives upon arrival at church is the 'order of worship.' Perhaps you may think that prayer is worship or that singing is worship. While prayer may be connected to worship and singing may lead to worship, worship can happen without prayer and without singing. Worship can happen before the sins are forgiven. Worship happens immediately and spontaneously and with no other preceding event or action, upon recognition of whom someone is and that they deserve our reverence. For example in western culture, people's behavior changes the instant someone of authority or prominence enters the room e.g. physician judge, pastor, mayor or governor. Attendees are asked to stand and do so, no questions asked. Likewise, our worship must be immediate because God is worthy.

The Nature of Worship

Where praise is external, worship is internal.

Again, Sorge explains, "One distinctive of praise concerns its extroverted nature. It is characterized by celebration and exhilaration." He continues: He who has merely contemplated the wonders of God has not yet entered into praise."[73]

We know that our actions are not separate from our thinking. Praise is only meaningful as action, when we contemplate the goodness of God, the character of God, and the acts of God, which is worship.

Some churches attract people by emphasizing technology – such as providing multiple flat-screens for people to watch religious videos during the service, or people paint and engage in the creation of artwork while the singers sing. I would hope our approach to worship centers on the awesomeness of God. True worship doesn't need a gimmick or bait. We are drawn to worship when we yield to His Lordship, His majesty, the brightness of His glory.

Abraham fell on his face and God talked to him saying...(Gen:17)

And Moses made haste, and bowed His head to the earth and worshiped (Exodus 34:8).

And Jehoshaphat bowed His head to the ground and all Judah and the inhabitants of Jerusalem fell before the Lord and worshiped the Lord (II Chron. 20:18).

While praise is the fruit of our lips, the, clapping, dancing, singing, playing on the instruments, and waving a banner – all physical demonstrations; worship is bowing down in adoring contemplation of who God is.

The Attitude of Worship

The attitude of worship is

- o submissiveness
- o lowliness
- o the human spirit exalting God
- o awe, fear, amazement
- o reverential or respectful

Reverence is necessary for proper worship over externals, such as dimmed lights, and other aesthetics. The proper reverent attitude comes from the heart of the individual. An individual will reverence God at the point of realizing the love of God is imminent.[74]

The Posture of Worship

The scriptures define the posture of worship in, Psalm 95:6 *"Come let us worship and bow down, let us kneel before the Lord our maker"* and, "*Psalm 99:5 Exalt the LORD our God and worship at his footstool; he is holy.*

Satan knew the significance of worship and commanded Jesus to *"Fall down and worship me" (Matt 4:9).* The devil knows that bowing esteems another higher than one's self. He wanted Jesus to acknowledge him as the higher power as he had attempted to establish against God, with no success.

The Gospel of *Mark, 3:11 says, "And unclean spirits, when they saw him, fell down before him, and cried, saying, Thou art the Son of God."* This passage falls under the category of a wowee! passage. Unclean spirits bowed in recognition of Jesus.

Keep in mind that the Word of God distinguishes worshiping in Spirit and in **Truth**. Consider yourself warned that there are other forms of worship which have no basis in truth. Yes the unclean spirits bowed, but they were incapable of worshiping in truth. The unclean spirits recognized Jesus as the Son of God – which is the truth – but they were incapable of worshiping Him in the right Spirit; they could not walk in truth. The evil spirits worked to expose the Kingship of Jesus before His time, thus Jesus silenced them, and they were subject to His command.

The idea of bowing down can have either a negative or positive correlation: For example: if someone was to tell you to "get on your knees" that directive could mean submission, humility, or humiliation; it would mean "acknowledge me for being better or greater than you" and work not just to humble someone, but to humiliate that person by paralyzing the person's power. . Either you would submit to reverencing someone one who deserves it, or you are being forced or controlled.

God does not control us. He wants us to submit to Him – because he is great, greater, and greatest! AND because He wants to reside in our praise and in our worship. God is not trying to distance Himself from us. He seeks relationship with us, His creation.

In some cultures it is customary to bow to another person in greeting. In Japan, the forwardness of one's bow reflects status. Those higher in status bow less deeply to those lower in status. Therefore, bowing too deeply to lower status Japanese by westerners is considered bad form. Among the Mossi of Burkina Faso, the most servile gesture is the poussi-poussi…[75] At one time it was customary for Chinese to bow in greeting but has now evolved to a polite nod. Western practices have influenced proper manners in the East. The simple act of bowing one's head, bowing the upper body, or bowing prostrate typifies self denial and humility.

The English word 'humble' means "close to the ground." Bowing to the ground is still acceptable if one is physically able. Psalm 95:6," *Come let us worship and bow down; let us kneel before the Lord our maker."*

Belief in Worship

As a child I was taught to kneel before the Lord. This is not to judge someone who ultimately stands before God, but back in those days the altar was a place for bowing down. Those old saints made us call Jesus over and over - sometimes for hours. And while you were calling Jesus, Jesus, Jesus, as fast as you could, they would be hollering, *put your mind on Him*! and all sorts of cheers to bring you 'through.' Today, things are done hurriedly without respect to real contemplation of God. Really, what is important here is not the length of time before God, but a heart for Him. Worship begins the moment we believe.

The Word of God records many times when people came to Jesus and worshiped saying "Lord I believe." There is the story of the blind man who was healed by Jesus and ultimately cast out of the synagogue:

> *Jesus heard that they had cast him out; and when he had found him, he said unto him, Dost thou believe on the Son of God?*
> *He answered and said, Who is he, Lord, that I might believe on him?*
> *And Jesus said unto him, Thou hast both seen him, and it is he that talketh with thee.*
> *And he said, Lord, I believe. And he worshiped him. (John 9:35-38)*

There was the time the disciples were in a ship and a storm rose against their ship. Peter walked on the water toward Jesus and then became afraid and began to sink:

> *And Peter answered him and said, Lord, if it be thou, bid me come unto thee on the water.*

> *And he said, Come. And when Peter was come down out of the ship, he walked on the water, to go to Jesus. But when he saw the wind boisterous, he was afraid; and beginning to sink, he cried, saying, Lord, save me. And immediately Jesus stretched forth his hand, and caught him, and said unto him, O thou of little faith, wherefore didst thou doubt?*
>
> *And when they were come into the ship, the wind ceased. Then they that were in the ship came and worshiped him, saying, Of a truth thou art the Son of God.*

Who He is in Worship

Mark 9 gives the account of the scribe whose son had a deaf and dumb spirit which tormented him. He brought his son to Jesus: "*Jesus said unto him, If thou canst believe, all things are possible to him that believeth. And straightway the father of the child cried out, and said with tears, Lord, I believe; help thou mine unbelief'(vv. 23, 24).* In all of these examples, worship happened at the moment of belief in the Lordship of Jesus.

Contemplating God

Worship is to lose oneself in awesome wonder of God; to yield, mind, body, and soul in total adoration. Worship is so complete in the spirit realm. The worshiper's comfort zone is forfeited in favor of the presence of the Lord. Worship begins with the immediate recognition that the Holy One is here. Contemplation begins immediately when someone you love indescribably and immeasurably enters. According to R.A. Torrey,

> Worship is the soul bowing itself in adoring contemplation before the object worshiped. To worship God is to bow before God in adoring contemplation of Him. The word worship is commonly used in a very loose and unscriptural manner-for example, we speak of the whole service of

> the Lord's Day morning and evening as 'public worship,' but there is a great deal in it that is not worship. Reading and meditating on Bible is not worship but certainly leads to worship, as we learn more about the things of God. Listening to a sermon is not worship. It may be and should be accompanied by worship, but it is not worship. (Again) Singing is not necessarily or generally worship. There are hymns that, if sung intelligently and in the proper spirit, would be worship, but they are comparatively few in the hymnology of the day. Worship, as said, is the soul bowing before God in adoring contemplation of Him"[76]

You may have heard the story of Jesus and the woman at the well of Jacob who was living according to a life style that either suited her or was convenient. Jesus knew she had had some moral and self control issues with men. She slept around with other people's husbands. She was a career 'other woman.' She was scandalous. She was not in that spiritual place where she would immediately recognize Jesus. From the passages below, the woman was not far off because she correctly perceived that she was talking to a prophet, and revealed in the conversation that she had the expectation that a savior was coming, and she was prepared to learn of Him.

Accordingly, when Jesus revealed that He was the One, she worshiped. She worshiped because she received the idea of the "living water" which Jesus offered, then went from a place of obscurity and doing her dirt in darkness, straight into town to tell everybody who would listen, *"Come see a man…"* No doubt the woman related what had happened with passion and conviction to convince the town's people that she was not talking about 'the man' that she'd slept with the night before. I believe, "*come see a man*" was a manner of praise following her worship because praise is lauding God for what He has done, who He is, and complimenting His character. She had already recognized and accepted Jesus for who He said He was and proceeded to witness with the fruit of her lips.

'Water' in the passage, was a metaphor for purification – and satisfaction (e.g. "*…whosever drinketh of the water that I shall give him shall never thirst").* Her worship began at the point of recognition that the Savior was there. She activated (praise) by leaving her water pot (v.26) and going into town to rave about Jesus. How is it that she could say, "come see a man" to the town's people when they all knew that she had seen her share of them?

This time it was different. Consider the conversation:

> *There cometh a woman of Samaria to draw water; Jesus saith unto her, Give me to drink.*
> *(For his disciples were gone away into the city to buy meat.)*
> *Then saith the woman of Samaria unto him, How is it that thou, being a Jew, askest drink of me, which am a woman of Samaria? For the Jews have no dealings with the Samaritans.*
> *Jesus answered and said unto her, if thou knewest the gift of God, and who it is that saith to thee, Give me to drink; thou wouldest have asked of him, and he would have given thee living water. (John 4: 7- 14)*

Clearly, from v. 15 the woman's life was not easy. She didn't want to have to keep climbing that mountain to fetch water, to wash clothes, to cook and clean, and to drink.

I believe life was brutal and inconvenient for her. She had met her share of men, probably just from going to that well. Men passing by on the way to town needed a cool drink, along with their animals. Other times in the bible we see that women were drawing water from wells. There was a lot of 'action' going on at these wells. The well is where Moses met his wife Zipporah, where Abraham sent a servant to find a wife for Isaac, and where Jacob fell in love with Rachel. (Gen. 29)

Jesus offered the woman a change when He said:*"Woman, believe me, a time is coming when you will worship the Father neither [merely] in this mountain nor [merely] in Jerusalem. A time will come, however, indeed it is already here, when the true (genuine) worshipers will worship the Father in spirit and in truth (reality)" [AMP].*

This woman's life was not only changed but she told of the change. She lauded, she exclaimed, and then proclaimed. She praised as she spoke of Jesus, but she worshiped when she recognized or reverenced the Lord Messiah. This is where worship begins: in the realization of who God is.

Another beautiful example of worship was the story of the woman with the Alabaster box. In both accounts, there is no mention of the women's names. But this woman had apparently heard or seen Jesus enter Simeon the Leper's house. I get the sense that not much was a secret in those villages. Everybody was privy to everyone else's business. It is not recorded whether this woman spoke any words but we know that she entered the house after hearing that Jesus would be eating there and stood behind Him weeping. The woman wiped Jesus' feet with her hair and poured oil upon his head.

She was not a groupie – she was a worshiper who sought her time with the Lord. She honored Him with something she valued most and could have sold for money. This was love - beyond words. Her actions entailed worship.

By comparison, the host Simeon the Leper (along with the disciples and on-lookers) sat in judgment of the woman with the alabaster box because of her past sins [Luke 7:39]. How hypocritical! First, Simeon was a leper AND a Pharisee. He was a societal outcast of the lowest rank. Lepers were customarily condemned to exile among the dead, and Pharisees were the unofficial hypocrites (politicians) who were liked only by like-minded individuals. Yet Jesus sat at supper with Simeon who Jesus 'outted' as a horrific host. Jesus had just performed some amazing miracles; including raising a woman's son from the dead on the way to Simeon's house and Simeon had the audacity to devalue the presence of the Lord, Jesus. Jesus looked beyond all of their faults, hence the reason He is so worthy of our worship.

Faith in Worship

Faith in worship is critical because without faith it is impossible to please God.

- Faith*less*ness essentially cancels the act of worship.
- Without faith there is no worship: "*He that comes to Him must **believe** that He is and that He is a rewarder of those that diligently seek Him" (Hebrews 11:16).*

Faith says that though we cannot see God we believe everything about Him, and He rewards us with Himself and the fullness of joy.

An excellent demonstration of faith in worship is the story of Nicodemus. Nicodemus was short in stature but tall in social status. Nicodemus heard Jesus was passing, saw the throngs of people, and decided to climb a sycamore tree. I love how Jesus has us in mind when we make the effort to be near Him. He called Nicodemus down from the sycamore tree so He could be with Him. Nicodemus climbed down. Note: Nicodemus had to come down. He was trying to see Jesus, but he was too high. I picture Nicodemus having an extraordinary height of 5 feet. At 5 feet, he was too high. In order to worship, he had to come down.

Chapter 16

Who We Worship

God, only.

> *Thou shalt have no other gods before me.*
> *Thou shalt not make unto thee any graven image, or any likeness of anything that is in heaven above, or that is in the earth beneath, or that is in the water under the earth. (Exodus 20:2-4)*
> *And Jesus answered and said unto him, Get thee behind me, Satan: for it is written, Thou shalt worship the Lord thy God, and him only shalt thou serve (Luke 4:8).*

These passages designate worship as exclusive for God. We must not bow ourselves to any person, nor our heads, nor raise our hands to any other person or thing.

If you are a person living outside a country that permits freedom of religious expression, the Word of God says that you may be persecuted for His sake.

Still, do not bow down to their gods.

You may be imprisoned, as were the disciples and the apostles, for the sake of your belief in Christ.

Do not bow down.

You may face the blackest prospect of being murdered for the sake of Christ.

Do not bow down.

The society where you live may have instituted laws to force you to bow or to honor their god; do not bow down or speak the name of their god.

The biblical precedence for this is Daniel chapter 3. There was a command that all the people, nation, and languages fall down and worship the golden image which King Nebuchadnezzar had made. Shadrach, Meshach, and Abednego refused and were thrown into a fiery furnace. The king, looked into the furnace and noticed the three men were walking around accompanied by a fourth person that looked like the Son of God.

How is it that the king, a worldly man and idol worshiper knew what the Son of God looked like? No one had seen Jesus. As God revealed Himself, the king acknowledged the God of Daniel. He proceeded to decree that anyone who spoke against the God of Shadrach, Meshach, and Abednego would be cut into pieces and their houses made a dunghill. How extreme! But once King Nebuchadnezzar recognized the Son of God, he had a change of heart and proceeded to make an "as for me and my house we will serve the Lord" move. The power that he once used to accomplish evil was now used for the glory of God.

Chapter 17

Recognizing God as Truth

In nearly every instance in the bible where someone met Jesus, there was change. Often worship happened even if sins were yet to be forgiven.

We return to the woman in Luke 7:44 – 47 who happened to be present when Jesus went to a Pharisee's house for a meal. The woman followed Jesus and stood behind Him weeping. As she wept, her tears fell on Jesus feet. She stooped and began to wipe the tears with her hair and pour perfume on Jesus' feet. The perfume is said to have been expensive. The scriptures state the woman was a sinner. Jesus honored her love for Him and forgave her sins which were many.

Most people don't like to be bothered with other folks' feet – especially feet that have been through dust and dirt and most likely with corns and blisters. It was common in those days to offer to wash someone's feet as an extension of hospitality and out of necessity – maybe for sanitation purposes, but the Pharisee that invited Jesus didn't offer Him any water at all! The Pharisee was not just a poor host; he used the encounter with the woman as an opportunity to criticize Jesus and to belittle the woman in his heart. But the ever loving Lord Jesus sent the woman away in peace.

R.A Torrey writes, "The result of true worship is that the Father God is satisfied and the worshiper is satisfied."[77]

The O.T. records that Israel wanted a king. God permitted his people to have a king, but none of those kings were the true king. All of those kings were men with faults. God's chosen people continued to wait for the promised One down through forty-two generations. The woman at the well had heard that the One was coming. The woman with alabaster box was overcome and overjoyed to be in the presence of the promised One. Both women worshiped with brokenness and a contrite heart.

The Book of Revelations includes some of the most magnificent examples of worship. In the fourth chapter, John is in the Spirit when he sees a vision resembling the One seen by the prophet Ezekiel, with the same imagery: including a throne made of precious stones surrounded by a rainbow and brilliant Light. In his vision John sees beasts and the twenty four Elders who fall down and worship, casting down their crowns (v.10) they worship and then they praise, saying, "Thou are worthy to receive glory and honour and power: for thou hast created all things, and for thy pleasure they are and were created." At the moment the prophet Ezekiel sees the likeness of the Glory of the Lord, He falls on his face to worship as does John, weeping. Also, three times the twenty four Elders fall down from their seats and worship, casting down their crowns. By these actions they demonstrated that they were in awe of God. They demonstrated worship.

Both visions contain spirit and truth. Both visions have within them aspects attributable only to God: fire and smoke, rushing wind, or thunder and lightning and a voice. Though it is likely the two writers responded to the spectacle of their visual experience in the Spirit, the vision was not a prompting for worship. In worship, the worshiper needs no prior perception nor is there a requisite of reasoning in reference to the awesomeness of God. It was the splendor of the Lamb who was slain; the glory of the One who sat upon the throne. The writer of Revelations needed no affirmation from Ezekiel. His experience was entirely personal, immediate, and based on his revelation of God.

In worship God extends to us trust. God trusts us with knowing Him in every way and depending on our faith, He will reveal himself the more. That's what these visions represented: revelation from the revelator.

Do you think God will invite a non worshiper into His house? Think about it. What will you do for eternity if not worship Him around the Throne?

The bible says that God is a Spirit, and they that worship Him must worship Him in spirit and in truth. The nature of God necessitates a moving in the Spirit realm.

> *A time will come, however, indeed it is already here, when the true (genuine) worshipers will worship the Father in spirit and in truth (reality); for the Father is seeking just such people as these as His worshipers. (John 4:22-24 AMP)*
>
> *God is a Spirit (a spiritual Being) and those who worship Him must worship Him in spirit and in truth (reality).*

To further elaborate, Jesus spoke the words in the verses above after speaking to the woman at the well. Jesus and the woman, a Samaritan, had a conversation about water. It was a grueling part of her daily life to draw water from the well for her needs and apparently others. Jesus told her He could give her living water which she interpreted as him saying she wouldn't have to go through the tedious task of drawing water every day. The woman surmised that Jesus was a prophet when He told her about what she did in her spare time – or her promiscuity. Everyone else in town condemned her for her race and because of her occupation. The woman knew something was different about the man with whom she spoke. After Jesus enlightened the woman that her worship would not be limited to the mountain where her ancestors had worshiped, she knew He was the One.

From the moment the Samaritan woman met Jesus, she was changed and worshiped in truth.

Chapter 18

Why Worship?

We Were Created to Worship Him
Because the Father Seeks Such
In God We Trust
Glory of God
To be in the Presence of God

We Were Created to Worship Him

> *Everyone who is called by My name, whom I have created for My glory; I have formed him, yes, I have made him. Let all the nations be gathered together, And let the people be assembled. (Isa. 43:7, NKJV)*

And,

> *O come, let us* ***worship*** *and bow down: let us kneel before the LORD our maker. (Psa.95:6)*

Because the Father Seeks Such.

> *But the hour cometh, and now is, when the true worshipers shall worship the Father in spirit and in truth: for the Father seeketh such to worship him.*

> *God is a Spirit: and they that worship him must worship him in spirit and in truth.*
> *(John 4:24, 25)*

> The above passage is an all-in-one verse. It tells the 'who, the what, and the how' of worship. Who? God.
> What? A Spirit.
> How? In spirit and in truth.

The word 'must' speaks to the fact that we don't get a choice in how we worship. 'Must' is absolute. 'Must' is a demand. We must worship God because he said so, in spirit and in truth.

In God we Trust

> *But if ye say unto me, We trust in the LORD our God: is not that he, whose high places and whose altars Hezekiah hath taken away, and hath said to Judah and Jerusalem, Ye shall **worship** before this altar in Jerusalem? (II Kings 18:2).*

To Glorify God

> *And Jesus said unto him, Thou hast both seen him, and it is he that talketh with thee.*
> *And he said, Lord, I believe. And he worshiped him.*
> *And Jesus said, For judgment I am come into this world, that they which see not might see; and that they which see might be made blind. (John 9:35-37)*

I love that God invites us to have a personal encounter with Him, which attests to the fact that He is living. Therefore our worship is not synonymous with objectifying a being or an object of our imaginations.

Because God is Holy

Earlier, the section on praise elaborated on the holiness of God. Holiness is founded on the same principles related to the absolute holiness and perfection of God: *Ascribe to the LORD the glory due his name; bring an offering and come before him. Worship the LORD in the splendor of his holiness" (IChron.16:29, NIV).*

That He is glorified and that He is holy are the foremost attributes. To glorify means to make Him known; while holiness refers to His essence.

We are to make known His splendor, His sovereignty, His superiority, His supremacy. His glory is pure and absolute as God self-described.

To glorify God is to express or imitate the likeness of God within the limitations of our humanness. His likeness is His image. This is to say if God is good, then we need to be good; if God is holy, then we need to be holy; if He is merciful in judgment, we need to be merciful. The list goes on in terms of his attributes and character.

We are not gods, nor can we ever measure up to Him. Measuring up – that is, equaling God in no way is our objective. We are trying to please him to the extent that He will look on us and receive us back into communion with Him until He comes for us. He wants to see a reflection of Himself in us. For example when a mother gives birth, the first witnesses look upon the child to see what features reflect the father or mother or someone else in the family. It pleases the father and or the mother to know the child looks like him or her.

Chapter 19

Who and What Not to Worship

Other gods
Angels
Idols
People

Other gods, idols

> *Thou shalt have no other gods before me (Ex. 20:3).*
>
> *Do not follow other gods to serve and worship them; do not provoke me to anger with what your hands have made. Then I will not harm you (Jer.25:6, NIV).*
>
> *It shall come about if you ever forget the LORD your God and go after other gods and serve them and worship them, I testify against you today that you will surely perish*
> *(Deut. 8:19).*

The worship of other gods is as prevalent today as during biblical times. In fact, there are references throughout scripture of people worshiping idols with the same diligence as those who worship the true and Living God. Apostle Paul criticized the Greeks for senseless idol worship:

> *Paul then stood up in the meeting of the Areopagus and said: "people of Athens! I see that in every way you are very religious (superstitious, KJV). For as I walked around and looked carefully at your objects of worship, I even found an altar with this inscription: TO AN UNKNOWN GOD. So you are ignorant of the very thing you worship – and this is what I am going to proclaim to you.*

This is why we must embed the truth about who God is our souls. Western idealistic thought declares that the United States, for example, is a Christian nation. We know this to be untrue and that as a nation, the United States has become increasingly secularized and idolatrous.

It would be awesome if everyone accepted Jesus Christ as Lord and worshiped Him as Savior but sadly, reality eludes the present spiritual condition of the United States and the world. Every day we see the signs of the spread of Islam and eastern belief systems. These idolatrous beliefs are working to destroy world peace and the Kingdom of Christ. An example of the depth of idolatry is Hinduism. In the Hindu religion "It is believed that there are 330 million gods in the Hindu Dharma. There are as many Hindu gods as there are devotees to suit the feelings, moods, and social background of the devotee, though not really the sign of ignorance…"[78] Worshiping other gods is becoming more popular and more public.

Paul observed the Athenians occupying their time being fascinated with 'myth de jour' he *Acts 17:21-23 (ESV).* (I get the sense that Apostle Paul was of the opinion that the Athenians were stupid in their superstition.)

Do not be fooled into thinking that the term 'spiritual' is truth. This is why we must worship in spirit *and* in truth: because there is the truth and then there is deception. There is truth and there is perversion. As stated in the section on Praise, God forbids the worship of living things or objects other than Him. We are not to worship angels, or things or even ordinances.

Worshiping other gods or idols is the act of turning away from following after the True and Living God, in favor of turning *to* other gods. Other gods may not have a name or shape or be formally organized in its devotion, but whatever we turn *to* in place of God becomes 'other gods' or idols.

The first commandment that God gave Moses was "*Thou shalt have no other gods before me*" *(Ex. 20:3)*. God said He will not share His glory with another. Glory or esteem is bestowed upon God through worship and by way of praise. Bowing down is reserved for the true and Living God. Apostle Paul warns of a deception:

> *Let no man beguile you of your reward in a voluntary humility and worshiping of angels, intruding into those things which he hath not seen, vainly puffed up by his fleshly mind,*
>
> *And not holding the Head, from which all the body by joints and bands having nourishment ministered, and knit together, increaseth with the increase of God. (2:18 – 19, NKJV)*

Verses 18 – 19 were directed to the church and the church at Laodicea in reference to the worshiping of Angels. This church was also referenced in Revelations, 3:13-15. This church was a lukewarm church and God was not pleased. They were carnal-minded and materialistic and possibly a bit stuffy. This church was so caught up in themselves and the things of the world that they had been tricked into worshiping angels. This goes back to the state of our thought life. We must focus our attention on the God-head and the things which God instructs us to think, and we can avoid being deceived.

Angels

Angels are <u>not</u> to be worshiped in any form. Though angels have the ability to help us, we are not to worship them. Some people are serious about praying to angels to the point of collecting and carrying around little figurines or collecting a glass menagerie of angels. The figurines can do nothing and were made with hands. Those things have no power or ability. Angels do not have a will of their own. They must also operate according to the Will of God.

Angels are,

Ministering spirits and servants of God. Angels were created by God to be worshipers and servants of God (Heb. 1:11).

> *And again, when he bringeth in the first begotten into the world, he saith, And let all the angels of God worship him.*
> *And of the angels he saith, Who maketh his angels spirits, and his ministers a flame of fire.*
> *But unto the Son he saith, Thy throne, O God, is forever and ever: a sceptre of righteousness is the sceptre of thy kingdom. (Hebrews, 1 – Also, Psa. 104:4))*

Apostle Paul taught, "*For by Him all things were created, both in the heavens and on earth, visible and invisible, whether thrones or dominions or rulers or authorities (a reference to angels)—all things have been created by Him and for Him" (Col. 1:16).*

→Please read Psalm 148.

Facts About Angels:

- The bible records how angels could easily be mistaken for something to be worshiped because of the radiance of their appearance. John saw what was probably the spectacle of the angel and fell down to worship: "*So I threw myself down at his feet to worship him, but he said, Do not do this! I am only a fellow servant with you and your brothers who hold to the testimony about Jesus. Worship God, for the testimony about Jesus is the spirit of prophecy" (Rev.19:10).*
- Angels cannot marry or reproduce but were created by God to worship and praise Him, as well as carry out tasks: "*For in the resurrection they neither marry, nor are given in marriage, but are as the angels of God in heaven" (Matt. 22:28).*

- Angels are charged with keeping us safe (Psa. 91:11); to be messengers (Gen. 16:9; Judges 6:20; Luke 1 28 – 30) and to destroy and do battle (I Chr. 21:15; Matt 26:23): *"Do not let anyone who delights in false humility and the worship of angels disqualify you from the prize. Such a person goes into great detail about what he has seen, and his unspiritual mind puffs him up with idle notions" (Col. 2:18).*
- Angels are subject to fall from grace as are we. Angels are no more qualified at any time to sit on the right hand of God, than humans. The Devil – before he became the devil was an angel. Demons were angels, until they fell from grace due to going along with Lucifer in his attempted coup d'état, they lost their positions as angels. *"How art thou fallen from heaven, O Lucifer, son of the morning! how art thou cut down to the ground, which didst weaken the nations!" (Isa. 14:12).*
- We shall judge the angels*: "Do you know not that we shall judge angels? How much more, things that pertain to this life?" (1Cor. 6:3, NKJV)*
- The Devil fell because he tried to take the place [glory] from the Most High God, and works to influence followers of Christ to defect and do the same thing? *"For thou hast said in thine heart, I will ascend into heaven, I will exalt my throne above the stars of God: I will sit also upon the mount of the congregation, in the sides of the north: I will ascend above the heights of the clouds; I will be like the most High" (Isa. 14: 11-14).*
- Angels spend a good amount of time worshiping God around the throne: *"And all the angels stood round about the throne, and about the elders and the four beasts, and fell before the throne on their faces, and worshiped God" (Rev. 7:11).*

People

Regardless of a person's position we should not bow down to people: *"And as Peter was coming in, Cornelius met him, and fell down at his feet, and worshiped him. But Peter took him up, saying, Stand up; I myself also am a man" (Acts10:25, 26,).*

Be mindful that Romans 13 says to give honor to whom honor is due within the context of people of power and position in the community; however, the Word of God also states that we are to esteem others high than ourselves (Phil 2:3). We are to be respectful and caring in our connection with others. We are to have a special love for those in the household of faith but we do not bow to any person. Some churches practice the custom of standing when the Bishop enters or to rise for a judge in a courtroom. People rise for the president of the United States as he enters. This gesture is showing respect for position. This is not the same as worship.

Ordinances

According to the Amplified bible, ordinances have to do with ceremonies or rituals for the sake of ritual without the accomplishment of purifying the heart unto holiness. This passage has to do with people thinking they are holy because of religiosity. Again acts and ordinances for the sake of religiosity are absent of grace through faith.

> *Which was a figure for the time then present, in which were offered both gifts and sacrifices, that could not make him that did the services perfect, as pertaining to conscience;*
> *Which stood only in meats and drinks, and divers washings, and carnal ordinances, imposed on them until the time of reformation*
> *But Christ being come an high priest of good things to come, by a greater and more perfect tabernacle, not made with that is to say not of this building; (Heb. 9:9-11)*

Talents or abilities

Talents and abilities were installed in us by God to be used for His Glory. Every time I sit at the organ I find myself bowing my head and pleading to the Holy Ghost for His anointing – I offer God all that He has placed in me to praise, and I put the flesh under subjection. Any compliment or accolades truly belong to Him.

I praise God for giving me a voice, and the gift of music. I love God for giving us all talents. Yet, I have heard people say, "I have no talent." Everyone has a talent. Everyone. Talent to express ourselves creatively is after the likeness of El-ohim, the Creator. If we are exceptional in our abilities and people are touched by what we do, then we should continue to reflect the Christ in us. We are not special or better than anyone else. We are not indispensible, nor should we ever have the attitude that the church can't go on without us. It is an honor and a privilege to be used. Never become lifted in pride or allow people to inflate your opinion of yourself. Be sure to remain small in His sight and that of those you serve. *"Know ye that the Lord he is God: it is he that hath made us, and not we ourselves; we are his people and the sheep of his pasture" (Psa. 110:3); "Not that we are sufficient of ourselves to think anything as of ourselves; but our sufficiency is of God" (II Cor. 35).*

Chapter 20

The Benefits of Worship

Peace
Liberty
Joy
Fulfillment

I don't know one good reason why someone would not want to be in the presence of a Living, God. Worshiping God and being in His presence is so much better than any other good thing on earth that brings us pleasure. Like human relationships, talking on the phone, texting, emailing is great as far as communication, but there is no substitute for a personal encounter where you can possibly embrace the person. It is the individual's company that draws you closer and increases your devotion.

Peace in Worship

There is nothing like peace. I find myself pursuing peace continuously. Mostly, I find peace in God; in His Word, in praising and in worshiping Him. The peace that Jesus gives is so much deeper than just the absence of sirens, gun fire, and people cussing and hollering in the streets all hours of the night. Peace is tranquility, or being free from agitation of mind and spirit. Life around you may be bedlam, but in worship you can be in a world within a world where the peace of God resides; that place where the Righteous can run into and find safety. In that place you may sigh or smile, but one thing you will do for sure is love a completely satisfying love. You may be exhilarated, but you will surely love. God will return that love with Himself. In this place of peace you can block out the voices of people who won't leave you alone; you can comfortably place them in God's hands, everything – that's everything that concerns you: your day to day welfare, what you will eat, what you will wear, your emotions, your desires, your mistakes, AND your *intentions* - your sleeplessness, your everything. Take a moment and meditate on the Living God and what you have learned about Him. Think about Him purposefully. Lay before Him and adore Him.

There is Liberty in Worship

The Bible says, Where the Spirit of the Lord is, there is liberty (II Cor. 3:17).

And,

> *Stand fast therefore in the liberty where Christ has made us free, and be not entangled again with the yoke of bondage (Gal. 5:1).*

The freedom spoken of here is a freedom not unto maliciousness but unto righteousness under grace versus law.

Joy and Gladness in Worship

> *Whom having not seen, ye love; in whom, though now ye see him not, yet believing, ye rejoice with joy unspeakable and full of glory: (I Peter 1:8)*

There is a joy that comes as a result of our faith. No doubt, it was much easier for the people who were able to behold Jesus' face or touch Him or to be in His presence as He taught by the way; but our worship is based solely on our belief that He is, even though we cannot see Him. We recognize and accept His Lordship – His kingship, and His position as God, by faith.

What Will Worship do?

Worship transforms (II Corinthians 3:18 – NASB, KJV)

Worship develops in us "such traits as forgiveness, tenderness, justice, righteousness, purity, kindness and love."[79]

- Satisfaction. Jesus said to the woman at the well that by worshiping Him in spirit and in Truth, she would never thirst. To us He is saying to worship Him will satisfy our most basic needs. This is in contrast to living in transgression - or sin, where there is perpetual dissatisfaction, constant searching and yearning.
- Worship intensifies our desire for the things of God
- Worship increases our understanding of God.
- Our spirit becomes sensitive to the heart of God.
- Worship fortifies our walk with God.
- Worship heightens, enlivens, enlightens

Chapter 21

What Happens in Worship

Recognition of the Lordship
Humility
Obedience
Spirit and Truth
Our Daily Walk, Giving (including tithing)

Recognizing the Lordship of Jesus

When we know God for who He is, we will worship. One of the reasons people have such difficulty worshiping is unbelief. This unbelief could be because the person is seeking to answer every question concerning God. This is why we worship in Spirit. We cannot reduce God to our intellect. If we want relationship with God we must believe what the Word of God says about him: questioning nullifies faith.

The bible records that the first person to worship Jesus – that is, recognize His Lordship, was His mother; not after she saw Him as a babe in her arms, wrapped in swaddling clothes, nor after she watched him grow. Mary began to worship and recognize the Lordship of Jesus while He was in her womb. Later, when He would tell her "*I must be about my father's business,*" she accepted his saying rather than get in the way of His divine mission.

Paul (as Saul then) tried to ignore God and commenced to persecuting the people of the early church. He was knocked down off his horse en route to advance his agenda, and left blinded by God's glory. He not only worshiped, but became the greatest champion of the Lordship of Jesus Christ.

Earlier we addressed Jesus' encounter with the woman at the well. Jesus states, *"If thou knewest the gift of God, and who it is that saith to thee, Give me to drink; thou wouldest have asked of him, and he would have given thee living water."* This verse affirms the principle that to worship Him we must know Him. This knowing is not a knowing as in 'familiarity,' but rather an intimate knowing to the point where knowing has affected the heart.

> *But the hour cometh, and now is, when the true worshipers shall worship the Father in spirit and in truth: for the Father seeketh such to worship him.*

> **Worship doesn't need to be taught**
> *But the anointing which ye have received of Him abideth in you and ye need not that any man teach you: but as the same anointing teacheth you of all things and is truth, and is no lie and even as it hath taught you, ye shall abide in Him. (I John 2:27)*

The true worship of which Jesus spoke had nothing to do with race or ethnicity as it had in the past. The race issue was still fresh in the woman's mind because, as a Samaritan, she was forbidden to talk to Jews. Up until that point the Jews worshiped the God of Abraham but had not fully received Jesus as Lord. They received His miracles but did not readily accept Him as Lord – or as Truth, for that matter. The worship of these individuals I have mentioned began with recognition of the personality of Jesus, followed by obedience.

Humility, Obedience

In I Samuel 15, Saul, the first King of Israel was a warrior. God told him to 'utterly destroy all that they (Amalekites) have, and spare them not; but slay man, woman, infant and suckling, ox and sheep, camel and ass.' The Amalekites were enemies of God and idol worshipers. King Saul decided to spare 'Agag, [their king] and the best of the sheep, and of the oxen, and of the fatlings, and the lambs, and all that was good, and would not utterly destroy them as instructed. King Saul conjured up an excuse later and said that it was the people who decided to save some of the cattle for the purpose of sacrifice. God was not pleased and had this to say to Saul through Samuel,

> *And Samuel said, Hath the LORD as great delight in burnt offerings and sacrifices, as in obeying the voice of the LORD? Behold, to obey is better than sacrifice, and to hearken than the fat of rams.*
>
> *For rebellion is as the sin of witchcraft, and stubbornness is as iniquity and idolatry. Because thou hast rejected the word of the LORD, he hath also rejected thee from being king (vss. 22, 23).*

King Saul never could have worshiped in Spirit and in Truth because in verse 15 he had already disavowed God by referring to Him as 'the Lord Thy God.' His heart was far from recognizing the Lordship of God for himself.

When we obey God we are right thinking. When we obey God, pride is nonexistent. *James 4:6 says, "God resists the proud, but gives grace to the humble."* The bible speaks about *"Casting down imaginations, and every high thing that exalts itself against the knowledge of God, and bringing into captivity every thought to the obedience of Christ" (II Cor.* 10:5). Even if you defy your heart's desire for God by disobeying God – you will not venture far. Your heart will eventually prevail over the urge to fulfill the things of the flesh.

Worship and praise begins in the mind. What we think about has much to do with our level of praise and worship. Long after the initial recognition of the Lordship of God, we should continue to think about things that are true, things that are honest, things that are just, things that are pure, things that are lovely, and things that are of good report. (Phil. 4:8) Worship becomes easier and more automatic for a mature Christian, possessing the mind of Christ: *"Let this mind be in you, which was also in Christ Jesus" (Phil 2:5).*

We must be obedient in praise and in worship. You may be well meaning in an action but obeying is better than sacrifice. In this context offering praise or worship is nullified when the heart is not cleansed from disobedience and turning from God.

In some cases, we may find ourselves justifying or rationalizing our disobedience. When God says something, He has all angles covered. He does not need us to 'help out' or figure things out. 1 Samuel records that the Ark of the Lord came into the camp and the people began to rejoice and play on all manner of instruments in before the Lord. They praised in such a way that the Ark of God began to shake. Uzzah put forth his hand to steady it. God's anger kindled against Uzzah, and he smote him. Uzzah's intentions may have been well meaning, but obedience is foremost. For this reason, it follows that when the Holy Spirit is at work in someone we mustn't feel the need to fetch a fan, some water or touch the person who is under the anointing. We don't need to try to guard or protect the person or intervene. As with the instances King Saul and Uzzah, getting between God and His Will, can be costly.

What is Truth?

The word 'truth' has a variety of connotations, such as honesty, good, faith… agreement with fact or reality in particular. The term has no single definition about which a majority of philosophers and scholars agree… there are differing claims on such questions as to what constitutes truth" and whether it is subjective, relative, objective, or absolute." The word 'true' is from old English having to do with good faith; "faith, word of honor, religious faith, belief or loyalty, honesty, good faith. 'Truth' involves both the quality of faithfulness, fidelity, loyalty, sincerity, veracity, and that agreement with fact."[80] For something to be true means anything oppositional, is a lie.

The working tenet in worship as it pertains to truth is that,

- God Himself is truth ("let God be true and every man liar").
- God is absolute truth and in Him is no approximation or partiality;
- Jesus is Truth personified.

Apostle John repeatedly refers to truth and acknowledges that Jesus is full of Grace and Truth (1:14). Jesus describes himself as the "way, the truth, and the life and that no man has access to the Father except by him (v.4, 6). John *14:17* states in the words of Jesus*: "Even the Spirit of truth whom the world can not receive, because it seeth Him not, neither knoweth Him: but ye know him; for he dwelleth with you and shall be in you."* [81]

Also, the Holy Spirit is the Spirit of truth (Spirit of Jesus).

> *Even the Spirit of truth; whom the world cannot receive, because it seeth him not, neither knoweth him: but ye know him; for he dwelleth with you, and shall be in you (v.17).*

> *Howbeit, when he, the Spirit of truth, is come, he will guide you into all truth: for he shall not speak of himself; but whatsoever he shall hear, that shall he speak: and he will shew you things to come (John 16:13).*

Theories on truth such as Coherence, Constructivist, and Pragmatic, all of which hold that truth is verified and confirmed by result of putting one's concepts into practice.[82] As it relates to the passages above, one must activate truth in one's life by faith. Truth is not limited to what we speak. Truth in the Spirit, in fact, is neither what we can verify, nor what can be substantiated by man's parameters - for we walk by faith and not by sight. We accept the truth as declared in the Word of God.

Worshiping through Giving (including tithing)

We must live in truth by faith. This is where obedience becomes joined with truth.

One area – which may be the last that believers have difficulty being obedient - is giving. If we are going to live and worship God in Spirit and in truth, we have to live the WHOLE truth – without the use of excuses like 'all they want is money' or 'the pastor is taking all the money' or 'I ain't got it like that.' Be obedient to the Word of God and then trust God to be true to His Word.

We cannot do the equivalent of a 'purse snatch' and still worship in truth. Unlike a thief,

I picture a robber as an unsophisticated, low-down-dirty-in-your-face-necklace-snatching – robber. God trusts us to give back what belongs to Him. Giving God tithe and offerings from our substance means we reciprocate His trust: "*Give the Lord the glory due unto his name: bring an offering and come before: worship the Lord in the beauty of holiness" (I Chron. 16:29).*

Daily walking in truth means:

- We apply the Word of Truth in life choices and to how we treat others
- Living our lives with integrity
- Telling the truth at all times
- Honesty with God concerning our giving. Tithing demonstrates our willingness to give back to God what already belongs to Him. Tithing evidences integrity. Obedience in giving says that we trust God. If we obey all other edicts of the Word of God, but rebel when it comes to bringing in the tithes and offerings into the storehouse, then we fall short of worshiping in Spirit and in Truth.

In his *Theological Dictionary*, Walter Elwell claims: "truth is also a quality used to describe utterances from the Lord. The church (body of believers) of the Living God is the Pillar and Ground of the Truth. There are philosophies that hold only mathematical propositions are true and all other propositions are completely dispensable (pluralist). This truth is described as deflamatory."[83]

For,

- The Lord's covenant and testimony are truth (Psalm 25:10)
- The Word of the Lord and His works are Truth (Psalm 33:4)
- The truth is the promises of God.
- In the Glory of God is truth (John 1:14)

Functions of Truth

- Truth protects [Shield and Buckler] (Psalm 89:14)
- Truth will judge (Psalm 96:13)
- Sanctifies (John 17:17)
- Liberates (Joh8:32)
- Guides (John 16:13)
- Endures Forever (Psalm100:5) [84]

Holiness as Characteristic of Worship

Holiness is connected to obedience in all things, including our obedience, our praise and our worship. Psalm 96:9 states,

> *O worship the Lord in the beauty of holiness: fear before him, all the earth.*

Also,

> *Give unto the Lord the glory due unto his name; worship the Lord in the beauty of holiness (Psa. 29:2).*

> Most importantly, the Word of God states, *"Be ye holy, for I am Holy" (I Peter 1:16).*

After reading the above passages you may ask, do I have to be saved in order to worship, and what should my relationship be with God? The answer is that at the moment you believe in your heart and confess with your mouth that Jesus is Lord, the bible states that you are saved. The people that met Jesus believed and He made them whole. When they recognized Him, they believed as indicated by their submissiveness in worship. The act of worship is the spirit's denial of self in complete favor of God's deity. Worship is our obeisance. Worship is the pleasure of our weakness beneath His strength. Ultimately, true worship is to honor the holiness, apartness, righteousness, light, and goodness of God by presenting him ourselves as holy.

The Presence and Glory of God
What is the Glory of God?

Most importantly, 'glory' is honor or distinction extended by common consent. 'Glory' is found in great beauty, magnificence, or resplendence. God's glory goes beyond description of physical attribute and is the manifestation of the essence of God. The brilliance or brightness of His being, beyond what the human eye can behold or contain. Glory is a distinguished quality or asset; something marked by beauty, perfection or resplendence.[85]

Strong's Concordance names several biblical uses for 'Glory' [#3519]:

1. Abundant riches
2. Honour, splendor, glory
3. Honour, dignity, reputation, reverence

Also the Hebrew term for this usage is "Kabowd' (ka-bode); whereas the Greek is translated "dokeo" [Strong's 1380] meaning 'think,' 'judge' or 'please.'[86] More specifically, the 'glory' of God is related to the splendor produced by the absolute purity and perfection of His essence and reputation.

The Word of God says in the book of Isaiah 43:7, **that we were created for God's glory** [reputation]**:** *Even everyone that is called by my name: for I have created him for my glory. I have formed him, yea, I have made him.*

The glory referred to in v.7 is the glory that we give unto God; it is the reverence, honor due him. The bible states that His glory is expressed in all that He created, in His Son, in mankind, and in His power. We give God glory (honor, reverence) so we can see His Glory (essence of His being). God says, *"I am the Lord: that is my name and my glory will I not give to another, neither my praise to graven images" (Isa. 43:10).*

We can give glory to God in different ways: through praise, by exhibiting the light that He places in us and by living in the image of God, which is His holiness, to name a few. When we glory in God we are witnessing. Our worship AND our praise are our witness. Thus there are 3 types of glory:

1. as in the honor or distinction one bestows upon another or that is assumed as a result of character or action of notoriety such as extraordinary achievement; to express delight
2. as in one's position
3. as in the essence of one's being

God defines His glory as His goodness. Moses asked, "*I beseech [beg] you, shew me your glory.*" Moses may have wanted to see God in person, in all of His splendor, but God responds "I *will make all my goodness* pass *before you* "(v.19, ch.33)

I find in my reading a universal consensus among scholars, theologians, preachers and thinkers that we are in search of two things: purpose, and knowing God. Some of us want to know Him up close and personal and to experience His glory. Still, a single definition belies 'glory.' Like many terms, glory is distinguished by its usage. My contribution to this discourse is that the glory of God - aside from what we can bestow - is the **visible manifestation of the Presence of God as Spirit, in the exquisite brightness of His Light, Love, Power, and Goodness; the glory of God is all of these apparent attributes and characteristics compounded and then magnified beyond measure at once**; in addition, the glory is absolute and complete. It is like mixing together the elements needed to make the most powerful bomb known to man and then activating the detonator.

The bible says God is a consuming fire. The children of Israel saw the Glory in the pillar of fire; they witnessed the fire on the mountain top where Moses talked with God (Ex.33). They were awestruck by the glory glowing on Moses' face; they saw the glory fill the house so that that the priest could no longer see to render service. So God has indeed manifested His glory in the eyes of humankind throughout time.

What does the Glory of the Lord Look Like?

Good question. The Glory of the Lord is not an ancient bearded man with white hair, bushy eyebrows and a tan sitting on a high back chair whistling winds into clouds all day. I believe no one now or historically can know what the glory of the Lord looks like because the bible records that when the Glory of the Lord appeared, it did so in a cloud every time so there was a covering. Each time God had to protect people from Himself. Moses was only permitted to see the hind part of God's glory as it passed before him.

When the people of Israel <u>saw</u> the glory, they saw a <u>representation</u> of God's glory.

The magnitude of God's Glory is beyond our comprehension as well as our capacity to behold. During Jesus' transfiguration, Peter, James and John saw Moses and Elias talking. Peter, being Peter, began talking about building tabernacles. God appeared in a cloud and spoke from heaven of His Son. They fell before Jesus, fearful and trembling.

We know that pure, incomprehensible light is associated with the Glory of God. If you want to get a small sense of beholding the Glory of God, gaze into the sun on a bright, clear day. Look up into it and try to hold that gaze. Within a few minutes your eyes will tear and your will lose focus. You may even experience some pain.

We return to the example of Moses as he requested three things of God: Moses sought earnestly for God to show him his way, to know God, and to be shown God's glory. Moses had inquired of God as to who would go with him and God answered, "My Presence [essence] will go with thee." In Moses' final requests, "I beseech thee, shew me thy glory." Beseech is to beg urgently, to request earnestly, to make supplication. God's Presence had been with the children of Israel since leaving Egypt in the form of a cloud and a pillar. Moses wanted more. He and God talked regularly as man to man. But Moses wanted more than the voice and the signs. Moses wanted to see God's glory.

Why did Moses request to see God's glory and not God?

How did Moses come to know there was such a thing as glory?

If I had wanted to see someone and really experience a moment with that person, I wouldn't ask to see some synthesis of the person; I would ask to see the person – face to face.

Moses had a rapport with God; he experienced the holiness of God and was never the same. God showed Moses His hind part, but protected Moses with His hand as He passed by. When Moses descended from the mountain his skin shone (34:30 – 35). God's glory was reflected in Moses' skin and the people were unable to look upon him without a veil. The conversation went as such:

> *If you are pleased with me, teach me your ways so I may know you and continue to find favor with you. Remember that this nation is your people." {14} The LORD replied, "My Presence will go with you, and I will give you rest." {15} Then Moses said to him, "If your Presence does not go with us, do not send us up from here. {16} How will anyone know that you are pleased with me and with your people unless you go with us? What else will distinguish me and your people from all the other people on the face of the earth?" {17} And the LORD said to Moses, "I will do the very thing you have asked, because I am pleased with you and I know you by name." {18} Then Moses said, "Now show me your glory." {19} And the LORD said, "I will cause all my goodness to pass in front of you, and I will proclaim my name, the LORD, in your presence. I will have mercy on whom I will have mercy, and I will have compassion on whom I will have compassion (Ex. 33:13-19 NIV).*

> *Then the LORD came down in the cloud and stood there with him and proclaimed his name, the LORD. And he passed in front of Moses, proclaiming, "The LORD, the LORD, the compassionate and gracious God, slow to anger, abounding in love and faithfulness, maintaining love to thousands, and forgiving wickedness, rebellion and sin. Yet he does not leave the guilty unpunished; he punishes the children and their children for the sin of the fathers to the third and fourth generation. Moses bowed to the ground at once and worshiped. (Ex. 34:45-8)*

The intimacy between God and Moses is arguably matched only by Jesus, such as the transfiguration in Matt 17:1, 2:

> *And after six days Jesus taketh Peter, James, and John his brother, and bringeth them up into an high mountain apart,*
>
> *And was transfigured before them: and his face did shine as the sun, and his raiment was white as the light.*

Moses sought to know every aspect of God. Thus, he communed with God continually. Moses was that friend of God that knew God as self existent (I Am, that I Am); as Elohim (Creator) he knew the purity of God (Holiness); the love of God; the mercy of God, the Grace of God, His grace, goodness and Truth (vss. 6&7). Moses praised then worshiped by bowing down to the earth.

Moses' knowing of the attributes of God was beyond intellectual knowledge. He spoke the reality of these attributes to God in his worship. God had instructed Moses to perform a task, which was to bring the people up to drive out the enemies of God from the land which He had promised them. Moses said to God, "*See thou sayest unto me bring thee up this people: and thou hast not let me know whom thou wilt send with me.*"

It is impossible to have a sustained love or appreciation for someone unless you know them through a series of encounters over a period of time. Today, encounters happen via a range of social networking sites, text messaging, emailing and maybe an occasional greeting card or letter – but nothing compares to a personal, face to face encounter where you see someone's face, hear their voice and exchange a touch or embrace.

Getting back to the account of Moses' conversation with God, up until that point Moses had been obedient according to his faith, but in v.13 he expresses a desire to know God in the company of His physical being. By v. 18, Moses becomes more impassioned. He knew God well enough to know he could never see God. Moses and God talked on a regular basis, and I believe God's voice was, in fact, audible at that time. Moses already knew the Presence of God was with the

Israelites and himself because God had manifested His Presence by way of the cloud by day and a pillar of fire by night in leading them to the promise land. Make no mistake; the glory cloud and the pillar of fire were anything but ordinary occurrences. Moses was no longer satisfied with the Presence of God covered by a cloud. Moses wanted more. He wanted God to reveal His visible nature.

God agreed to show His essence, but would provide the protection of His hand. The glory of God was so great and so intense that the light was transferred to Moses' face. Now Moses had to cover his face to protect the people as God had done for him. Awesome! Moses fell to the earth and worshiped. Within that worship was fear and trembling. Within that worship was awe. Within that worship the acknowledgement of the magnitude of God.

More on the Shekinah Glory

Just as 'worship' is linked to the earth - or bowing toward the earth, the 'presence of God' is 'the interior' or indwelling, or His manifest presence. Many teachers and scholars agree that the Presence of God is everywhere; that God is omnipresent.

"Shekinah" refers to the residence or dwelling, and has come [sic] to mean the visible majesty of the divine presence. All description of the Shekinah says that it was a most brilliant and glorious light enveloped in a cloud. The Jews described the Shekinah as God's visible presence in the Holy of Holies sitting between the cherubim..."[87] When the cloud filled the house, the Glory filled the house.

> *And it came to pass, when the priests were come out of the holy place, that the cloud **filled** the house of the Lord,*
>
> *So that the priests could not stand to minister because of the cloud: for the glory of the Lord had **filled** the house of the Lord.*

And,

> *Now when Solomon had made an end of praying, the fire came down from heaven and consumed the burnt offering and the sacrifices; and the glory of the Lord filled the house.*
> *And the priests could not enter into the house of the Lord, because the glory of the Lord had filled the house. And when all the children of Israel saw how the fire came down, and glory of the Lord upon the house, they bowed themselves with their faces to the ground upon the pavement, and worshiped and praised the Lord, saying for he is good; for his mercy endureth for ever (II Chron. 7:1-3).*

Also in the book of Acts the presence of God was manifested in the wind that filled the house

(Acts 2) on the day of Pentecost. Notice that any time there was the Glory or the Presence of God, the house was filled. Filling indicates nothing else can fit; there is satisfaction as a result of completeness. With God all things are complete, perfect and absolute.

Summary

Everyone Must Worship

Whether a person chooses to do so or not, everyone will worship the true and living God here on earth or in the Day of Judgment:

> *For this reason also, God highly exalted Him, and bestowed on Him the name which is above every name, so that at the name of Jesus every knee will bow, of those who are in heaven and on earth and under the earth, and that every tongue will confess that Jesus Christ is lord, to the glory of God the Father (Phil.2:9-11, NASB).*

> *I have sworn by myself, the word is gone out of my mouth in righteousness, and shall not return, that unto me every knee shall bow, every tongue shall swear (Is. 45:23).*

These passages indicate that we will all bow. AND we will all confess (praise) the Lordship of Jesus Christ. We want to strive to worship Him now so that the time of judgment will be a time of triumph.

Keep Your Worship Sacred

Lastly, we must be careful not to attribute commonalities to worship. What is done in worship should be set apart. This is serious! The application of slang terminology in language and acts not ordained by God unto Himself should not be used in worship. We worship by bowing down the head, bowing the face, bowing the knees, or laying prostrate. That's it. We don't burn incense or objectify our worship. We don't bow before images of Jesus or Mary or angels.

The Danger of not Worshiping God as God when We Know Him

> *Because that when they knew God they glorified Him not as God neither were thankful; but became vain in their imagination and their foolish heart was darkened, professing themselves to be wise they became…who changed the truth of God into a lie and worshiped and served the creature more than the Creator who is blessed forever, Amen. For this cause God gave them up to vile affections. And even as they did not like to retain god in their knowledge, God gave them over to a reprobate mind to do those things which are not convenient. (Rom. 1:21-28)*

Book Summary

The word 'passion' is increasingly becoming one of the most frequently overused words in the English dictionary (alongside 'iconic," ubiquitous' and 'quintessential.'). To have passion means we possess an excitement or zeal. The old saints used to say, "on fire for God" meaning get excited, make some noise, let the dead bury the dead.

It is time that the church, catch on fire. This is not the time to become complacent or routine in our approach to worship. Our ever-increasing faith and love for God must be manifested by way of a passion to praise and a will to worship.

Passion. Passion is any powerful or compelling emotion or feeling, such as love or hate; a strong amorous feeling or desire; love; ardor; a strong or extravagant fondness, enthusiasm, or desire for anything; the object of such a fondness or desire; an outburst of strong emotion or feeling.[88]

This discussion began with a question: Is praise what you do? I endeavored to candidly answer the question with an examination and application of biblical truth.

When you think of yourself praising, are you *doing* anything, and if so, *what* are you doing? Who or what are the focus of your praise and your worship?

'Praise' and 'worship' are two of the most relevant topics in the life of the church that addresses whether it is functioning in animated fashion in the body of believers of Jesus Christ. The body of believers must show the breath of God which is the Spirit of God manifested through our praise. We must be in action, full of energy and passion. We must show evidence of our devotion through our worship. Remember that praise is that outward visible, audible favorable expression toward God; while worship expresses obedience by bowing down.

The existence of God is where our praise begins. We should praise Him because of who He is, His names, His character and attributes.

In contrast, praise is different from prayer or the spiritual gifts; all of which work together, but are distinct from one another.

God says we are to worship Him only and that He will not share His glory with another. He will not share His glory with another god, another person, another activity, angels, our beloved spiritual leaders nor Jesus' mother, Mary. We praise and we worship God, and God and God alone, for beside Him is no other.

We must commend God for His mighty acts, His attributes, and His names.

Calling God by His names, deposits praise in context. Perhaps you don't know Him as Jehovah-tsidkenu, but you know that when He saved you, He became your righteousness; you may not know Him by the name Jehovah-shammah, but you can testify that He is a present help in the time of trouble and if you don't know Him as anything else, know that He is Lord – for "*every knee shall bow and every tongue shall confess that he is Lord over all*" *(Romans 14:11)*.

"Thank you Jesus," "yes Lord" and "hallelujah" are nice praise phrases but not enough. We want to always seek a deeper, more intimate praise unto God. There is so much more to God and about God that we can declare. We can recognize Him as the Lamb who is worthy, as in Revelations: *"Saying with a loud voice, Worthy is the Lamb that was slain to receive power, and riches, and wisdom, and strength, and honour, and glory, and blessing" (Rev. 5:12)*. We can tell Him that He is Holy, *"And the four beasts had each of them six wings about him; and they were full of eyes within: and they rest not day and night, saying Holy, holy, holy, Lord God Almighty, which was and is, and is to come" (Rev. 4:8)*.

We can call Him by His names, as in the Amen: *"And the four and twenty elders and the four beasts fell down and worshiped God that sat on the throne, saying, Amen; alleluia" (Rev. 19:4)*. We can call Him the first and the last: *And when I saw him, I fell at his feet as dead. And he laid his right hand upon me, saying unto me, fear not; I am the first and the last: (Rev.*

1:17), and *"I am Alpha and Omega, the beginning and the end, the first and the last" (Rev. 22:13)*.

Praise begins with God, Himself. As He identifies Himself, He demonstrates the manner in which we should praise Him. All of us must praise. Pastors must praise, Bishops must praise, Prophets and Apostles must praise. Musicians must praise with the fruit of their lips. No one is exempt. We must teach the children to praise. Praise is not an option. Our church leaders – especially pastors are the most effective praise leaders. Allow the people to hear you and see you with hands upraised or to bow down or lay broken before God.

★★★★★

Why write a book about praise? There is nothing that will ever take the place of the Word of God. No one can argue or improve the unadulterated Word of God. I have written about praise to encourage the saints in these last days to draw nigh to God and to have constant communication with Almighty God in prayer and praise.

The aim of this book was to distinguish Praise from Worship so that we give God all that is due unto Him the way the bible says to do it.

Our relationship with God is necessitated by every available means of communication with Him; including praise, worship, and the spiritual gifts. Our praise and our worship make up our way of life, not our religion. Also, we want to praise and worship so that we can delight ourselves in Him and in His Glory.

Knowing God is not about sensations or feelings. We don't receive the reality of a true and living God based on emotions or a sign, but by faith. This book lets believers and seekers know that we can be excited about God, and that there is joy in knowing the living God.

We can encourage ourselves through praise; we can have victory when we praise.

The methods of praise are varied and broad. We are not limited to a response of clapping. Clapping is good, but there is so much more that is our privilege.

There will be distractions - such as television and all that technology offers - to occupy our time. Younger people who are in pursuit of education may encounter other philosophies and lifestyle points of view. I encourage you to hold fast to what you know to be true about God for He is Truth. Profess God and then hold on to that profession.

God is calling us to return to the expressed likeness of His image. He is seeking a holy people to worship Him in Spirit and in truth.

How can you get started if you have not begun? Praise and Worship are not difficult actions; nor should you be afraid. Please, begin to put the principles of this book into practice immediately. Find a secret closet, bus stop, apartment, bathroom stall, the woods or any place where you can commune with God. Get to church early, say as little as possible to people (without being rude) as you make your way to the altar to bow before the Lord, your God. You can praise there or worship there. Direct your thoughts to Him. Contemplate him until your heart becomes contrite and broken. Tremble before Him. Let no one stop you or distract you. Open up to God. Be weak before His strength. Glorify His name and His Essence. If you have done this, you have willed to worship and you have begun a path to develop a passion for praise.

In the book of Revelations, there is a lot of praising going on. I hope the praises we offer on earth is just a rehearsal for that day when we will all join in with the twenty-four Elders, the heavenly hosts, and those who will overcome by the word of their testimony. Church, we should begin rejoicing that we are in number that no man can number. Begin to cry Holy, Holy, Holy…worthy to receive Glory and honor, wisdom and power. Worthy is the Lamb that was slain, for He is the Alpha and Omega, the First and the Last. Praise ye the LORD!

Somehow being where I've been elevates the senses to where the surroundings become more vivid. Time allows you to notice that what you dismissed as hills are layers of mountains; some jagged while others loom blue in the distance. My experiences have triggered a keen sense of the setting sun's hues that tempt me to peel it and taste its tangy sweetness. I hear the sound of a mosquito over traffic, the distinct language of heaven's creatures, chatting and interacting which keeps me mindful of the supremacy of our God.

As I began this project, it was not my desire to share the bleak aspects of my life; but I did so to encourage you not to give up. Just as praise must be personal, as these writings progressed, it became more of a personal testimony (witness/praise) of the great things that God has done. We do not know what will bring us to that place of praise.

While writing this, I learned that the earth is not void of praise and that not all believers in Jesus Christ are lumbering in limbo or in need of spiritual resuscitation. All over the world people are lifting up the name of Jesus in exuberant fashion.

So why write this book?

Again, this book was written to encourage believers and those who may not yet have intimate relationship with God. Also, for those of you who are discouraged and experiencing the trying of your faith, this book purposed to assist in directing your thoughts to the methods by which we can have assurance in God. As we go through trials and tribulations, our praise and our worship can lead to deliverance.

Our passion for praise must first develop as individuals, and then as a corporate body. Hopefully, you worship at a church where the Spirit of the Lord is welcome to pour out upon the collect as it worships and praises God. I pray you are not bound by obligation or tradition, for tradition's sake. I pray you know the importance of praise and worship as conduits to a closer walk with God.

By now you know that we are His creation, and we were created to bring forth praises as His witnesses. Be clear about what you are doing when you praise. Dance is praise, singing is praise, lifting up hands or raising a banner are praise, but worship is found only in humbly bowing down the head or knees. Moreover, the acts of praise and worship must be directed vertically toward God.

I have written this while taking my life one day at a time. Some days I am grasping for the hope that I encourage in others. I am destitute of daily necessities, but still passionate in seeking the face of God. Every day I probe to know God more and more. I talk to Him about who He is. I talk to Him about His acts. I want His glory and I want His embrace. I have trouble believing for me sometimes. Events and people are beyond my control, but if I can make it to that next moment or that next day while keeping my focus heavenward, then I will make heaven. Yet, if I experience no change, I will keep trusting and hollering out to God. I vow to continue sending up bold, favorable expression in word, in song (tehillah), on the instruments (zamar), and with the waving of my hands (towdow).

I pray that you will continue to draw close to God and allow your passion for praise to develop, and your will to worship until your spirit appreciates wholeheartedly, the matchless magnitude of the True and Living God.

L.

Notes

1 C. Austin Miles, 1912, "In the Garden"

2 Butler, Trent C. Editor. Entry for "Praise." Holman Bible Dictionary. http://www.studylight.org/dictionaries.hbd/view.cgi?n=5086. 1991

3 Ibid.

4 *Strong's Exhaustive Concordance: New American Standard Bible.* 1995. Updated ed. La, Habra: Lockman Foundation. http://www.biblestudytools.com/concordances/strongs- exhaustive-concordance/.

5 Ibid.

6 Ibid

7 Author, unknown

8 Columbia Electronic Encyclopedia - ebsco - Columbia Electronic Encyclopedia, 6th Edition - http://web.ebscohost.com

9 Matthew Henry Complete Commentary on
http://www.blueletterbible.org/Comm/mhc/Psa/Psa_133.cfm

10 Aquinas Thomas. "Nature of God." *Stanford Encyclopedia of Philosophy.* Web.

11 Ibid.

12 Deem, Richard, "*The Evidence for God from Science*," http://www.godandscience.org/

13 Begley, Sharon. "Science Finds God." *Newsweek.com*, 20 July 1998, Web. 44

14 http://westernamezion.org/aboutus.html

15 Elwell, Walter A. "Entry for 'Comfort'". *"Evangelical Dictionary of Theology"* 1997.

16 Denton, Michael "*Evolution: A Theory* in *Crisis*" (Adler & Adler, Chevy Chase, 1985) 250

17 Luther, Martin, "*Table Talks*, vol. 54, 1rst Edition" (Fortress Press, Minneapolis ;1967)

18 Winfrey, Oprah. *Oprah Winfrey Show*, CBS Television. Feb. 2008. Television.

19 H. Spurgeon, Charles,"Open Praise and Public Confession,"
(Sermon, Metropolitan Tabernacle, Newington, October 11, 1883)

20 Lutzer, Erwin, "*Nothing Else Matters*"
(sermon, as broadcast on *Running to Win, Radio, September 30, 2012)*

21 Hagee, John, "The Lord's Prayer: Thy Will be Done." Sunday Morning Worship. Cornerstone Church, San Antonio TX, aired July 20,2014, Sermon

22 Ibid.

23 *Scofield Study Bible* (Oxford University Press, 2005)

24 Franklin, Jentezen "*Judging Yourself Unworthy*," Sunday Morning Worship, Free Chapel, aired July 20

25 Sorge, Bob, "*Exploring* Worship: A *Practical Guide to Praise and Worship*," (Oasis House, Lee's Summit, 1987)

26 Matthew Henry, *"Matthew Henry Commentary," (*Zondervan, Grand Rapids, 2010)

27 Lewis, C.S., *"Reflections on the Psalm*" (Harcourt Inc., Orlando, 1958)

28 Marshal, W.S., arr. By Jefferson, J. Cleveland, "*Blessed Quietness," 1937, A.M.E.* Zion Bicentennial Hymnal, 226, print

29 Harrington, Karl P. "*The Lord is in His Holy Temple,"* 1865, *A.M.E.* Zion Bicentennial Hymnal, #685, print

30 www.steelers.com/history/terrible-towel.html/

31 Wesley, John, Funk, Joseph, "*O For Thousand Tongues To Sing,"* 1739, A.M.E. Zion Bicentennial Hymnal, 1999, print

32 College Sports fans.com, *nd*

33 Frey, William, "The Functional Anatomy of Humour" *np.* Also: International Journal of Humor Research; vol 7, issue 2, p. 111-126, DOI: 10.1515/humr.1994.7.2.111, July 2009

34 Wikipedia.com, orig. published as Miceli, M.; Castelfranchi, C. (2003*). "Crying: Discussing its Basic Reasons and Uses*". *New Ideas in Psychology* (3): 247–73. doi:10.1016/j.newideapsych.2003.09.001.

35 Alan Wolfelt, "*The Power of Tears*" article, pub. By More to life bible study, http://www.moretolifetoday.com/bible%20Study_power%20of%20Tears.pdf

36 'Brady, Sheryl, "*Theres a Story Behind My Praise,"* Judahfest, St. James COGIC, Chicago, 2007, sermon

37 Torrey, R.A., *What the Bible Teaches Updated Edition (*Whitaker House, New Kensington, 1996) 36-40

38 Berkhoff, Louis "*Sanctification*" http://www.bibleteacher.org/berkmos.htm, nd

39 Charnock, Stephen, *The Attributes of God*, (Baker Books, Ada, 1996) np

40 Louis Berkhof, *Systematic Theology* 6th *edition* (Banner of Truth, Carlisle, 1959) 73

41 From: "*Who is the Lord that I Should Obey Him"?* www.bunyanministries.org/expositions/attributes/02_Holiness.pdf, accessed June 2014

42 Discovering Light article, "*What is Light*"? Oracle Think Quest.org

43 *Strong's Concordance* (Hendrick's Publishers, Inc., Peabody, MA, 2009) 1

44 A.W. Tozer, *The Attributes of God vol 1: A Journey into the Father's Heart,* (Wingspread Publishers, Camphill, 2003)6

45 Charles Spurgeon, *The Attributes of God,,"http://www.preceptaustin.org/the_attributes_of_god_-_spurgeon.htm, accessed, June 2014*

46 Witherington, Bill, "*What is the Character of God," article, September 1, 2006, http://benwitherington.blogspot.com/2006/09/what-is-character-of-god.html*

47 Tozer, A.W., *The Attributes of God vol 1: A Journey into the Father's Heart,* (Wingspread Publishers, Camphill, 2003)

48 *Matthew Henry, Complete Commentary on the Whole Bible, Commentary on Psalm 9, pub.* domain

49 Spangler, Ann, *Praying the Names of God (*Zondervan, Grand Rapids, 2004) 16

50 Ellinger, Karl, *Hebraica Stuttgartensia edition of the Hebrew Masoretic Text (*German Bible Society, 1997*)*

51 Ibid.

52 *Hebraica Stuttgartensia edition of the Hebrew Masoretic Text, Strong's Concordance (Hendrickson Pub.,* August 2006)

53 Encyclopedia Judaica, Strong's Concordance; "Yehovah's Shekinah Glory, Hope of Isarel.org

54 Sproul, R.C. *Can I Know God's Will?* (Reformation Trust, Lake Mary, Fl, 2009) 14

55 Holman Illustrated Dictionary, Revised Edition, October 2003, p. 1529, print

56 http://www.reference.com/browse/(pantomime), accessed July 2014

57 unknown

58 Strong's Concordance #4057, Shalom Center.org

59 Meyer, Joyce *Battlefield of the Mind: Winning the Battle in Your Mind* (Warner Books, New York, 1995)

60 Glory. (Strong's 1391, 5193, 1392). In Thayer's Greek Lexicon: New American Standard Bible.
Retrieved from http://biblehub.com/concordance/g/glory_of_god.htm

61 Edwards, Jonatthan, *From" The Works of Jonathan Edwards, Vol. 1 Section 1 A Treatise on Religious Affections" (*Banner of Truth, Carlisle, 1961)

62 Torrey, R.A.,*What the Bible Teaches Updated Edition (*Whitaker House, New Kensington, 1996)

63 Holman, Illustrated Bible Dictionary, p. 1319

64 Barber, John, PhD Luther and Calvin "*Music and Worship' Reformed Perspectives Magazine*, vol. 8, Jul. 8, 2006

65 Evangelical Lutheran Church In America "*Why is there Music in the Liturgy*?" http://www.saintjamesfay.org/music/,accsessed July 2014

66 "This Far by Faith, People of Faith: Thomas Dorsey." PBS Documentary, television

67 Walker, Chris, *Top 13 Reasons Unchurched People Choose a Church,* Web. October 17, 2010, http://www.evangelismcoach.org/2010/top- reasons-unchurched-people-choose-a-church/ (Orig. Research conducted by Ranier, in 1999)

68 Warren, Rick, "*The Purpose Driven Church*"(Zondervan, Grand Rapids, 1999)

69 Bevere, Lisa, Speaker. "*Forward Conference 2014*." Daystar T.V. 26June 2014. Television

70 Houghton, Israel and Lindsay Aaron, "If Not for Your Grace," *A Deeper Level*, Integrity/Columbia, 2007, CD

71 Sorge, Bob, *Exploring Worship: A Practical Guide to Praise and Worship* (Oasis House, Lee's Summit, 1987) 75

72 David B. Givens, Ph.D, Center for Non-verbal Studies, 1999 – 2005

73 Sorge, Bob, *Exploring Worship: A Practical Guide to Praise and Worship* (Oasis House, Lee's Summit, 1987)

74 Taylor, Gene. "Reverence in Worship" http://www.centervilleroad.com/articles/reverence.html, accessed 2012
Centerville Church, n.d.

75 B. Givens, David, Ph.D, Center for Non-verbal Studies, 1999 – 2005

76 Torrey, R.A., *What the Bible Teaches* (New Kensington, Whitaker House, 1996) 564

77 Torrey, R.A.*What the Bible Teaches Updated Edition (*Whitaker House, New Kensington, 1996)

78 Venkatesan, Manisha, "*India"* Prezi.com, n.d. June 2013

79 *"Determine if You Worship in Spirit & in Truth:The Purpose of Our Worship of God," Bible lesson 1, accessed, May 2014*

80 Encyclopedia.org

81 Ewell, Walter, *Baker's Evangelical Diction of Theology, 2nd Edit.* (Ada, Baker Publishing Group, 2001)

82 Ewoldt, Bob, Homepage. *What is Truth?* http://bobewoldt.com/what-is-truth/acccsessed July 2013

83 Walter Elwell, *Dictionary of Theology 2nd Edit.* (Ada, Baker Publishing Group, 2001)

84 Ibid.

85 Webster Collegiate Dictionary

86 Strong's.com, Strong's biblical concordance

87 The Glory of God (Part I) Richard T. Rittenbaugh

88 Dictionary.com